IN CHARGE

Mastery
of
College Reading
and
Writing

D0144320

IN CHARGE

Mastery of College Reading and Writing

Jo An Simmons, Editor

Lloyd Thomas and Marianne Boretz,
Assistant Editors

Harcourt Brace Jovanovich, Publishers

San Diego New York Chicago Atlanta Washington, D.C.
London Sydney Toronto

This book grew out of a project sponsored by Dean Juan Francisco Lara, Office of Academic Interinstitutional programs, University of California, Los Angeles and by Chancellor Leslie Koltai, Los Angeles Community College District.

Copyright © 1986 by Harcourt Brace Jovanovich, Inc.
All rights reserved. No part of this publication may be reproduced or transmitted in any form or by any means, electronic or mechanical, including photocopy, recording, or any information storage and retrieval system, without permission in writing from the publisher.

Requests for permission to make copies of any part of the work should be mailed to: Permissions, Harcourt Brace Jovanovich, Publishers, Orlando, Florida 32887.

ISBN: 0-15-541330-9
Printed in the United States of America

ACKNOWLEDGMENTS

We are grateful to the following instructors whose combined experience from varied campuses, and whose creativity, expertise, and passionate convictions produced the curriculum portfolio on which **In Charge** is based:

Bruce Anders	**West Los Angeles College**
Barbara Bilson	**Santa Monica College**
Muriel Blatt	**Los Angeles Harbor College**
Marianne Boretz	**Los Angeles City College**
James Frisby	**Los Angeles Southwest College**
William Landau	**Los Angeles Pierce College**
Edythe McGovern	**Los Angeles Valley College**
Ronald Migaud	**Compton College**
Wylene Moore	**Los Angeles Trade-Technical College**
Rose Najar	**East Los Angeles College**
Jo An Simmons	**Los Angeles City College and UCLA**
Lloyd Thomas	**Los Angeles Mission College**

We are also grateful to the National Writing Project, UCLA's Office of Academic Interinstitutional Programs and the Los Angeles Community College District for funding the seminar that produced the curriculum portfolio. We acknowledge the lively sentence-combining instruction of Judy Markline (Hancock College), the model reading aids demonstrated by Thomas Bean (CSU, Fullerton), and the groundwork laid by Mina Shaughnessy. For the intellectual underpinnings of our new approach, we are indebted to Frank Smith (University of Victoria), Stephen D. Krashen (USC), and Patricia Simmons Taylor (UCLA's Office of Academic Interinstitutional Programs). From the same office, we thank Antonia Turman for her careful manuscript work and Dean Juan Francisco Lara for sponsoring the seminar and the book.

FOREWORD

The purpose of **In Charge** is to prepare students for freshman English and other academic classes. Unlike the traditional remedial text, **In Charge** integrates reading, writing, and thinking. To span the infamous gap between remedial and university transfer curricula, this text engages students in academic ways of thinking and writing and in reading selections that are challenging but manageable. Appropriate for any community college population, **In Charge** pays special attention to the needs and interests of minority and ESL students. The intended course level is just below freshman English; the intended students are intermediate, rather than basic writers, students who read on the ninth to eleventh grade levels. The text offers intensive learning to students in a hurry to reach their academic goals.

Experimental Nature

The text grew out of a new curriculum for an experimental, five-hour-a-week preparatory course. The text tries out the ideas curriculum designers had in response to these questions:

- Would a meaning-centered approach break through the tedium seemingly inherent in remediation?
- Could there be an alternate to the goose-step of programmed texts which so often deprive students of purpose and context, of motivation to read and write, or of excitement about ideas?
- Could a different approach to grammar bypass the students' sense of having been through all this before without success?
- Could applications of language acquisition theory help more minority students who speak a dialect and more ESL students qualify for freshman English?
- Shouldn't reading be restored to the writing classroom since it is intimately related to writing skill, generates content for writing, and is the basis of writing assigned in other classes?
- Could the intended students who are more unread than dysfunctional in reading profit from reading aids developed by the University of California/California State University Learning from Text Project?

As a result the text has these special features:

Meaning-Centered Approach

The book focuses on meaning. Instead of isolated prescriptive bits and pieces, this book connects the reading, writing assignments, and grammar instruction to a meaningful context. Students learn to extract meaning from what they read; to recognize and reproduce in their own writing the rhetorical ways meaning is created and organized; and to discover their own meaning vis-à-vis a subject as they write. Writing assignments call for academic ways of exposing meaning: problem-solving, defining, synthesizing material from several sources, analyzing, comparing, contrasting, and summarizing. The students' own writing is responded to as real writing with a meaningful content, not just as practice for correctness. The sentence manipulations and imitations are connected to the chapter's theme. Preliminary results from classrooms using these meaning-centered materials show increased morale and learning.

Integration of Reading and Writing

All the writing/thinking tasks revolve around a core of readings, selections from first-rate writers. Such selections certainly stretch the reach of students at this reading range but students in previous experimental sections have managed them. Students are directly helped by such reading/study aids as anticipation-response guides to pique their interest in a selection, graphic organizers to help them see the hierarchy of ideas in a piece, and by a Mina Shaughnessy scheme for vocabulary study. Additional reading instruction includes how to read actively and critically by marking a book Mortimer Adler-style and how to use reading journals. Some teachers in previous experimental sections have assigned full-length books like William Zinsser's **Willie and Dwike** or Richard Rodriguez's **Hunger of Memory** in addition to the text. The saturation in reading leads to multiple assignments: assignments for fluency, assignments that directly and indirectly teach correctness, paragraph assignments that lead up to longer assignments, assignments that simulate the academic writing of freshman English. These simulated versions with their models and guides provide an intermediate step between writing from personal experience and expository writing.

A New Approach to Teaching Fluency, Correctness, and Style

A new approach is needed for the student who may be able to learn rules for a grammar test but who can't permanently house these rules in his own writing. The student without a fund of patterns, constructions, and words already on call must interrupt his putting thoughts down on paper to search his conscious mind for some rule; as a result, his articulation of thoughts gets cut off and little gets written. To assimilate rules and fill in some of the missing patterns, **In Charge** combines direct instruction with indirect language acquisition. This approach utilizes the findings of Frank Smith, Stephen Krashen, Patricia Simmons Taylor, and others on acquiring literacy through reading, creative imitation, and sentence manipulation. Smith and Krashen find that literacy (here, I mean chiefly writing skill) is acquired through reading for meaning, rather than learned skill by skill through drill and explanation. Taylor's work indicates that creative imitation complements and furthers this process of assimilation. Just as students are subconsciously depositing writing features in their brains as they read, they are also hoarding for later withdrawal features of the model they imitate. To speed acquisition, the text provides quality readings, abundant sentence manipulation, and imitation of paragraphs, rhetorical patterns, and sentences. In each type of imitation, students substitute their own content for that of the original. This technique allows students to experiment safely with more sophisticated and stylish constructions than they might use on their own and to enjoy writing like the "pros" they are imitating. They experience the success that comes from concentrating on a few aspects of writing with the model taking care of the others.

The direct instruction aims at sentence mastery. By equipping students to avoid error, it attacks the roots of error. The four "Managing Sentences" sections help students match their sentence structure with their intentions; students learn the signal words, their meaning, and the punctuation that will convey the desired relationship between their ideas. Students thus increase their options and avoid sentence errors. Of course some errors will persist, both on the sentence level and with the conventions of English. To get at these errors, students will need to use a slim handbook such as Pearlman and Pearlman's **Guide to Rapid Revision** as they revise and edit their drafts. Since instructors have their preferred ways of responding to drafts and guiding revision (individual conferences, peer groups, etc.), the text does not include any specific revision apparatus.

Workability

Do these special features work? You can help us answer this question. Besides a formal experiment with matching control and experimental sections which is now under way, we are interested in your individual results and reactions. Whether you are an instructor or a student, please fill out the evaluation at the end of the book. Let us know whether **In Charge** gives students greater mastery of college reading and writing.

Jo An Simmons

* * *

I dedicate this book to

Jim Simmons--an excellent teacher, wise mentor, and superb husband

J.S.

TABLE OF CONTENTS

The chapters below also contain various preparations for and responses to the ideas in the readings and numerous writing practices leading up to a major writing assignment.

Chapter

5. **ETHNIC IDENTITY AND AMERICANIZATION**

Winners in their school's Reading Olympics, these two girls are receiving the reading encouragement which the writers of this chapter either missed and/or recommend. Norma Briceno and Celina Barber, who in the last school year read 67 and 56 books respectively, were also rewarded by their parents, Norma with a watch and Celina with a party. Principal Carmen Gardner, who awarded another 125 trophies at her inner city 66th Street School, Los Angeles, claims that this competition has helped raise test scores and self-esteem.

© Los Angeles Times

CHAPTER 1

READING FOR PLEASURE AND POWER

by

Lloyd Thomas

Contributors:

Marianne Boretz

James Frisby

Rose Najar

Jo An Simmons

OVERVIEW

The first three readings are excerpts from the autobiographies of three American writers—Richard Wright, Richard Rodriguez, and Eudora Welty. The pieces describe the role that reading played in their personal and academic lives. The fourth selection, by Dr. Stephen D. Krashen of USC, examines the relationship between students' reading and writing.

WHAT TO LOOK FOR

In the first three articles, read to see

- what difficulties, if any, these writers had with reading and how they overcame them
- why they read
- what impressed them about what they read
- the encouragement or lack of encouragement they received concerning their reading
- what effect reading had on the person they became
- what doors reading opened for each writer

In the fourth article, read to see what the relationship is between reading and skill in writing.

CHAPTER PLAN

"The Library Card," excerpt from **Black Boy,** by Richard Wright

Excerpt from **Hunger of Memory,** by Richard Rodriguez

"Learning to Listen," excerpt from **One Writer's Beginnings,** by Eudora Welty

"What is Known About Learning to Write," excerpt from **Writing: Research, Theory and Application,** by Stephen D. Krashen

Major Writing Assignments

"THE LIBRARY CARD"

Richard Wright

Born in Natchez, Mississippi, Richard Wright (1908-1960) spent his childhood moving throughout the South while his mother looked for work. After completing the ninth grade, Wright migrated to Memphis, then to Chicago, and finally to New York. He published his first book, **Uncle Tom's Children,** at the age of thirty and wrote his most famous novel, **Native Son,** two years later. These books made Wright the most prestigious black writer in the United States. Wright's autobiography, **Black Boy,** from which the following chapter is taken, appeared in 1945. The next year Wright moved to Paris, where he resided for the rest of his life. In "The Library Card" Wright explains how he devised a clever trick to gain access to library books.

One morning I arrived early at work and went into the bank lobby where the Negro porter was mopping. I stood at a counter and picked up the Memphis **Commercial Appeal** and began my free reading of the press. I came finally to the editorial page and there was an article dealing with one H. L. Mencken. I knew by hearsay that he was the editor of the **American Mercury,** but aside from that I knew nothing about him. The article was a furious denunciation of Mencken, concluding with one, hot, short sentence: Mencken is a fool.

I wondered what on earth this Mencken had done to call down upon him the scorn of the South. The only people I had ever heard denounced in the South were Negroes, and this man was not a Negro. Then what ideas did Mencken hold that made a newspaper like the **Commercial Appeal** castigate him publicly? Undoubtedly he must be advocating ideas that the South did not like. Were there, then, people other than Negroes who criticized the South? I knew that during the Civil War the South had hated northern whites, but I had not encountered such hate during my life. Knowing no more of Mencken than I did at that moment, I felt a vague sympathy for him. Had not the South, which had assigned me the role of a non-man, cast at him its hardest words?

Chapter XIII from BLACK BOY: A Record of Childhood and Youth by Richard Wright. Copyright 1937, 1942, 1944, 1945, by Richard Wright. Reprinted by permission of Harper & Row, Publishers, Inc.

Now, how could I find out about this Mencken? There was a huge library near the riverfront, but I knew that Negroes were not allowed to patronize its shelves any more than they were the parks and playgrounds of the city. I had gone into the library several times to get books for the white men on the job. Which of them would now help me to get books? And how could I read them without causing concern to the white men with whom I worked? I had so far been successful in hiding my thoughts and feelings from them, but I knew that I would create hostility if I went about this business of reading in a clumsy way.

I weighed the personalities of the men on the job. There was Don, a Jew; but I distrusted him. His position was not much better than mine and I knew that he was uneasy and insecure; he had always treated me in an offhand, bantering way that barely concealed his contempt. I was afraid to ask him to help me to get books; his frantic desire to demonstrate a racial solidarity with the whites against Negroes might make him betray me.

Then how about the boss? No, he was a Baptist and I had the suspicion that he would not be quite able to comprehend why a black boy would want to read Mencken. There were other white men on the job whose attitudes showed clearly that they were Kluxers or sympathizers and they were out of the question.

There remained only one man whose attitude did not fit into an anti-Negro category, for I had heard the white men refer to him as a "Pope lover." He was an Irish Catholic and was hated by the white Southerners. I knew that he read books, because I had got him volumes from the library several times. Since he, too, was an object of hatred, I felt that he might refuse me but would hardly betray me. I hesitated, weighing and balancing the imponderable realities.

One morning I paused before the Catholic fellow's desk.

"I want to ask you a favor," I whispered to him.

"What is it?"

"I want to read. I can't get books from the library. I wonder if you'd let me use your card?"

He looked at me suspiciously.

"My card is full most of the time," he said.

"I see," I said and waited, posing my question silently.

"You're not trying to get me into trouble, are you, boy?" he asked, staring at me.

"Oh, no, sir."

"What book do you want?"

"A book by H. L. Mencken."

"Which one?"

"I don't know. Has he written more than one?"

"He has written several."

"I didn't know that."

"What makes you want to read Mencken?"

"Oh, I just saw his name in the newspaper," I said.

"It's good of you to want to read," he said. "But you ought to read the right things."

I said nothing. Would he want to supervise my reading?

"Let me think," he said. "I'll figure out something."

I turned from him and he called me back. He stared at me quizzically.

"Richard, don't mention this to the other white men," he said.

"I understand," I said. "I won't say a word."

A few days later he called me to him.

"I've got a card in my wife's name," he said. "Here's mine."

"Thank you, sir."

"Do you think you can manage it?"

"I'll manage fine," I said.

"If they suspect you, you'll get in trouble," he said.

I'll write the same kind of notes to the library that you wrote when you sent me books," I told him. "I'll sign your name."

He laughed.

"Go ahead. Let me see what you get," he said.

That afternoon I addressed myself to forging a note. Now, what were the names of books written by H. L. Mencken? I did not know any of them. I finally wrote what I thought would be a foolproof note: **Dear Madam: Will you please let this nigger boy**--I used the word "nigger" to make the librarian feel that I could not possibly be the author of the note--**have some books by H. L. Mencken?** I forged the white man's name.

I entered the library as I had always done when on errands for whites, but I felt that I would somehow slip up and betray myself. I doffed my hat, stood a respectful distance from the desk, looked as unbookish as possible, and waited for the white patrons to be taken care of. When the desk was clear of people, I still waited. The white librarian looked at me.

"What do you want, boy?"

As though I did not possess the power of speech, I stepped forward and simply handed her the forged note, not parting my lips.

"What books by Mencken does he want?" she asked.

"I don't know, ma'am," I said, avoiding her eyes.

"Who gave you this card?"

"Mr. Falk," I said.

"Where is he?"

"He's at work, at M------ Optical Company," I said. "I've been in here for him before."

"I remember," the woman said. "But he never wrote notes like this."

Oh, God, she's suspicious. Perhaps she would not let me have the books? If she had turned her back at that moment, I would have ducked out the door and never gone back. Then I thought of a bold idea.

"You can call him up, ma'am," I said, my heart pounding.

"You're not using these books, are you?" she asked pointedly.

"Oh, no, ma'am. I can't read."

"I don't know what he wants by Mencken," she said under her breath.

I knew now that I had won; she was thinking of other things and the race question had gone out of her mind. She went to the shelves. Once or twice she looked over her shoulder at me, as though she was still doubtful. Finally she came forward with two books in her hand.

"I'm sending him two books," she said. "But tell Mr. Falk to come in next time, or send me the names of the books he wants. I don't know what he wants to read."

I said nothing. She stamped the card and handed me the books. Not daring to glance at them, I went out of the library, fearing that the woman would call me back for further questioning. A block away from the library I opened one of the books and read a title: **A Book of Prefaces.** I was nearing my nineteenth birthday and I did not know how to pronounce the word "preface." I thumbed the pages and saw strange words and strange names. I shook my head, disappointed. I looked at the other book; it was called **Prejudices.** I knew what that word meant; I had heard it all my life. And right off I was on guard against Mencken's books. Why would a man want to call a book **Prejudices**? The word was so stained with all my memories of racial hate that

I could not conceive of anybody using it for a title. Perhaps I had made a mistake about Mencken? A man who had prejudices must be wrong.

When I showed the books to Mr. Falk, he looked at me and frowned.

"That librarian might telephone you," I warned him.

"That's all right," he said. "But when you're through reading those books, I want you to tell me what you get out of them."

That night in my rented room, while letting the hot water run over my can of pork and beans in the sink, I opened **A Book of Prefaces** and began to read. I was jarred and shocked by the style, the clear, clean, sweeping sentences. Why did he write like that? And how did one write like that? I pictured the man as a raging demon, slashing with his pen, consumed with hate, denouncing everything American, extolling everything European or German, laughing at the weaknesses of people, mocking God, authority. What was this? I stood up, trying to realize what reality lay behind the meaning of the words...Yes, this man was fighting, fighting with words. He was using words as a weapon, using them as one would use a club. Could words be weapons? Well, yes, for here they were. Then, maybe, perhaps, I could use them as a weapon? No. It frightened me. I read on and what amazed me was not what he said, but how on earth anybody had the courage to say it.

Occasionally I glanced up to reassure myself that I was alone in the room. Who were these men about whom Mencken was talking so passionately? Who was Anatole France? Joseph Conrad? Sinclair Lewis, Sherwood Anderson, Dostoevski, George Moore, Gustave Flaubert, Maupassant, Tolstoy, Frank Harris, Mark Twain, Thomas Hardy, Arnold Bennett, Stephen Crane, Zola, Norris, Gorky, Bergson, Ibsen, Balzac, Bernard Shaw, Dumas, Poe, Thomas Mann, O. Henry, Dreiser, H. G. Wells, Gogol, T. S. Eliot, Gide, Baudelaire, Edgar Lee Masters, Stendhal, Turgenev, Huneker, Nietzsche, and scores of others? Were these men real? Did they exist or had they existed? And how did one pronounce their names?

I ran across many words whose meanings I did not know, and I either looked them up in a dictionary or, before I had a chance to do that, encountered the word in a context that made its meaning clear. But what strange world was this? I concluded the book with the conviction that I had somehow overlooked something terribly important in life. I had once tried to write, had once reveled in feeling, had let my crude imagination roam, but the impulse to dream had been slowly beaten out of me by experience. Now it surged up again and I hungered for books, new ways of looking and seeing. It was not a matter of believing or disbelieving what I read, but of feeling something new, of being affected by something that made the look of the world different.

As dawn broke I ate my pork and beans, feeling dopey, sleepy. I went to work, but the mood of the book would not die; it lingered, coloring everything I saw, heard, did. I now felt that I knew what the white men were feeling. Merely because I had read a book that had spoken of how they lived and thought, I identified myself with that book. I felt vaguely guilty. Would I, filled with bookish notions, act in a manner that would make the whites dislike me?

I forged more notes and my trips to the library became frequent. Reading grew into a passion. My first serious novel was Sinclair Lewis's **Main Street.** It made me see my boss, Mr. Gerald, and identify him as an American type. I would smile when I saw him lugging his golf bags into the office. I had always felt a vast distance separating me from the boss, and now I felt closer to him, though still distant. I felt now that I knew him, that I could feel the very limits of his narrow life and this had happened because I had read a novel about a mythical man called George F. Babbitt.

The plots and stories in the novels did not interest me so much as the point of view revealed. I gave myself over to each novel without reserve, without trying to criticize it; it was enough for me to see and feel something different. And for me, everything was something different. Reading was like a drug, a dope. The novels created moods in which I lived for days. But I could not conquer my sense of guilt, my feeling that the white men around me knew that I was changing, that I had begun to regard them differently.

Whenever I brought a book to the job, I wrapped it in newspaper—a habit that was to persist for years in other cities and under other circumstances. But some of the white men pried into my packages when I was absent and they questioned me.

"Boy, what are you reading those books for?"

"Oh, I don't know, sir."

"That's deep stuff you're reading, boy."

"I'm just killing time, sir."

"You'll addle your brains if you don't watch out."

I read Dreiser's **Jennie Gerhardt** and **Sister Carrie** and they revived in me a vivid sense of my mother's suffering; I was overwhelmed. I grew silent, wondering about the life around me. It would have been impossible for me to have told anyone what I derived from these novels, for it was nothing less than a sense of life itself. All my life had shaped me for the realism, the naturalism of the modern novel, and I could not read enough of them.

Steeped in new moods and ideas, I bought a ream of paper and tried to write; but nothing would come, or what did come was flat beyond telling. I discovered that more than desire and feeling were necessary to write and I dropped the idea. Yet I still wondered how it was possible to know people sufficiently to write about them? Could I ever learn about life and people? To me, with my vast ignorance, my Jim Crow station in life, it seemed a task impossible of achievement. I now knew what being a Negro meant. I could endure the hunger. I had learned to live with hate. But to feel that there were feelings denied me, that the very breath of life itself was beyond my reach, that more than anything else hurt, wounded me. I had a new hunger.

In buoying me up, reading also cast me down, made me see what was possible, what I had missed. My tension returned, new, terrible, bitter, surging, almost too great to be contained. I no longer felt that the world about me was hostile, killing, I knew it. A million times I asked myself what I could do to save myself, and there were no answers. I seemed forever condemned, ringed by walls.

I did not discuss my reading with Mr. Falk, who had lent me his library card; it would have meant talking about myself and that would have been too painful. I smiled each day, fighting desperately to maintain my old behavior, to keep my disposition seemingly sunny. But some of the white men discerned that I had begun to brood.

"Wake up there, boy!" Mr. Olin said one day.

"Sir!" I answered for lack of a better word.

"You act like you've stolen something," he said.

I laughed in the way I knew he expected me to laugh, but I resolved to be more conscious of myself, to watch my every act, to guard and hide the new knowledge that was dawning within me.

If I went north, would it be possible for me to build a new life then? But how could a man build a life upon vague, unformed yearnings? I wanted to write and I did not even know the English language. I bought English grammars and found them dull. I felt that I was getting a better sense of the language from novels than from grammars. I read hard, discarding a writer as soon as I felt that I had grasped his point of view. At night the printed page stood before my eyes in sleep.

Mrs. Moss, my landlady, asked me one Sunday morning:

"Son, what is this you keep on reading?"

"Oh, nothing. Just novels."

"What you get out of 'em?"

"I'm just killing time," I said.

"I hope you know your own mind," she said in a tone which implied that she doubted if I had a mind.

I knew of no Negroes who read the books I liked and I wondered if any Negroes ever thought of them. I knew that there were Negro doctors, lawyers, newspapermen, but I never saw any of them. When I read a Negro newspaper I never caught the faintest echo of my preoccupation in its pages. I felt trapped and occasionally, for a few days, I would stop reading. But a vague hunger would come over me for books, books that opened up new avenues of feeling and seeing, and again I would forge another note to the white librarian. Again I would read and wonder as only the naive and unlettered can read and wonder, feeling that I carried a secret, criminal burden about with me each day.

That winter my mother and brother came and we set up housekeeping, buying furniture on the installment plan, being cheated and yet knowing no way to avoid it. I began to eat warm food and to my surprise found that regular meals enabled me to read faster. I may have lived through many illnesses and survived them, never suspecting that I was ill. My brother obtained a job and we began to save toward the trip north, plotting our time, setting tentative dates for departure. I told none of the white men on the job that I was planning to go north; I knew that the moment they felt I was thinking of the North they would change toward me. It would have made them feel that I did not like the life I was living, and because my life was completely conditioned by what they said or did, it would have been tantamount to challenging them.

I could calculate my chances for life in the South as a Negro fairly clearly now.

I could fight the southern whites by organizing with other Negroes, as my grandfather had done. But I knew that I could never win that way; there were many whites and there were but few blacks. They were strong and we were weak. Outright black rebellion could never win. If I fought openly I would die and I did not want to die. News of lynchings were frequent.

I could submit and live the life of a genial slave, but that was impossible. All of my life had shaped me to live by my own feelings and thoughts. I could make up to Bess and marry her and inherit the house. But that, too, would be the life of a slave; if I did that, I would crush to death something within me, and I would hate myself as much as I knew the whites already hated those who had submitted. Neither could I ever willingly present myself to be kicked, as Shorty had done. I would rather have died than do that.

I could drain off my restlessness by fighting with Shorty and Harrison. I had seen many Negroes solve the problem of being black by transferring their hatred of themselves to others with a black skin and fighting them. I would have to be cold to do that, and I was not cold and I could never be.

I could, of course, forget what I had read, thrust the whites out of my mind, forget them; and find release from anxiety and longing in sex and alcohol. But the memory of how my father had conducted himself made that course repugnant. If I did not want others to violate my life, how could I voluntarily violate it myself?

I had no hope whatever of being a professional man. Not only had I been so conditioned that I did not desire it, but the fulfillment of such an ambition was beyond my capabilities. Well-to-do Negroes lived in a world that was almost as alien to me as the world inhabited by whites.

What, then, was there? I held my life in my mind, in my consciousness each day, feeling at times that I would stumble and drop it, spill it forever. My reading had created a vast sense of distance between me and the world in which I lived and tried to make a living, and that sense of distance was increasing each day. My days and nights were one long, quiet, continuously contained dream of terror, tension, and anxiety. I wondered how long I could bear it.

* * *

READING JOURNALS

In your college work (as in life generally) it is important to know what you really think and important to record your understanding of and reaction to what you are learning. Many professional writers (and ordinary people who write well) keep journals. These are informal private records of thoughts and experiences that the writer finds important. Perhaps you have kept journals for high school or other college courses. The journal you will write now is different. Here you should write about what you read. You can certainly write summaries of the reading or copy down the direct words of the author that you feel are important (if you do, be careful to use quotation marks in order to distinguish someone else's words from your own). But the most valuable way to use your journal is to find out what you yourself think about what you read. Is there wisdom here that you can apply to your own life? Have you experienced anything like the situation described? Do you know people or places like those being described? Have you heard these ideas before or are they radically different from yours? Asking yourself questions such as these and writing down your responses in a reading journal can improve your reading comprehension and add a great deal to your education.

When you write your journal, write to express your feelings and thoughts. Don't worry about the "mechanics" of English writing--spelling or punctuation or grammar. Write so you can explore your thoughts on paper and so that you can have a record of what you really think. Don't be surprised if you start out with one opinion and end up with something quite different.

Student Sample

Here is a sample student journal entry which may give you an idea of how to write in your own reading journal:

I admired Richard Wright for his curiosity about H. L. Mencken. If it wasn't for Mencken's book, Richard Wright might never have found his true inner feelings about himself and the life he led. The only life Richard Wright knew was to cater to the whites and stay on good terms with them. He learned long ago never to hope or express his true feelings. By reading books Richard Wright found out there was another side of life he never knew existed. By reading books he found out he was able to show his true feelings. Richard Wright knew he couldn't continue living the life he had, so he left the South, scared, but knowing there was a better life ahead for him.

From my own experience, I can relate to Richard Wright. He wasn't satisfied with the life he led, so he took a chance and headed to the North, not sure if he had made the right decision. I've given up working full time at a very secure and well-paid job to continue my education. It was a very big step for me, and like Wright, I'm not sure if it was the right decision, but I'm determined to succeed, and I know I'm going to reach my main goal in life.

QUESTIONS FOR DISCUSSION AND WRITING

The following questions can be used for class discussion, for individual or group writing assignments, and for entries in a reading journal. Follow your teacher's instructions.

1. Wright's encounter with Mencken's ideas and his further reading opened up a new world to him. What similar experience have you had?

2. What book has ever captured your imagination or been especially memorable to you?

3. In this story, Wright is impressed because Mencken uses "words as weapons." Can you give other examples of when words are used as weapons? In an argument? In the Declaration of Independence?

4. Wright wanted Mencken's books so badly that he was willing to endure the humiliating treatment of the librarian. Describe the sacrifices you have made to get something you wanted badly.

5. Wright's reading was the first step to a new and better life for him. As the biographical description on page 3 indicates, Wright eventually left the South for places of greater opportunity and reached his full potential as a successful writer.

   At the period of his life that we've just read about, however, reading brought him some pain and frustration. Through reading, he became aware to the full extent of the injustice against blacks and of the limited possibilities he had living in the South. Reading brought him a problem to solve and negative feelings to resolve.

Reading can sometimes be upsetting to the college students too.

- o Has new knowledge made you aware of painful problems or situations?
- o Have instructors or texts challenged ideas or values dear to you?
- o Do you ever feel as angry or frustrated as Wright did?

The good that comes out of this situation is growth. Whether we keep our original ideas or values, modify them, reformulate them on a more mature level, or reject them, we grow by examining them.

- o What experiences have you had along these lines and how have you handled them?

6. Describe what you admire (or object to) in Wright's story and relate it to an incident in your own life.

VOCABULARY

Richard Wright speaks of figuring out what new words mean by looking at their surrounding words and meanings, their context.

Look at the contexts of the following words from "The Library Card" and write down what you think they mean:

addle

hostile

discerned

naive

tentative

repugnant

MODEL SUMMARY

In "The Library Card" Richard Wright described his struggles to gain access to the inspiring and troubling world of books. As a Negro in the South, Wright was prevented from checking out library books himself. So he enlisted the help of another minority member, Mr. Falk, a Roman Catholic, who let Wright use his card in order to get books. In order to keep the librarian from getting suspicious, Wright forged a letter from Mr. Falk in which he refers to himself as a "nigger." Wright was willing to use this insulting, racist word in order to conceal his own role in the plot to get books out of the library.

Wright wanted to read certain books by H. L. Mencken because the Southern culture which oppressed Wright also hated Mencken. Wright saw Mencken as a potential ally in his struggle to grow intellectually and personally. When Wright finally did get a hold of Mencken's **Book of Prefaces,** he was led into the world of great writers like Sinclair Lewis, Theodore Dreiser, Joseph Conrad, Fyodor Dostoevski and others. Wright admired Mencken because he used "words as a weapon" and he enjoyed "fighting with words." Wright respected Mencken because he had found a way to fight back against an oppressive culture and free himself.

Wright read Lewis and Dreiser and many of the other writers; he also tried to write himself. His reading had a paradoxical effect on him. On the one hand, the fact that other people could write books showed Wright that it was possible to exist on a creative and personally satisfying level. On the other hand, because Wright sensed a great gap between his station in life and that of the writers, he felt depressed, and he doubted whether he would ever attain the position of a creative professional person.

ACQUIRING STYLE THROUGH CREATIVE IMITATION

From the schoolboys of ancient Greece and Rome to modern writers like Dylan Thomas and Alex Haley, people have found that imitating a model passage has been a shortcut to good writing style. This kind of imitation, different from mere copying, can be creative whether you follow the model closely or loosely.

Original Passage

That night in my rented room, while letting the hot water run over my can of pork and beans in the sink, I opened **A Book of Prefaces** and began to read. I was jarred and shocked by the style, the clear, clean, sweeping sentences. Why did he write like that? And how did one write like that? I pictured the man as a raging demon, slashing with his pen, consumed with hate, denouncing everything American, extolling everything European or German, laughing at the weaknesses of people, mocking God, authority. What was this? I stood up, trying to realize what reality lay behind the meaning of the words...Yes, this man was fighting, fighting with words. He was using words as a weapon, using them as one would use a club. Could words be weapons? Well, yes, for here they were. Then, maybe, perhaps, I could use them as a weapon? No. It frightened me. I read on and what amazed me was not what he said, but how on earth anybody had the courage to say it. (p. 4)

Imitation

That evening in the dimly lit garage, while sipping a lukewarm cup of coffee, I watched my brother work on my VW engine. I was impressed and amazed by the quickness and sureness of his hands. Could I ever handle a socket wrench like that? How could he remove the air filter so quickly? I saw my brother as a surgeon with car tools, unfastening bolts, adjusting fan belts, consumed with a desire to save the aging engine, hating grease and grime, admiring clean spark plugs, exposing faulty wiring everywhere he found it. He saved that engine's life. I leaned over the motor, imagining that I was an assistant surgeon, trying to appreciate the years of experience which lay behind my brother's confidence with car engines...Yes, he was doing open-engine surgery on that engine, open-heart surgery with a wrench and a greasy shop rag. Could an engine be just like a human heart? Well, yes, for that motor was just as clogged up as many hearts.

Your Imitation

Look at the original passage and the imitation above. Then write your own imitation of the Wright passage on your own paper. Keep the form the same but change the subject matter just as Lloyd Thomas has done in his imitation.

PROBLEM-SOLVING: EXAMINING ALTERNATE POSSIBILITIES

Richard Wright takes us into his thinking as he examines possible solutions to problems:

Problem: Which of the white men available to him would most likely help him obtain library books?

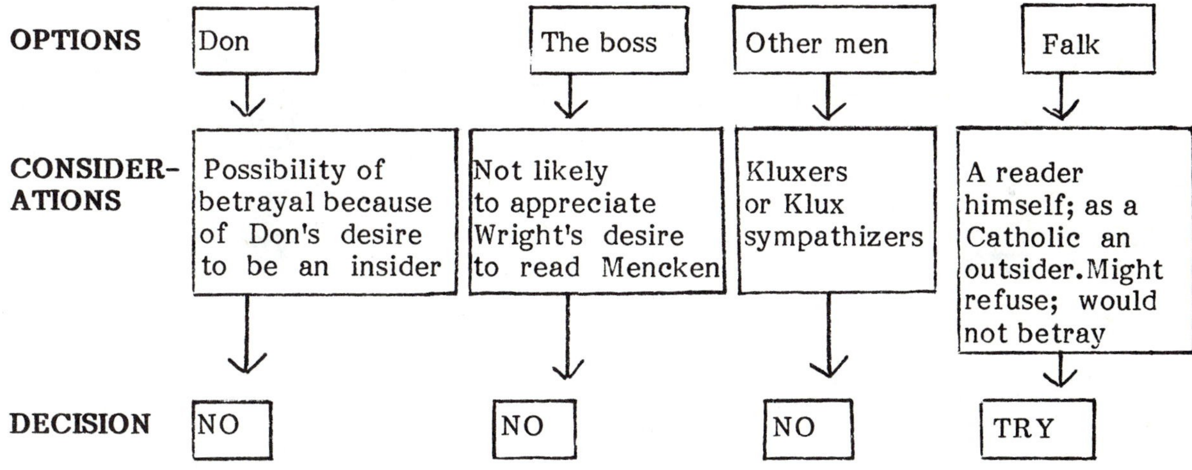

Fill in the boxes of the partial graphic organizer below. Put in the three types of submission and coping that he considers.

Problem: Now that reading has made Wright aware of the restricted life possible for him in the South, he must decide how to handle his anger and his options.

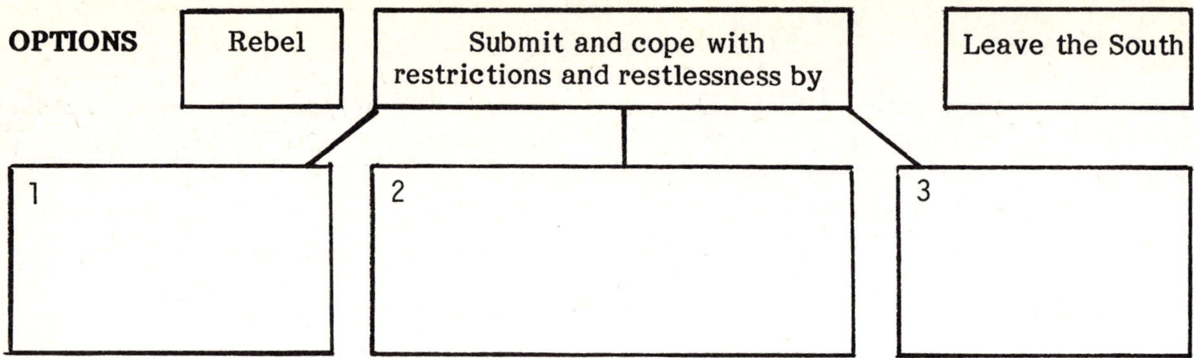

Write a paragraph reconstructing your own thinking in solving a problem. Fill in the graphic organizer below, adding boxes as needed.

Perhaps you had to decide whether or not to speak to your supervisor about a problem at work (an unrealistic workload, an uncooperative employee, etc.). Use the graphic organizer to make your decision.

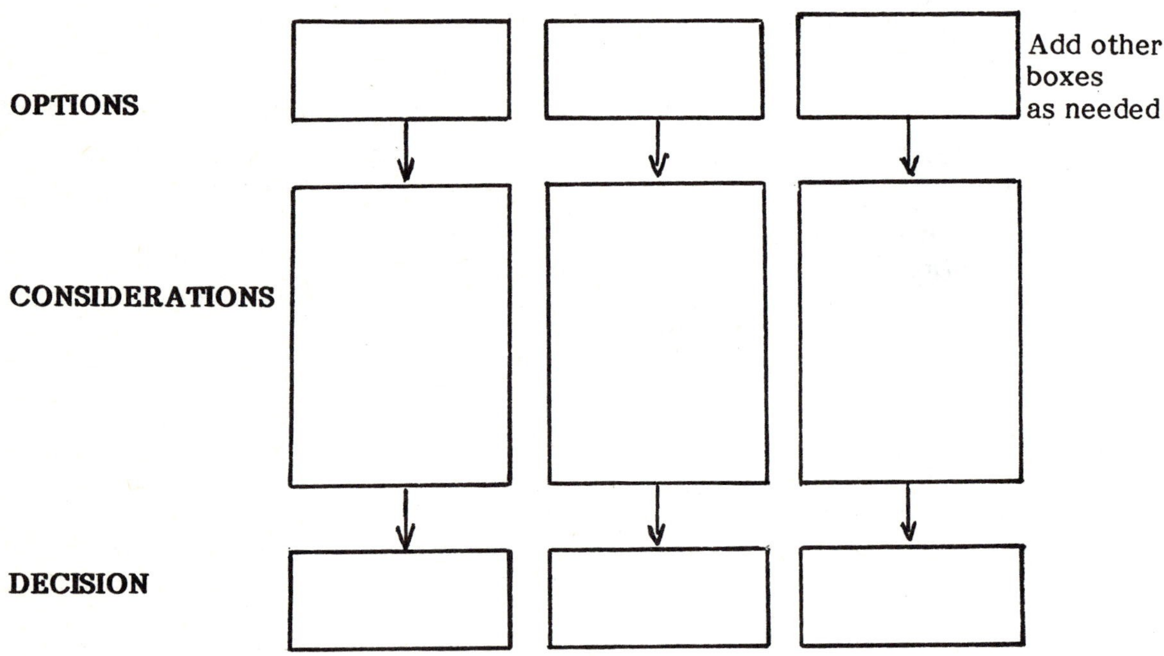

You could use a similar technique to decide problems such as whether to take an additional class next semester, whether to take a vacation in Hawaii next summer, or whether to apply for a new car loan.

We all do this kind of thinking informally: the process of elimination leads us to our best options. In your other classes you will recognize this examination of possiblities in its more formal dress of "analysis." One example is the elimination of possible causes or substances in a laboratory experiment.

SENTENCE-COMBINING EXERCISE FOR WRIGHT'S "THE LIBRARY CARD"

Each of these short sentences summarizes important ideas in the Wright story. By combining them into longer sentences, you can compose the opening paragraph of a critical response to the story.

1. Wright wants to read books by Mencken.
   He can't get books from the library by himself.
   Blacks aren't allowed to check books out of the library.

2. Wright doesn't trust many people.
   He asks Mr. Falk for help.
   Falk is a Roman Catholic.

3. Wright has to forge a letter to get the books he wants.
   He tricks the librarian.

4. Wright says Mencken uses words like weapons.
   He fights with words.
   Wright would like to fight against his oppressive Southern culture.

5. Wright admires Mencken.
   Wright respects Mencken.
   Wright wants to imitate Mencken.

6. Wright is dissatisfied.
   He feels depressed.
   His world isn't like the world he reads about in books.
   He decides to go north.

IMITATION OF INTRODUCTORY PARTICIPIAL PHRASES

Add your own imitations to each of the three original sentences written by Wright.

1. Knowing no more of Mencken than I did at that moment, I felt a vague sympathy for him.

   Inhaling the tantalizing aromas from the kitchen, I felt a great respect for the cook.

2. In buoying me up, reading also cast me down, made me see what was possible, what I had missed.

   In inspiring me, the lecture also discouraged me, made me see what I was supposed to learn, what I had failed to grasp.

3. Steeped in new moods and ideas, I bought a ream of paper and tried to write, but nothing would come, or what did come was flat beyond telling.

   Armed with skill and knowledge, I tried to get a job, but nothing was available or what was available was menial beyond description.

IMITATION OF PARALLEL GRAMMATICAL UNITS

Add your own imitations, paying special attention to the underlined parallel constructions.

1. I doffed my hat, stood a respectful distance from the desk, looked as unbookish as possible, and waited for the white patrons to be taken care of.

   I looked at the exam question, uncapped my pen, carefully jotted down a brief outline, and then wrote the best composition of my life.

2. I pictured the man as a raging demon, slashing with his pen, consumed with hate, denouncing everything American, extolling everything European or German, laughing at the weaknesses of people, mocking God, authority.

   I pictured Abraham Lincoln as a moral giant, protecting the union, denouncing slavery, praising all who wished to be free and independent, mocking those who lived off the work of slaves.

3. That winter my mother and brother came and we set up housekeeping, buying furniture on the installment plan, being cheated and yet knowing no way to avoid it.

   That spring, my wife and I set up housekeeping, buying furniture at Sears, going into debt and yet knowing no way to avoid it.

4. I smiled each day, fighting desperately to maintain my old behavior, to keep my disposition seemingly sunny.

   I practiced soccer each day, trying wholeheartedly to win a position on the team, to keep my self-respect.

Excerpt from

A HUNGER OF MEMORY

Richard Rodriguez

Richard Rodriguez was raised in Sacramento, the son of working-class Mexican immigrant parents. In two decades he journeyed from a mostly Spanish environment to being a highly prized "minority student," writing his dissertation on English Renaissance literature in the reading room of the British Museum. **A Hunger of Memory** is the story of this educational journey—an intellectual autobiography of a scholarship boy. It describes the "troubling passage from the intimate Spanish of the family to the 'public' English of schools and universities and the consequences of that transforming displacement."

From an early age I knew that my mother and father could read and write both Spanish and English. I had observed my father making his way through what, I now suppose, must have been income tax forms. On other occasions I waited apprehensively while my mother read onion-paper letters air-mailed from Mexico with news of a relative's illness or death. For both my parents, however, reading was something done out of necessity and as quickly as possible. Never did I see either of them read an entire book. Nor did I see them read for pleasure. Their reading consisted of work manuals, prayer books, newspapers, recipes. . . .

In our house, each school year would begin with my mother's careful instruction: "Don't write in your books so we can sell them at the end of the year." The remark was echoed in public by my teachers, but only in part: "Boys and girls, don't write in your books. You must learn to treat them with great care and respect."

OPEN THE DOORS OF YOUR MIND WITH BOOKS, read the red and white poster over the nun's desk in early September. It soon was apparent to me that reading was the classroom's central activity. Each course had its own book. And the information gathered from a book was unquestioned. READ TO LEARN , the sign on the wall advised in December. I privately wondered: What was the connection

---

Reprinted from Hunger of Memory by Richard Rodriguez, copyright (c) 1981 by Richard Rodriguez. Reprinted by permission of David R. Godine, Publisher, Boston.

between reading and learning? Did one learn something only by reading it? Was an idea only an idea if it could be written down? In June, CONSIDER BOOKS YOUR BEST FRIENDS. Friends? Reading was, at best, only a chore. I needed to look up whole paragraphs of words in a dictionary. Lines of type were dizzying, the eye having to move slowly across the page, then down, and across. . . . The sentences of the first books I read were coolly impersonal. Toned hard. What most bothered me, however, was the isolation reading required. To console myself for the loneliness I'd feel when I read, I tried reading in a very soft voice. Until: "Who is doing all that talking to his neighbor?" Shortly after, remedial reading classes were arranged for me with a very old nun.

At the end of each school day, for nearly six months, I would meet with her in the tiny room that served as the school's library but was actually only a storeroom for used textbooks and a vast collection of **National Geographics**. Everything about our sessions pleased me: the smallness of the room; the noise of the janitor's broom hitting the edge of the long hallway outside the door; the green of the sun, lighting the wall; and the old woman's face blurred white with a beard. Most of the time we took turns. I began with my elementary text. Sentences of astonishing simplicity seemed to me lifeless and drab: "The boys ran from the rain . . . She wanted to sing. . . The kite rose in the blue." Then the old nun would read from her favorite books, usually biographies of early American presidents. Playfully she ran through complex sentences, calling the words alive with her voice, making it seem that the author somehow was speaking directly to me. I smiled just to listen to her. I sat there and sensed for the very first time some possiblity of fellowship between a reader and a writer, a communication, never **intimate** like that I heard spoken words at home convey, but one nonetheless **personal.**

One day the nun concluded a session by asking me why I was so reluctant to read by myself. I tried to explain; said something about the way written words made me feel all alone--almost, I wanted to add but didn't, as when I spoke to myself in a room just emptied of furniture. She studied my face as I spoke; she seemed to be watching more than listening. In an uneventful voice she replied that I had nothing to fear. Didn't I realize that reading would open up whole new worlds? A book could open doors for me. It could introduce me to people and show me places I never imagined existed. She gestured toward the bookshelves. (Bare-breasted African women danced, and the shiny hubcaps of automobiles on the back covers of **Geographic** gleamed in my mind.) I listened with respect. But her words were not very influential. I was thinking then of another consequence of literacy, one I was too shy to admit but nonetheless trusted. Books were going to make me "educated." **That** confidence enabled me, several months later, to overcome my fear of the silence.

In fourth grade I embarked upon a grandiose reading program. "Give me the names of important books," I would say to startled teachers. They soon found out that I had in mind "adult books." I ignored their suggestion of anything I suspected was written for children. (Not until I was in college, as a result, did I read **Huckleberry Finn** or **Alice's Adventures in Wonderland.**) Instead, I read the **The Scarlet Letter** and Franklin's **Autobiography.** And whatever I read I read for extra credit. Each time I finished a book, I reported the achievement to a teacher and basked in the praise my effort earned. Despite my best efforts, however, there seemed to be more and more books I needed to read. At the library I would literally tremble as I came upon whole shelves of books I hadn't read. So I read and I read and I read: **Great Expectations;** all the short stories of Kipling; **The Babe Ruth Story;** the entire first volume of the **Encyclopaedia Britannica** (A-ANSTEY); the **Iliad; Moby Dick; Gone with the Wind; The Good Earth; Ramona; Forever Amber; The Lives of the Saints; Crime and Punishment; The Pearl.** . . . Librarians who initially frowned when I checked out the maximum ten books at a time started saving books they thought I might like. Teachers would say to the rest of the class, "I only wish the rest of you took reading as seriously as Richard obviously does."

But at home I would hear my mother wondering, "What do you see in your books?" (Was reading a hobby like her knitting? Was so much reading even healthy for a boy? Was it the sign of "brains"? Or was it just a convenient excuse for not helping around the house on Saturday mornings?) Always, "What do you see . . . ?"

What **did** I see in my books? I had the idea that they were crucial for my academic success, though I couldn't have said exactly how or why. In the sixth grade I simply concluded that what gave a book its value was some major idea or theme it contained. If that core essence could be mined and memorized, I would become learned like my teachers. I decided to record in a notebook the themes of the books that I read. After reading **Robinson Crusoe,** I wrote that its theme was "the value of learning to live by oneself." When I completed **Wuthering Heights,** I noted the danger of "letting emotions get out of control." Re-reading these brief moralistic appraisals usually left me disheartened. I couldn't believe that they were really the source of reading's value. But for many more years, they constituted the only means I had of describing to myself the educational value of books.

In spite of my earnestness, I found reading a pleasurable activity. I came to enjoy the lonely good company of books. Early on weekday mornings, I'd read in my bed. I'd feel a mysterious comfort then, reading in the dawn quiet—the blue-gray silence interrupted by the occasional churning of the refrigerator motor a few rooms away or the more distant sounds of a city bus beginning its run. On weekends I'd go the public library to read, surrounded by old men and women. Or, if the weather was fine, I would take my books to the park and read in the shade of a tree. A warm summer evening was my favorite reading time. Neighbors would leave for vacation and I would water their lawns. I would sit through the twilight on the front porches or in backyards, reading to the cool, whirling sounds of the sprinklers.

I also had favorite writers. But often those writers I enjoyed most I was least able to value. When I read William Saroyan's **The Human Comedy**, I was immediately pleased by the narrator's warmth and the charm of his story. But as quickly, I became suspicious. A book so enjoyable to read couldn't be very "important." Another summer I determined to read all the novels of Dickens. Reading his fat novels, I loved the feeling I got—after the first hundred pages—of being at home in a fictional world where I knew the names of the characters and cared about what was going to happen to them. And it bothered me that I was forced away at the conclusion, when the fiction closed tight, like a fortune-teller's fist—the futures of all the major characters neatly resolved. I never knew how to take such feelings seriously, however. Nor did I suspect that these experiences could be part of a novel's meaning. Still, there were pleasures to sustain me after I'd finish my books. Carrying a volume back to the library, I would be pleased by its weight. I'd run my fingers along the edge of the pages and marvel at the breadth of my achievement. Around my room, growing stacks of paperback books reenforced my assurance.

I entered high school having read hundreds of books. My habit of reading made me a confident speaker and writer of English. Reading also enabled me to sense something of the shape, the major concerns of Western thought. (I was able to say something about Dante and Descartes and Engels and James Baldwin in my high school term papers.) In these various ways, books brought me academic success as I hoped that they would. But I was not a good reader. Merely bookish, I lacked a point of view when I read. Rather, I read in order to acquire a point of view. I vacuumed books for epigrams, scraps of information, ideas, themes—anything to fill the hollow within me and make me feel educated. When one of my teachers suggested to his drowsy tenth-grade English class that a person could not have a "complicated idea" until he had read at least two thousand books, I heard the remark without detecting either its irony or its very complicated truth. I merely determined to compile a list of all the books I had ever read. Harsh with myself, I included only those books over a hundred pages in length. (Could anything shorter be a book?)

There was yet another high school list I compiled. One day I came across a newspaper article about the retirement of an English professor at a nearby state college. The article was accompanied by a list of the "hundred most important books of Western Civilization." "More than anything else in my life," the professor told the reporter with finality, "these books have made me all that I am." That was the kind of remark I couldn't ignore. I clipped out the list and kept if for the several months it took me to read all of the titles. Most books, of course, I barely understood. While reading Plato's **Republic,** for instance, I needed to keep looking at the book jacket comments to remind myself what the text was about. Nevertheless, with the special patience and superstition of a scholarship boy, I looked at every word of the text. And by the time I reached the last word, relieved, I convinced myself that I had read **The Republic.** In a ceremony of great pride, I solemnly crossed Plato off my list.

* * *

ACQUIRING STYLE THROUGH CREATIVE IMITATION

Original Passage

From an early age I knew that my mother and father could read and write both Spanish and English. I had observed my father making his way through what, I now suppose, must have been income tax forms. On other occasions I waited apprehensively while my mother read onion-paper letters air-mailed from Mexico with news of a relative's illness or death. For both my parents, however, reading was something done out of necessity and as quickly as possible. Never did I see either of them read an entire book. Nor did I see them read for pleasure. Their reading consisted of work manuals, prayer books, newspapers, recipes.

Imitation of Rodriguez's Opening Paragraph

From an early age I knew that my brother made his living playing basketball. I had observed him practicing what, I now suppose, must have been free-throws. On other occasions, I stared respectfully while my brother practiced jump-shots. For my brother, however, practicing basketball was something done out of necessity. He was a professional.

Now write your own imitation in the space provided

QUESTIONS FOR DISCUSSION AND WRITING

The following questions can be used for class discussion, for individual or group writing assignments, and for entries in a reading journal. Follow your teacher's instructions.

1. Describe the ways in which Rodriguez's parents either encourage or discourage his love of reading.

2. Give at least two examples of how Rodriguez's teachers influence him.

3. Do you believe Rodriguez really enjoys all the books he reads? Which books does he specifically say that he enjoyed reading? Which books does he confess he didn't understand at all?

4. Explain the last two sentences "And by the time I reached the last word, relieved, I convinced myself that I had read The Republic. In a ceremony of great pride, I solemnly crossed Plato off my list."

VOCABULARY

Richard Rodriguez tells of how he had to look up whole paragraphs of words in the dictionary.

1. Look up "bookish." In what sense is "bookish" a negative word?

2. Look up "epigrams." If Rodriguez vacuumed his books for epigrams, was he getting the big picture or central meaning of the reading?

3. Look up "irony." Did Rodriguez's teacher really mean that his students ought to go out and read 2,000 books?

4. Look up "paradox." Rodriguez writes of "the lonely good company of books." How would you explain the paradox that reading can be lonely but books can, at the same time, be good company?

SENTENCE-COMBINING SUMMARY

By combining the short sentences below which are grouped by braces, you will develop a summary of Rodriguez's article. (You don't have to do anything with sentences 2, 6, 8, 13, 15 and 17.) After you are satisfied with your combinations, write sentences 1-18 in paragraph form.

1. { Rodriguez's parents are bilingual.
   They do not read books for pleasure.

2. This attitude influences him at first.

3. Rodriguez doesn't enjoy reading.
He has to look up words in the dictionary.

4. He feels reading is a "chore."
Reading makes him feel "lonely."

5. Finally, he meets an interested teacher.

She makes Rodriguez aware of the "possiblity of fellowship between a reader and a writer."

She helps Rodriguez realize that reading "would open up whole new worlds."

6. This idea excites the young student.

7. Rodriguez tries to read lots of famous books.
He reads Dickens, Kipling, Twain, Melville, and Homer.
Rodriguez starts a "grandiose reading program."

8. Unfortunately, he still doesn't get any real pleasure from reading.

9. He reads books trying to discover their themes.
He reads books for their moral value.

10. His parents don't understand why he reads so many books.
Rodriguez isn't exactly sure what he sees in books.

11. He reads all the time.
He loves reading.
Books are still mysterious to him.

12. He doesn't see how books can be "enjoyable" and "important" at the same time.
He feels that books which he has fun reading can't really be that important.

13. In high school, he reads even more books.

14. His tenth-grade teacher says a person needs to read at least two thousand books before he can have "a complicated thought."
His English teacher speaks half jokingly.
Rodriguez reads with grim determination.

15. In a way his reading program was ill-conceived.

16. He read out of a sense of duty.
He didn't understand his teacher completely.

17. However, there were benefits.

18. He got pleasure from his reading.
Reading helped him learn to write.
Reading helped him become a better student.

IMITATION OF INTRODUCTORY PHRASES

By studying and imitating the following grammatical and syntactical patterns, you will increase the fluency and style of your own writing. Write your own imitations as directed by your teacher.

Introductory phrases which act as transitions:

From an early age I knew that my mother and father could read and write both Spanish and English.

From an early age I dreamed of traveling to Europe.

On other occasions I waited apprehensively while my mother read onion-paper letters airmailed from Mexico.

On other occasions I read magazines in the library.

In spite of my earnestness, I found reading a pleasurable activity.

In spite of my nervousness, I found giving a speech a pleasure.

REPETITION AND PARALLELISM

Never did I see either of them read an entire book. Nor did I see them read for pleasure.

Never did I see my brother open a textbook. Nor did I see him receive a diploma.

I never knew how to take such feelings seriously, however. Nor did I suspect that these experiences could be part of a novel's meaning.

I never knew how much work a term paper involved. Nor did I suspect how proud I would be of my finished paper.

APOSTROPHES

The apostrophe may be used to show possession (The car of Henry may be shortened to read: Henry's car).

The apostrophe may be used to show the contraction of two words: can not—can't, it is—it's, should not—shouldn't.

Possessive pronouns don't take apostrophes:
My, our, his, her, their, whose, its, your, mine, ours, hers, theirs, yours.

Practice

Change the following words from Richard Rodriguez's Hunger of Memory:

- **from contractions to complete words OR**
- **from showing possession with an apostrophe to showing possession with a phrase and vice versa OR**
- **explain why no change is needed.**

1. a relative's illness
2. they do not
3. the nun's desk
4. the classroom's central activity
5. its own book
6. I'd feel
7. who is
8. the old woman's face
9. didn't
10. hadn't
11. its value
12. the themes of the books
13. its theme
14. reading's value
15. I'd
16. the more distant sound of a city bus
17. I would set
18. a fortune-teller's fist
19. novel's meaning
20. I'd

"LEARNING TO LISTEN"

Excerpt from

ONE WRITER'S BEGINNINGS

Eudora Welty

Eudora Alice Welty was born on April 13, 1909, in Jackson, Mississippi, the daughter of Christian, an insurance company executive, and Chestina Welty. She attended Mississippi State College for Women from 1926-1927 and received a B.A. from the University of Wisconsin in 1929. She attended Columbia University School of Advertising from 1930 to 1931. During the early years of the Depression, she worked on newspapers and radio stations in Mississippi, then as a publicity agent for the state office of the WPA (Works Progress Administration).

Her first published book was **A Curtain of Green**, a collection of short stories, in 1941. Welty's awards and honors include the Pulitzer Prize, the O. Henry Award, the Gold Medal for the Novel from the Academy and Institute of Arts and Letters, and a National Book Award nomination.

Eudora Welty is the author of 22 books; she still lives in Jackson, in her father's house on Pinehurst Street, which was built in 1925.

I learned from the age of two or three that any room in our house, at any time of day, was there to read in, or to be read to. My mother read to me. She'd read to me in the big bedroom in the mornings, when we were in her rocker together, which ticked in rhythm as we rocked, as though we had a cricket accompanying the story. She'd read to me in the diningroom on winter afternoons in front of the coal fire, with our cuckoo clock ending the story with "Cuckoo," and at night when I'd got in my own bed. I must have given her no peace. Sometimes she read to me in the kitchen while she sat churning, and the churning sobbed along with **any** story. It was my ambition to have her read to me while **I** churned: once she granted my wish, but she read off my story before I brought her butter. She was an expressive reader. When she was reading "Puss in Boots," for instance, it was impossible not to know that she distrusted **all** cats.

Excerpt from One Writer's Beginnings by Eudora Welty. Copyright (c) 1983, 1984 by Eudora Welty. Reprinted by permission of Harvard University Press.

It had been startling and disappointing to me to find out that story books had been written by people, that books were not natural wonders, coming up of themselves like grass. Yet regardless of where they came from, I cannot remember a time when I was not in love with them—with the books themselves, cover and binding and the paper they were printed on, with their smell and their weight and with their possession in my arms, captured and carried off to myself. Still illiterate, I was ready for them, committed to all the reading I could give them.

Neither of my parents had come from homes that could afford to buy many books, but though it must have been something of a strain on his salary, as the youngest officer in a young insurance company, my father was all the while carefully selecting and ordering away for what he and Mother thought we children should grow up with. They brought first for the future .

Besides the bookcase in the livingroom, which was always called "the library," there were the encyclopedia tables and dictionary stand under windows in our diningroom. Here to help us grow up arguing around the diningroom table were the **Unabridged Webster**, the **Columbia Encyclopedia, Compton's Pictured Encyclopedia,** the **Lincoln Library of Information,** and later the **Book of Knowledge.** And the year we moved into our new house, there was room to celebrate it with the new 1925 edition of the **Britannica,** which my father, his face always deliberately turned toward the future, was of course disposed to think better than any previous edition.

In "the library," inside the mission-style bookcase with its three diamond-latticed glass doors, with my father's Morris chair and the glass-shaded lamp on its table beside it, were books I could soon begin on—and I did, reading them all alike and as they came, straight down their rows, top shelf to bottom. . .

To both my parents I owe my early acquaintance with a beloved Mark Twain. There was a full set of Mark Twain and a short set of Ring Lardner in our bookcase, and those were the volumes that in time united us all, parents and children . . .

I was presented, from as early as I can remember, with books of my own, which appeared on my birthday and Christmas morning. Indeed, my parents could not give me books enough. They must have sacrificed to give me on my sixth or seventh birthday—it was after I became a reader for myself—the ten-volume set of **Our Wonder World.** These were beautifully made, heavy books I would lie down with on the floor in front of the diningroom hearth, and more often than the rest, volume 5, **Every Child's Story Book,** was under my eyes. There were the fairy tales—Grimm, Andersen, the English, the French, "Ali Baba and the Forty Thieves"; and there were

Aesop and Reynard the Fox; there were the myths and legends, Robin Hood, King Arthur, and St. George and the Dragon, even the history of Joan of Arc; a whack of **Pilgrim's Progress** and a long piece of **Gulliver.** They all carried their classic illustrations. I located myself in these pages and could go straight to the stories and pictures I loved. . .

I believe I'm the only child I know of who grew up with this treasure in the house. I used to ask others, "Did you have **Our Wonder World**?" I'd have to tell them **The Book of Knowledge** could not hold a candle to it.

I live in gratitude to my parents for initiating me—and as early as I begged for it, without keeping me waiting—into knowledge of the word, into reading and spelling, by way of the alphabet. They taught it to me at home in time for me to begin to read before starting to school. I believe the alphabet is no longer considered an essential piece of equipment for traveling through life. In my day it was the keystone to knowledge. You learned the alphabet as you learned to count to ten, as you learned "Now I lay me" and the Lord's Prayer and your father's and mother's name and address and telephone number, all in case you were lost. . .

Ever since I was first read to, then started reading to myself, there has never been a line read that I didn't **hear.** As my eyes followed the sentence, a voice was saying it silently to me. It isn't my mother's voice, or the voice of any person I can identify, certainly not my own. It is human, but inward, and it is inwardly that I listen to it. It is to me the voice of the story or the poem itself. The cadence, whatever it is that asks you to believe, the feeling that resides in the printed word, reaches me through the reader-voice. I have supposed, but never found out, that this is the case with all readers—to read as listeners—and with all writers, to write as listeners. It may be part of the desire to write. The sound of what falls on the page begins the process of testing it for truth, for me. Whether I am right to trust so far I don't know. By now I don't know whether I could do either one, reading or writing, without the other.

My own words, when I am at work on a story, I hear too as they go, in the same voice that I hear when I read in books. When I write and the sound of it comes back to my ears, then I act to make my changes. I have always trusted this voice . . .

Long before I wrote stories, I listened for stories. Listening for them is something more acute than listening _to_ them. I suppose it's an early form of participation in what goes on. Listening children know stories are there. When their elders sit and begin, children are just waiting and hoping for one to come out, like a mouse from its hole . . .

When I was five years old, I knew the alphabet, I'd been vaccinated (for smallpox), and I could read. So my mother walked across the street to Jefferson Davis Grammar School and asked the principal if she would allow me to enter the first grade after Christmas.

"Oh, all right," said Miss Duling. "Probably the best thing you could do with her."

Miss Duling, a lifelong subscriber to perfection, was a figure of authority, the most whole-souled I have ever come to know. She was a dedicated schoolteacher who denied herself all she might have done or whatever other way she might have lived (this possibility was the last that could have occurred to us, her subjects in school). I believe she came of well-off people, well-educated, in Kentucky, and certainly old photographs show she was a beautiful, high-spirited-looking young lady --and came down to Jackson to its new grammar school that was going begging for a principal. She must have earned next to nothing: Mississippi then as now was the nation's lowest-ranking state economically, and our legislature has always shown a painfully loud reluctance to give money to public education. That challenge brought her.

In the long run she came into touch, as teacher or principal, with three generations of Jacksonians. My parents had not, but everybody else's parents had gone to school to her. She'd taught most of our leaders somewhere along the line. When she wanted something done—some civic oversight corrected, some injustice made right overnight, or even a tree spared that the fool telephone people were about to cut down—she telephoned the mayor, or the chief of police, or the president of the power company, or the head doctor at the hospital, or the judge in charge of a case, or whoever, and calling them by their first names, told them. It is impossible to imagine her meeting with anything less than compliance. The ringing of her brass bell from their days at Davis School would still be in their ears. She also proposed a spelling match between the fourth grade at Davis School and the Mississippi Legislature, who went through with it: and that told the Legislature . . .

Jackson's Carnegie Library was on the same street where our house was, on the other side of the State Capitol. "Through the Capitol" was the way to go to the Library. You could glide through it on your bicycle or even coast through on roller skates, though without family permission.

I never knew anyone who'd grown up in Jackson without being afraid of Mrs. Calloway, our librarian. She ran the Library absolutely by herself, from the desk where she sat with her back to the books and facing the stairs, her dragon eye on the front door, where who knew what kind of person might come in from the public? SILENCE in big black letters was on signs tacked up everywhere. She herself spoke in her normally commanding voice; every word could be heard all over the Library above a steady seething sound coming from her electric fan: it was the only fan in the Library and stood on her desk, turning directly onto her streaming face.

As you came in from the bright outside, if you were a girl, she sent her strong eyes down the stairway to test you: If she could see through your skirt she sent you straight back home: you could just put on another petticoat if you wanted a book that badly from the public library. I was willing; I would do anything to read.

My mother was not afraid of Mrs. Calloway. She wished me to have my own library card to check out books for myself. She took me in to introduce me and I saw I had met a witch. "Eudora is nine years old and has my permission to read any book she wants from the shelves, children or adult," Mother said. "With the exception of **Elsie Dinsmore,**" she added. Later she explained to me that she'd made this rule because Elsie the heroine, being made by her father to practice too long and hard at the piano, fainted and fell off the piano stool. "You're too impressionable, dear," she told me. "You'd read that and the very first thing you'd do, you'd fall off the piano stool." "Impressionable" was a new word. I never hear it yet without the image that comes with it of falling straight off the piano stool.

Mrs. Calloway made her own rules about books. You could not take back a book to the Library on the same day you'd taken it out: it made no difference to her that you'd read every word in it and needed another to start. You could take out two books at a time and two only: this applied as long as you were a child and also for the rest of your life, to my mother as severely as to me. So two by two, I read library books as fast as I could go, rushing them home in the basket of my bicycle. From the minute I reached our house, I started to read. Every book I seized on, from **Bunny Brown and His Sister Sue at Camp Rest-a-While** to **Twenty Thousand Leagues under the Sea,** stood for the devouring wish to read being instantly granted. I knew this was bliss, knew it at the time. Taste isn't nearly so important; it comes in its own time: I wanted to read **immediately.** The only fear was that of books coming to an end.

* * *

QUESTIONS FOR DISCUSSION AND WRITING

The following questions can be used for class discussion, for individual or group writing assignments, and for entries in a reading journal. Follow your teacher's instructions.

1. Unlike Wright who at nineteen began a program of reading serious writers or Rodriguez who as a boy read "important" books, Eudora Welty read for pleasure both non-serious books like **Bunny Brown and His Sister Sue at Camp Rest-a-While** and classics like **Twenty Thousand Leagues under the Sea.**

   To Welty what one reads isn't as important as the frequency of reading. "Taste isn't nearly so important; it comes in its own time."

   - How do you feel about "escape" reading—mysteries, romances, science fiction, juvenile fiction, comics or humor? Would you discourage a person from this kind of reading? (If you would, read the next article by Dr. Krashen to see the benefits such reading gives.)

2. As she reads, Eudora Welty "listens" to an inner voice. She hears the sounds of the words in her head.

   - Do you hear an inner voice as you read?

   Reading specialists warn us that reading aloud (vocalization) or making silent lip movements (subvocalization) cuts down on our reading speed. Speed readers, skimming along to get the gist of a piece, probably won't "hear" what they read. In speedreading a notice or newspaper article, they probably aren't missing anything by not "hearing."

   - What kind of reading is worth slowing down for and listening to?

   - How did "being read to" influence Rodriguez's and Welty's pleasure in reading?

   - When you write, do you hear an inner voice? As you add thoughts, do you go back to the beginning and "hear" how what you've just written fits in with what you started with? Many writers recommend this practice to keep thoughts and words in flow.

   When you're checking your final draft for errors, do you ever read it aloud? By doing this, students often catch problems that their eye may miss.

3. Describe the various types of help which Welty received from her parents, her teachers, and the librarian.

ACQUIRING STYLE THROUGH CREATIVE IMITATION

Think of a person—perhaps a relative, teacher, clergyman, neighbor—who has touched your life or that of your family or community. Instead of imitating the original description exactly, describe your person loosely following the Welty original or the imitation by Rose Najar as models.

Original Passage

Miss Duling, a lifelong subscriber to perfection, was a figure of authority, the most whole-souled I have ever come to know. She was a dedicated schoolteacher who denied herself all she might have done or whatever other way she might have lived (this possibility was the last that could have occurred to us, her subjects in school). I believe she came of well-off people, well-educated, in Kentucky, and certainly old photographs show she was a beautiful, high-spirited-looking young lady—and came down to Jackson to its new grammar school that was going begging for a principal. She must have earned next to nothing: Mississippi then as now was the nation's lowest-ranking state economically, and our legislature has always shown a painfully loud reluctance to give money to public education. That challenge brought her.

In the long run she came into touch, as teacher or principal, with three generations of Jacksonians. My parents had not, but everybody else's parents had gone to school to her. She'd taught most of our leaders somewhere along the line. When she wanted something done—some civic oversight corrected, some injustice made right overnight, or even a tree spared that the fool telephone people were about to cut down—she telephoned the mayor, or the chief of police, or the president of the power company, or the head doctor at the hospital, or the judge in charge of a case, or whoever, and calling them by their first names, told them. It is impossible to imagine her meeting with anything less than compliance. The ringing of her brass bell from their days at Davis School would still be in their ears. She also proposed a spelling match between the fourth grade at Davis School and the Mississippi Legislature, who went through with it: and that told the Legislature. . . .

Sample Imitation

Dr. Lacey, a compassionate, empathetic healer, personified the best in family medical practice in our small community. He was an unassuming, gentle physician who never seemed put upon by the continuous and sometimes unremitting demands of his patients of all ages. The son of a noted New England surgeon, Dr. Lacey had been drawn to the West's sunny climate and vast open stretches. A quietly jovial man given to occasional moments of meditative silence, he had come to our town in the early thirties to open a much-needed family clinic. He couldn't have earned much: our town was the smallest in the valley with its farming families earning less than the lush, fruit laden orchards surrounding the town might have suggested. That challenge--service with limited remuneration--brought him.

Over the years he touched the lives--as physician and advisor--of three generations of Santa Isabelans. My parents as well as everybody else's had been treated by him for everything from whooping cough to arthritis. Everyone in town had experienced his care in some form or another; he delivered babies and immunized them against every preventable disease, listened to countless heartbeats and pulmonary sounds, opened mouths, and heard ah's in every accent spoken by our ethnically diverse population. And at least half a dozen males who had survived premature birth under his care proudly bore the doctor's name, Frederick. When his busy office schedule permitted, Dr. Lacey met with grammar school classes, church groups, and ladies' clubs to talk about first aid, nutrition, or pre-natal care, whatever suited the needs and age of his audience. His name on a club meeting's program always guaranteed a larger than usual gathering. Wherever he went, whatever group he addressed, Dr. Lacey was regarded with respect and reverence; his words rang with biblical authority. He even proposed to a nearby Rotary Club that they set up a scholarship fund to send a local boy to medical school: that suggestion, enthusiastically taken up not only by the Rotarians but also by a neighboring Lions Club, showed everyone the good doctor's dedication to his calling.

"WHAT IS KNOWN ABOUT LEARNING TO WRITE"

Excerpt from

WRITING: RESEARCH, THEORY, AND APPLICATIONS

Stephen D. Krashen

Reading and Writing

A variety of studies indicate that voluntary pleasure reading contributes to the development of writing ability. Our study (Kimberling, Wingate, Rosser, DiChara and Krashen, cited in Krashen, 1978) examined this issue directly. Sixty-six USC freshmen were given a questionnaire and were asked to write an essay at home, which was evaluated by two raters. Only those essays judged to be "highly competent" and "of low competence" were retained for further analysis. The questionnaire asked students to indicate the amount of pleasure reading they had done at different times in their lives. We found very clear differences between good writers and poor writers--good writers reported more pleasure reading at all ages, and especially during high school years. In fact, not one poor writer reported "a lot" of pleasure reading during high school.

Woodward and Phillips (1967) surveyed 919 freshmen at the University of Miami. Good writers were defined as those who received grades of "A" or "B" in freshman writing, while poor writers received "D" or "E". Good writers reported more reading of the daily newspaper than poor writers (the only question that probed voluntary reading habits). There were no outstanding differences between the groups with respect to the amount of assigned reading done in high school, although more poor writers reported no assigned reading.

Applebee's survey (1978) of 481 good high school writers, winners of the 1967 NCTE achievement awards in writing, adds further evidence, although no control group was investigated. Applebee reported that "these successful writers were also regular readers. For voluntary reading, they reported an average of 14 books over the summer vacation, and another four books in their first eight to ten weeks of senior year" (p. 340).

Excerpt by permission of Dr. Stephen D. Krashen, © copyright 1984, Pergamon Press, Oxford, publisher.

Donalson (1967) compared "effective" and "ineffective" tenth-grade writers, writing quality in this case being determined by rating of three compositions by high school English teachers. Questionnaire results revealed that effective writers read "more widely and more frequently" (p. 40), reported more magazines in the home (C coefficient = .38) and owned more books (C = .23).

Ryan (1977) compared 54 "regular" and 55 "intensive" writers, that is, those in normal college freshmen writing classes and those who were assigned to special sections because of writing problems. After conducting home interviews, Ryan reported that the regular writers' homes had more books, and a greater variety of books. (This result is consistent with Donalson's finding of more magazines in the homes of effective tenth-grade writers, but is only weakly supported by Woodward and Phillips, who found that more poor writers reported no books in the home; equal numbers of good and poor writers reported many books in the home, however.) Ryan also reported that the parents of good writers had read to them more as children, and that these parents also read more themselves.

McNeil (in Fader, 1976) evaluated the results of a pleasure reading program ("Hooked on Books") on boys aged 12 to 17 in a correctional school in Michigan over a two-year period. He reported that the "readers" showed significantly greater writing fluency and wrote with greater complexity than did control subjects. The readers also gained in self-esteem as compared to controls, were less anxious about school, improved in attitudes toward reading and writing, and were superior in reading comprehension.

One study apparently did not find a pleasure reading-writing relationship. Illo (1976) reports that correlations between self-reported pleasure reading and freshman composition grades at Shippensburg State College seemed "weak and uncertain" (p. 134). Illo, however, does not provide more detail than this.

Several studies report statistically significant correlations between reading and writing ability (e.g., Grobe and Grobe, 1977, Mathews, Larsen, and Butler, 1945, both studies using college freshmen; Zeman, 1969, using second and third grade children; Evanechk, Ollil, and Armstrong, 1974, using sixth graders). This kind of result is to be expected if pleasure reading contributes to both good reading ability (as supported by McNeil, cited above) and good writing.

RESEARCH ON READING AND WRITING

study	subjects	findings
Kimberling et al.	college freshmen	good writers report more pleasure reading when younger
Woodward & Phillips	college freshmen	good writers read the newspaper more
Applebee	high school	NCTE winners do a great deal of pleasure reading
Donalson	high school	effective writers read more, own more books, report more magazines in the home
Ryan	college freshmen	good writers had more books in the home, were read to more
McNeil	age 12 to 17	boys who get "hooked on books" improve more in writing attitude
Illo	college freshmen	"weak and uncertain" correlations between outside reading and writing

* * *

QUESTIONS FOR DISCUSSION

1. Dr. Krashen surveys seven research studies on the relationship between pleasure reading and skilled writing. Give a one-sentence summary of this relationship as shown in most of the findings.

2. What is a "control group" in such a research study?

3. Do the experiences of Wright, Rodriguez, and Welty prove Krashen's thesis that "pleasure reading contributes to . . . good writing"?

MAJOR WRITING ASSIGNMENTS

1. Richard Rodriguez's family did not understand the importance of his reading to his educational success. Parents who have not been to college themselves sometimes do not realize how much reading is necessary, how much time is needed to complete college assignments, and how important is a quiet place to study. Occasionally, a student is made to feel antisocial by the family who misses his or her company.

   With the information you have from these four readings, describe what you would do to help your children become good students, from the time they are preschoolers to their college years. Give reasons for what you plan to do.

Guidelines

As you write, remember to come up with a detailed plan that covers the period from preschool through college, to incorporate what you understand from the readings into your plan, and to give reasons for the various parts of your plan.

The two questions that follow ask you to analyze the reading experiences of Wright, Rodriguez, and Welty. As directed by your teacher, choose the short version or the long version.

2. Short Version—People read for a variety of reasons—for self-improvement, power, pleasure, or for understanding themselves and the world around them. Write an essay in which you explain the reasons why Wright, Rodriguez, and Welty read and give examples.

Guidelines

Make sure you understand the reasons that each person reads, that you include all the reasons each mentions, and that you have enough examples.

3. Long Version—Write an essay showing what was different about the reading experiences of Wright, Rodriguez, and Welty. Cover at least three of the differences below:

   - why they read
   - what impressed them about what they read
   - what difficulties, if any, they had with reading
   - the degree of encouragment they received concerning their reading
   - the doors that reading opened for them
   - the effect reading had on the person they became

Guidelines

After you have decided the points of difference you are going to write about, reread the first three articles making notes on these points. Be sure to include at least three points.

CHAPTER 2

JAZZ:

A STUDY IN BLACK AND WHITE

by

Jo An Simmons

Resource:

Richard Collins

Art and Music Section
Los Angeles Public Library

OVERVIEW

All three readings involve a unique American creation—jazz music. The first introduces jazz and tells how it developed. The second shows a contemporary jazz duo, Willie Ruff and Dwike Mitchell, demonstrating jazz to the Chinese by improvising blues on Chinese melodies. The last reading, James Baldwin's short story, "Sonny's Blues," reveals what jazz has meant to members of the black community.

WHAT TO LOOK FOR

The first reading asks and answers two questions: What is jazz? and How did jazz develop? As you read, write in the answers to these questions.

What is jazz?
Jazz is music with these characteristics:
1.
2.
3.
4.
5.

How did jazz develop?
Jazz developed from
1.
2.
3.
4.
5.

The second reading brings the story of jazz up to the 1980's. Look for the description of the way the two contemporary jazz artists perform the blues and explain them.

The last reading, "Sonny's Blues," tells of Sonny's struggle with suffering and drugs and the part jazz plays in this struggle. Look for the importance of blues to Sonny.

CHAPTER PLAN

"Jazz: A Study in Black and White," by Jo An Simmons
Excerpt from Willie and Dwike, by William Zinsser
"Sonny's Blues," by James Baldwin
Major Writing Assignment

JAZZ:

A STUDY IN BLACK AND WHITE

Jo An Simmons

What's black and white and American all over? That blend of the American black's musical heritage from West Africa with the American white's musical heritage from Europe. Admired and imitated around the world, jazz is considered America's original art form and gift to music. Only here could jazz have been created. European jazz critic Joachim Berendt says:

> Jazz was born in the meeting between black and white. That is why it orginated where this meeting took place in the most intensive fashion: in the United States' South. Until this day, jazz is conceivable only in terms of this confrontation. It loses its fundamental rationale when one or the other element [black or white] is emphasized, as has been done.
>
> The contact between the races, which has been so important in the development of jazz, symbolizes that spirit of "togetherness" per se which characterizes jazz. (p. 12)

Today, almost seventy years after jazz officially began, it still entertains an audience. Jazz has taken many forms during its history: New Orleans style, Dixieland, Chicago style, big-band swing, be-bop, cool jazz, free jazz and third stream. Its older forms have as many fans as its newest one. A much larger audience hears jazz-influenced music in movies, on television, in popular songs, and in rock. Our music could never be the same after jazz. To know something about jazz is to know more about our country's story. It is to know more about blacks and whites. It is to know more about older generations through the music they loved.

What is Jazz?

That question has often been asked and ducked. When a sweet old lady asked musician Fats Waller this question, he sighed and said, "Madam, if you don't know by now, DON'T MESS WITH IT!" Other people have sighed trying to define jazz. One can get the essence of jazz more easily through hearing it than through verbal description. However, it is possible to name its characteristics:

1. Jazz has a rhythm all its own: it swings

Jazz rhythm is like European rhythm in having a foundation beat. The march tempo (2/4 time) and 4/4 time are basic to classic jazz. What makes jazz rhythms different from European and closer to West African are multiple rhythms going over, below, around, and in between the basic beat. It is also like West African rhythms in putting accents in unexpected places. Hispanic rhythms, especially the dance rhythms of Cuba, the West Indies and Brazil, play their part in creating a special jazz rhythm.

2. Jazz music is semi-improvised

Instead of playing the music just as it's written, jazz musicians get to make some of it up. This is called improvising. Sometimes, they make it up on the spot, spontaneously. Other times, they make it up during rehearsal and play it that way in performance. Some musicians never play or sing a solo the same way twice. This "live" quality makes jazz more exciting than "canned" music. When a singer starts to scat or an instrument takes off on a tangent to the melody or harmony, it's an adventure for everyone.

How much is arranged ahead of time was different in the days when some jazz players couldn't read music. Somehow they did their own thing but did it together. Lil Hardin, who later married Louis Armstrong, describes such an instance. Lil was on vacation from Fisk University where she was receiving training as a classical pianist. She left her vacation job of playing in a music store to try out for the job of jazz pianist.

> When I sat down to play I asked for the music and were they surprised! They politely told me they didn't have any music and furthermore never used any. I then asked what key would the first number be in. I must have been speaking another language because the leader said, "When you hear two knocks, just start playing."
>
> It all seemed very strange to me, but I got all set, and when I heard that two knocks I hit the piano so loud and hard that they all turned around to look at me. It took only a second for me to feel what they were playing and I was off. The New Orleans Creole Jazz Band hired me, and I never got back to the music store. . . . (Shapiro and Hentoff, p. 93)

3. <u>Jazz music has a haunting "blues" sound</u>

"Blues" has several meanings in jazz. The term means a particular song form invented by the American black (described in a later section); it refers to all the plaintive songs written in this form and to blue notes. Blue notes are the third, seventh and occasionally fifth notes of a scale. What makes them "blue" is their being lowered off pitch and their wavering between microtones. "The third and seventh of all Negro music from spirituals to hot jazz are not pitched steadily. They are as Abbé Niles has said, 'worried, wavering between flat and natural'" (Harop, in Gold, p. 23). "The precise pitch or intonation of blue notes is not fixed but varies according to the performer's expression, ranging to more than a semitone below true pitch" (**New Grove Dictionary,** p. 117). The combination of blue notes and standard European chords creates a new sound which expresses emotions well.

4. <u>Jazz has a lot of back-and-forth calling and responding between two instruments, two sections of the band, or between a singer and an instrument</u>

Call-and-response is both a black and white musical tradition. A leader or lead instrument makes a statement and a group or another instrument answers. You can hear call-and-response in work songs between the leader and the crew; in the drums and voices of West Africa; in lined-out hymn singing with the preacher saying the words before the congregation sings them; in song-sermons; and in spirituals.

One jazz soloist will comment on the phrases of the soloist who went before. They often try to "outdo" each other. Marshall Stearns describes one example:

> Following trumpeter Dizzy Gillespie, the saxophonist Charlie Parker astonished his colleagues at a Carnegie Hall concert in 1950 by repeating Gillespie's complicated phrases, wringing them out, and hanging them up to dry with additional embellishments—in the same time interval. No one else could have done it. (p. 16)

5. <u>Jazz musicians and singers play their instruments and use their voices in a freer way</u>

It's as if these musicians don't know the limits of their instruments or voices. They bend notes and experiment with new sounds. Many instrumentalists play their horns as if they were singing and many singers try to sound like an instrument. As a result, they achieve sounds that are individual to them and sometimes astounding to their listeners. Hoagy Carmichael describes his reaction the first time he heard Bix Beiderbecke play his trumpet with the Wolverines:

> I could feel my hands trying to shake and getting cold when I saw Bix get out his horn. Boy, he took it! . . .
> Just four notes. . . . But he didn't blow them—he hit 'em like a mallet hits a chime—and his tone, the richness. . . .
> I got up from the piano and staggered over and fell on the davenport. (pp. 6-7)

He also describes what happened when he and others heard Louis Armstrong playing with King Oliver:

> The King featured two trumpets, a piano, a bass fiddle and a clarinet. . . a big black fellow (then) . . . slashed into **Bugle Call Rag.**
>
> I dropped my cigarette and gulped my drink. Bix was on his feet, his eyes popping. For taking the first chorus was that second trumpet, Louis Armstrong.
>
> Louis was taking it fast. Bob Gilette slid off his chair and under the table. . . . Every note that Louis hit was perfection. (p. 53)

How Did Jazz Develop?

The blending of black and white music had a long, hidden history during slavery. Although jazz would become a lively river, it grew slowly from small mountain streams. As the glacier of racial separation began to melt after the Civil War, these streams ran faster and flowed together. Besides feeding jazz, many streams became rivers of their own. Before we look at these sources, let's look at the riverbed, the foundations of jazz.

The rock bottom of jazz is a blending of European melody, harmony, measure, and instruments with Afro-American and Hispanic rhythms, and Afro-American phrasing, blues, and improvisation.

Church Music

One source of jazz was church music. That seems a strange statement when you think of some of the settings of early jazz. In New Orleans, the red-light district, Storeyville, employed jazz pianists, and, in other cities, gangsters often owned the night clubs that promoted early jazz. The underworld may have paid jazz pipers, but it was the "otherworld" of church music that affected its tune.

In the early days of slavery, blacks and whites didn't worship separately. The camp meeting revival movement of the early 1800s brought blacks and whites together. Through this contact, blacks began to blend the European melody of hymns and psalm-singing with black rhythms. After prayer or praise meetings on a plantation, the blacks would hold a circle or ring shout. Worshippers would circle counterclockwise to the accompaniment of psalm-singing and the multiple rhythms of clapping and stomping.

A later blend, the song-sermon, offered a pattern for jazz. Song sermons are still sung. The preacher starts by setting a powerful beat and singing a "call"; the congregation shouts the "response." The preacher might ask, "What do you think of Jesus?" On that cue, the congregation cuts in, "He's all right!" All this time the preacher is improvising melody, repeating certain phrases and building intensity. The jazz band going back and forth between instruments, repeating, and improvising builds up the same intensity. Preachers often use a bluesy tone. Blues guitarist T-Bone Walker has said, "Lots of people think I'm going to be a preacher when I quit this business because of the way I sing blues. They say it sounds like a sermon" (Stearns, p. 98).

The next two blends—the jubilee and the spiritual—have more melody and add blue notes and rhythm to a type of white folk hymn. The jubilee is a shorter, cheerful, rhythmic song. "When the Saints Go Marching In" is a well-known jubilee. These lines from another jubilee can give you the feeling:

> "Sit down, servant." "I can't sit down . . .
> My soul's so happy that I can't sit down."

Spirituals have longer melodies and were traditionally sad and deeply religious. "Swing Low, Sweet Chariot," "He Never Said a Mumblin' Word," and "Nobody Knows the Trouble I Seen" express these qualities. It was the spiritual that came to reveal the depths, sorrows, and beauties of black people to white people all over the world. The Fisk University singers on tour to raise money were at first afraid to share spirituals with white audiences. They feared that the audience would laugh at the dialect and the slave origins. Instead, many in the audience cried. They were deeply moved by the lovely melody, the poetry, and the sorrowful situations in the music. Soon the Fisk singers were invited to sing for President Grant in the

White House, Queen Victoria in England, and the Czarina in Russia, with many concert stops in between. Spirituals introduced whites to a new dimension of the black person and of music:

> They had introduced half the world to certain characteristics of American Negro folk music—to the syncopated rhythm, the call and response form, the free weaving of improvised lines into the basic pattern of melody. They accustomed the ears of white listeners to the strange swoops and glides of slave singing and to the haunting off-pitch notes and quavers. All this paved the way for blues and jazz. (Erlich, p. 36)

Gospel songs, a later development, are composed music, rather than folk music. These songs are always joyous and share with jazz the same rhythms, phrasing, and blue notes. Mahalia Jackson, called the queen of gospel singers, was famous for the way she embellished blue notes. A member of the Sanctified Church in Mount Vernon described it: "Mahalia she add more flowers and feathers than anybody, and they all is exactly right." Mahalia, who died in 1972, has been followed by such notable gospel singers as Dorothy Love Coates, Marion Williams, the late Clara Ward, and Bessie Griffen. Gospel song became a school for jazz musicians such as Ray Charles and vibraharpist Milt Jackson and singers Sarah Vaughn, Dinah Washington, and Aretha Franklin.

Blues

The blues are a mainstream through jazz and a mighty river of their own. Jazz without blues is unimaginable; as blues singer Jimmy Rushing puts it, blues are "like the foundation of the building" to jazz.

The blues is a particular kind of musical form, having twelve measures or bars. It was created by black folksingers using European harmony, became both vocal and instrumental by the 1920s, was taken up by country and western music of the late twenties, and accounted for one-third of the rock-and-roll repertory of the 50s, 60s and 70s (Schuller and Williams, p. 2). The blues form has the blue tonality discussed earlier and takes its emotions, topics, and attitudes from the black experience. Early blues songs were about everyday life—its lonesomeness, its difficulties and its comic aspects. They were about "love and discrimination, prison and the law, floods and railroad trains, the future told by a gypsy, that evening sun and the hospital" (Berendt, p. 140). Modern blues singer Jimmy Rushing says that "Today, as it was then, the blues come back to a person's feelings, to his daily activities in life. But rich people don't know nothing about the blues, please believe me" (Erlich, p. 69). Blues can be sad or happy, slow or fast. What is special about the blues is the attitude toward troubles. The blues singer is not devastated by troubles. Drawing on the black experience, the singer finds a bittersweet humor and endures. This is illustrated in the verses from two blues songs below:

> If your house catch on fire, Lord, and there ain't no water around
> If your house catch on fire, Lord, and there ain't no water around
> Throw your trunk out the window, and let the shack burn down.
>
> or
>
> I'm goin' down and lay my head on the railroad track
> I'm goin' down and lay my head on the railroad track
> But if I see the train a-comin', I'm gonna jerk it back.

> The blues form has been called the primary artistic expression of a minority culture: it was created mainly by black working-class men and women, and through its simplicity, sensuality, poetry, humor, irony and resignation transmuted into aggressive declamation, it mirrored the qualities and attitudes of Black America for three-quarters of a century. (Oliver, p. 118)

Another special blues feature which is very important for jazz is the "break," a built-in place for improvisation. The break is a short musical passage played by one or more instruments, by the guitar or harmonica in the earliest days of blues. The blues break has been called the "germ cell of jazz improvisation as a whole" (Berendt, p. 139).

The man who first wrote down and published blues was W. C. Handy. He composed his blues from scraps of folk melodies he heard in his travels with an all-black minstrel group and later as the leader of his own band. He is famous for "The Saint Louis Blues," "Beale Street Blues," "Loveless Love Blues," "Aunt Hagar's Blues," "Memphis Blues," and others. His life, recorded in his autobiography, **Father of the Blues**, spans the history of jazz's development from his birth in 1873 to a special moment in 1954. Blind, and eighty-one years old, he sat in on the recording session that produced the album "Louis Armstrong Plays W. C. Handy." With tears of happiness, he said, "Truly wonderful! Truly wonderful! Nobody could have done it but my boy Louis!"

Outstanding old-time blues singers include Blind Lemon Jefferson, Big Bill Broonzy, Ma Raines, and Bessie Smith. More modern blues artists are Jimmy

Rushing, Jack Teagarden, Ray Charles, Ida Cox, Billie Holiday, Ethel Waters, Mildred Bailey, and Ella Fitzgerald.

Today and continually since the beginning of jazz, blues are being sung and played by blacks and whites. The old type of blues--folk blues, country blues and prison blues--and the new type--city blues, urban blues, jazz blues, rhythm and blues, and soul blues—can all be heard.

"It is worth repeating that the blues is the only original musical form of the century, that it is an American and specifically Afro-American contribution, that people all over the world have responded to it. In quantity it has accounted for a major portion of the world's music" (Schuller and Williams, p. 6).

Ragtime

Ragtime is another stream that fed jazz, in particular, jazz pianists and Dixieland music. Ragtime made a huge splash in the period from 1897 to 1917. After its introduction at several world's fairs, ragtime became the "in" music. It could be heard in minstrel shows, vaudeville acts, cabarets, circuses, beer halls, at dances and silent movies, and from player pianos in the parlors of many homes. (A player piano was a mechanical piano that played tunes on paper rolls.) People loved ragtime's upbeat, lively tunes and its danceable rhythms.

Ragtime has been called "white music played black." It blends composed pianistic music in the European tradition with a distinctive black rhythm. It is not improvised and is limited to mainly one mood—happy—although pieces like Scott Joplin's "Solace" have a lonesome quality. The complex rhythm is unmistakably black. In its simplest form, a rippling syncopated rhythm in the right hand is played against a steady beat in the left. (Syncopate means to accent the weak beat, rather than the strong.) On top of this, other rhythms can be added by suspending, accenting and getting-between-the-beat effects. The result is "a rare and sophisticated piano music that can be played well only by a few highly gifted virtuosos" (Stearns, p. 106).

The virtuoso who wrote the first rags was a black composer in Sedalia, Missouri, named Scott Joplin. Those who saw the 1974 movie **The Sting** heard his music performed by piano and orchestra. Other musicians both black and white wrote and performed their own rags: Tom Turpin, Louis Chauvin and Artie Mathews from St. Louis; Jelly Roll Morton from New Orleans; and the Harlem pianists James

P. Johnson, Fats Waller and Lucky Roberts. The last great authentic ragtime pianist, Eubie Blake, at age ninety was the hit of the 1973 "Newport in New York" Festival. "The Maple Leaf Rag," "That's A Plenty," and "The Muskrat Ramble" are still favorites in Dixieland music.

Brass Bands

The brass bands of New Orleans were a stream running directly into jazz. They brought together European instruments and band music marching to the beat of black rhythms, church music and ragtime, improvisation and the blues.

These marching bands were in demand for parades (especially for Mardi Gras), picnics, riverboat excursions, dances and funerals. Even before the Civil War, there were excellent black bands made up of black freedmen. These were often Creoles of mixed French, Spanish and African blood who had some musical training. Their descendants--musicians like Alphonse Picou, Sydney Bechet, Papa Celestin, Kid Ory, and Barney Bigard would later become jazz musicians. After the Civil War, all-black bands became popular not only for New Orleans civic affairs but for black funerals. Most blacks belonged to one or more lodges which helped defray funeral expenses. Funerals received the full treatment in celebration and might involve three or four bands, depending on the number of lodges the deceased belonged to. Trumpeter Bunk Johnson describes such a funeral:

> On the way to the cemetery with an Odd Fellow or a Mason--they always buried with music you see--we would always use slow, slow numbers such as "Nearer My God to Thee," "Flee as a Bird to the Mountains," "Come Thee Disconsolate." We would use most any 4/4, played very slow; they walked very slow behind the body.
>
> After we would get to the cemetery, and after that particular person were put away, the band would come on to the front, out of the graveyard. The lodge would come out . . . and then we'd march away from the cemetery by snare drum only, until we got about a block or two blocks from the cemetery. Then we'd go right on into ragtime--what people call today swing--ragtime. We would play "Didn't He Ramble,"--or we'd take all those spiritual hymns and turn them into ragtime--2/4 movements, you know, step lively everybody. "Didn't He Ramble," "When the Saints Go Marching In," that good old piece "Ain't Gonna Study War No More," and several others. . . .
>
> We'd have a second line there that was 'most equivalent to King Rex parade--Mardi Gras Carnival parade. The police were unable to keep the second line back--all in the street, all on the sidewalks. . . . We'd have some immense crowds following. They would follow the funeral up to the

> cemetery just to get this ragtime music comin' back . . . and the Law was trying not to gang the thoroughfare, but just let them have their way. There wouldn't be any fight or anything of the kind; it would just be dancin' in the street. Even police horses—mounted police—their horses would prance. Music done them all the good in the world. That's the class of music we used on funerals. (Album notes, **New Orleans Parade,** numbers 101-03)

The second line Johnson refers to is the line of children and dancers who strutted behind the band. That line provided jazz schooling for youngsters like Louis Armstrong.

Latin Music

Fresh liveliness entered jazz whenever its course and that of Latin music crossed. Latin music, primarily from Cuba, Brazil, and Mexico, also blended black and white musical heritages. This blend, however, had a different flavor since Spanish and Portuguese songs, dances, and harmonies replaced those of Northern Europe; Latin percussion instruments and rhythms were closer to their African beginnings; and some Amerindian, specifically Andean Indian influences, were felt.

Latin ingredients were present during the days of ragtime and New Orleans brass bands. Later, during the big band period of the '30s, Latin musicians like Mario Bauza and Juan Tizol were creating arrangements for Chick Webb and Duke Ellington. But Latin influence was greatest during the period from the 1940s to the present day. Some examples are Machito's Afro Cuban Band, whose drummer Tito Puente began a North American percussion revolution; Cubop or Afro-Cuban jazz of the '50s led by Machito; Dizzy Gillespie and his remarkable conga player Chano Pozo, and Stan Kenton; the quintet styles of Nat "King" Cole and George Shearing; Chico O'Farrill's mambo-jazz arrangements; the **bossa nova**, a Brazilian blend of samba and jazz; and finally, **salsa**, another blend of jazz and Cuban music.

But as early as 1917 all the streams had come together for the beginning of jazz. This happened when the Original Dixieland Jazz Band, a white band, became a sensation. Other black and white bands in New Orleans, Chicago, Saint Louis, Kansas City, and New York soon attracted audiences. It was the beginning of a floodtide for this delightful music, a floodtide that would circle the globe. It was a music that could express mischief, protest, high spirits, or sorrows in an honest way. It was a music that spoke to the human condition and looked at troubles with a spiritual eye and a bittersweet humor. It was a music black and white and loved all over.

Bibliography

Album Notes. **New Orleans Parade.** American Music Records, Nos. 101-03.

Berendt, Joachim. **The Jazz Book: From New Orleans to Rock.** New York: Laurence Hill, 1975.

Carmichael, Hoagy. **The Stardust Road.** New York: Rinehart, 1946.

Erlich, Lillian. **What Jazz is All About.** New York: Julian Messner, 1962.

Gold, Robert S. **Jazz Talk.** Indianapolis: Bobbs-Merrill, 1975.

Oliver,Paul. **The New Grove Dictionary of Music and Musicians.** Washington, D.C.: Macmillan, 1980.

Roberts, John S. **The Latin Tinge.** New York: Oxford University Press, 1979.

Schuller, Gunther, and Martin Williams. **Big Band Jazz.** Washington, D.C.: Smithsonian Collection of Recordings, 1983.

Shapiro, Nat, and Nat Hentoff. **Hear Me Talkin' to You.** New York: Rinehart, 1955.

Stearns, Marshall. **The Story of Jazz.** New York: Oxford University Press, 1958.

Zinsser, William. **Willie and Dwike: An American Profile.** New York: Harper and Row, 1984.

* * *

QUESTIONS FOR DISCUSSION AND WRITING

The following questions can be used for class discussion, for individual or group writing assignments, and for entries in a reading journal. Follow your teacher's instructions.

1. What new information did you get from this introduction to jazz and its beginnings? Did anything surprise you?

2. As you were reading, did you make any connections between jazz and music that you are more familiar with? What are they?

3. With the information you now have, you wouldn't have to duck the question, "What is Jazz?"

Your answer might look like this:

> Jazz is a type of music created in the United States which blends European and African musical elements. Jazz differs from other music in these ways: it has a distinctive rhythm and is partly improvised; it employs blues features, call-and-response patterns, and individual ways of phrasing and playing instruments. This blend was developed by American blacks and whites over the years from church music, the blues, ragtime, brass bands, and Latin music.

The definition above explains the term "jazz" by putting it in the category "type of music" and then naming the traits that differentiate jazz from other types of music. The definition goes on to trace jazz's development.

Another type of definition follows—one in which the general term "poverty" is explained.

> Poverty in America does not mean starvation. It does not mean utter destitution, hunger, or homelessness as it does for hundreds of millions of the poor of Asia, Africa, and Latin America. But it does mean substandard medical care, substandard education, and substandard cultural influences, all of which doom the children of the poor to remain poor unless blessed by extraordinary ability or great good fortune. It means a shorter life plagued by more frequent physical and mental disease; a smaller body and a less developed mind. And it means passing aimless days on street corners and the porches of rural shacks. It means stagnation.
>
> —Edward Brooke, from "Where I Stand"

Brooke makes the general term "Poverty in America" real for us by naming specific conditions and results of being poor.

This last definition is a technical definition written by a Harbor College student in Dr. Beverly Shue's microbiology class.

> Immunity is resistance to infection that one has or develops during life. The two types are natural and acquired. Natural immunity protects against infection at the time of birth and includes species immunity (protection because of being a homo sapiens) **racial** immunity (resistance in certain racial or ethnic groups resulting from genetics) **prenatal** immunity (protection gained during fetal life) and **individual** (resistance due to your own genetic individual physiology). **Acquired** immunity is resistance gained after birth and includes **accidental** immunity (which comes from having had an active infection process where lymphocytes are activated and antibodies are formed); **artificial** immunity (which results from vaccination where protection against a specific infection is sought); and **passive acquired** immunity (given when a person has a severe infection and is in high danger. This mostly involves toxic infections).

This technical definition has more facts per square inch than the other types. And these facts are very exact, dividing one kind of immunity thinly from another kind. Science and technology courses like electronics call for a careful reading of the textbook and a precise use of words.

Assignment

Using any one of these definitions as a model or combining features you like from all three, write your own definition. You could define another kind of music, or a general term or concept you are learning in another class.

ACQUIRING STYLE THROUGH CREATIVE IMITATION

Original Passage

Sound in jazz is—to give a few examples at random—the slow, expressive vibrato of Sydney Bechet's soprano sax; the voluminous, erotic tenor sax sound of Coleman Hawkins; the earthy cornet of King Oliver; the "jungle" sound of Bubber Miley; the elegant clarity of Benny Goodman's clarinet; the sorrow and lostness of Miles Davis or the victoriousness of Louis Armstrong; the lyrical sonority of Leslie Young; the gripping, concentrated power of Roy Eldridge or the clear glow of Dizzy Gillespie (Joachim Berendt, **The Jazz Book**, p. 122).

Imitation

Sounds in the desert are--to give a few examples at random—the harsh, humorous cawing of the ravens; the strange cry of the roadrunner; the soft, insistent hoot of the owl; the long wail and noisy yapping of the coyotes; the responsive barking of our dogs in protest to the coyotes; the hungry neighing of the neighbor's horse; and the wild moaning of the wind rattling the window panes.

Your Imitation

Try using the same pattern as the passages above but changing the content. For your content, you could describe sound in another kind of music like rock, new wave, gospel song, country music, etc., naming the special sound of individual performers. Or you might prefer to describe the sounds in your home, workplace, classroom, library, cafeteria, church, hospital, zoo, bus, neighborhood, etc. The original passage gives eight examples (with two double examples). See how many you can give. Try to use descriptive words like "earthy," "gripping," "clear."

VOCABULARY

Directions: **The word definitions with boxes teach various forms of the word. Fill in the desired forms next to the letters and blank lines as in #4.**

1. **Heritage** (noun) — something that belongs to a person by reason of birth; an inherited portion as national heritage of honor, pride, and courage

Verbs	Nouns	Adjectives	Adverbs
inherit	**heritage** **heredity** **inheritance** **heir, heiress**	a.________tary **inherited**	

2. **Scat singing** — substituting improvised nonsense syllables (hi dee hi, ho dee ho) for words in a song and attempting to sound like a musical instrument

3. **Off on a tangent** — suddenly leaving one course of action or thought and, turning to another

4. **Response** (noun) — an answer or reply; reaction to a stimulus

Verbs	Nouns	Adjectives	Adverbs
b. respond	**response**	c. responsive	d. responsively

5. **Intensity** (noun) — energy, strength, concentration of activity, thought or feeling as He went at the job with great intensity; an extreme degree as of cold or heat

Verbs	Nouns	Adjectives	Adverbs
	intensity	e.________	f.________ly
intensify	g.________	**intensive**	h.________ly

6. **Embellish** (verb) — to beautify, to ornament or to adorn

What noun comes from the word embellish?

i.____________________

7. **Repertory** (noun) — a particular collection of musical pieces, dramas or operas that an artist or group can perform

8. **Stagnation** (noun) — a state of inactivity, dullness, sluggishness; making no progress like a still pool of unmoving water--a stagnant mind or stagnant economy

Verbs	Nouns	Adjectives	Adverbs
j.__________	stagnation	k.__________	l.______ly

RESEARCH ASSIGNMENTS

Further Reading

For your own enjoyment and information, choose a book from the following list. Follow any directions your teacher may give.

Albertson, Chris. **Bessie.** New York: Stein and Day, 1972.

Armstrong, Louis. **Satchmo.** New York: Prentice-Hall, 1954.

Blesh, Rudi. **Shining Trumpets: A History of Jazz.** New York: DaCapo Press, 1975.

Blesh, Rudi, and Harriet Janet. **They All Played Ragtime.** New York: Knopf, 1950.

Charles, Ray, and David Ritz. **Brother Ray.** New York: Dial Press, 1978.

Chilton, John. **Who's Who of Jazz.** Philadelphia: Arlington House, 1972.

Dance, Stanley. **The World of Count Basie.** New York: Scribner's, 1980.

Dreggs, Frank, and Harris Lewine. **Black Beauty/White Heat: A Pictorial History of Classic Jazz.** New York: William Morrow, 1982.

Ellington, Duke. **Music is My Mistress.** New York: DaCapo Press, 1976.

Feather, Leonard. **The Encyclopedia of Jazz.** New York: Horizon Press, 1960.

__________. **The Encyclopedia of Jazz of the 60's.** New York, 1966.

__________. **The Encyclopedia of Jazz of the 70's.** New York, 1976.

__________. **The Book of Jazz.** New York: DaCapo Press, 1976.

__________. **Inside Jazz.** New York: DaCapo Press, 1977.

Gourse, Leslie. **Louis' Children: American Jazz Singers.** New York: William Morrow, 1984.

Handy, William. **Father of the Blues.** New York: Macmillan, 1941.

Hughes, Langston. **Famous Negro Music Makers.** New York: Mead, 1955.

Jones, LeRoi. **Blues People.** New York: William Morrow, 1963.

Lomax, Alan. **Mister Jelly Roll.** New York: Duell, Sloan, and Pierce, 1950.

Lyons, Len. **The 101 Great Jazz Albums.** New York: William Morrow, 1980.

Rose, Al. **Eubie Blake.** New York: Schirmer Books, 1979.

Ulanov, Barry. **A History of Jazz in America.** New York: Viking Press, 1952.

Waller, Maurice, and Anthony Calabrese. **Fats Waller.** New York: Schirmer Books, 1977.

Waters, Ethel, and Charles Samuels. **His Eye is on the Sparrow.** New York: Doubleday, 1950.

Research on a Jazz Performer—
Three-part Assignment:

1. Interview your relatives and friends concerning their memories of earlier jazz music and their favorite jazz artists. Listen to any records or tapes that they might have.

2. Choose a jazz artist from your interviews or from the list that follows. Find out as much as you can about that person. Start with Leonard Feather's **Encyclopedia of Jazz** and take notes on interesting facts.

3. Use this information for the assignment below:

   You are a disc jockey putting on a thirty-minute special about a particular jazz artist. Your program has no commercials and more talk than music. Write what you would say about the person and tell what musical selections you would play between comments. You can name the selections; if you run out of titles for seven selections, just write "record." For your assignment, write just what you would say on the program, beginning with "Good evening, jazz fans."

Model:

Good evening, jazz fans. Tonight's program features the life and music of the man who moved early jazz from Dixieland to the smooth, swinging style of the big bands. Known as the "Colored King of Jazz," this man assembled and trained a group of jazz giants. Among them were Louis Armstrong, Don Redman, Benny Carter and Coleman Hawkins. Who is this man? Fletcher Henderson.

Let's listen now to this 1924 recording of Fletcher Henderson and His Orchestra playing "Copenhagen."

COPENHAGEN

It was music like "Copenhagen" that kept people dancing at the Roseland Ballroom on Broadway. The Roseland on the Great White Way was the home of Henderson's music off and on for seventeen years. But it was not to head the second Negro orchestra to play all-season engagements at the Roseland that Henderson came to New York City. Born in Cuthbert, Georgia, in 1898, the son of a high school principal, Henderson had not intended to be a full-time musician. He had been a chemistry major at Atlanta University and came north for post-graduate work at New York University. He soon found that he needed to be a part-time musician to finance his stay. Through his friendship with W. C. Handy, Fletcher put his piano playing to use accompanying singers like Ethel Waters, Bessie Smith, and Ma Rainey and working in recording studios. His avocation soon became his vocation. From pianist, he would become a composer and arranger.

Let's listen now to one of his own compositions, "The Henderson Stomp."

HENDERSON STOMP

This band piece was revived in 1940 by Benny Goodman in an arrangement close to the original. What arranger Don Redman and Henderson were trying to achieve was the distinctive sound you heard in this piece. Part of the sound you heard was a call-and-response pattern between sections of the orchestra. In this and in our next selection you'll hear how Henderson treated these sections separately with the trumpets doing one thing, the trombones another, the saxophones still another and the rhythm section accompanying. Henderson's musicians functioned both as a team of swinging sections and as soloists making individual contributions.

We'll now hear "Hop Off" with six soloists.

HOP OFF

The Roseland was the scene of battles of jazz among the bands that played there—bands like the Dorsey Brothers, Casa Loma, Vincent Lopez, Jean Goldkette and the Buffalodians. When such a music-playing contest would start, Henderson would tell his men, "Come on—let's take charge." In the next selection, a Fats Waller piece arranged by Henderson, you'll see why his band couldn't be beat. Let's hear the "New King Porter Stomp."

NEW KING PORTER STOMP

With this selection and the upcoming record, Henderson had set the pattern for a swing band style that was copied by nearly everyone else. His style was heard over national radio broadcasts from the Roseland and musicians from other bands, both black and white, gathered round to listen both in dance halls and at his home.

In fact, it was Henderson's arrangement that made a little known but talented clarinetist the King of Swing. Yes, Benny Goodman continually credits Fletcher Henderson with his own overnight success. Our would-be chemist had changed the course of jazz.

Let's close with a final example, "Down South Camp Meetin'," written and arranged by Fletcher Henderson.

DOWN SOUTH CAMP MEETIN'

Tune in next week for another jazz special.

Guidelines for Writing

Audience: A make-believe radio audience

Purpose: To give listeners a picture of the jazz performer that has interesting facts and to make informed comments on the music.

Grading Criteria: You will be graded on how much interesting material you provide and how smoothly your facts and comments run together.

Your final draft is expected to be written in complete sentences and to observe correct spelling and information.

List of Jazz Performers

Louis Armstrong
Leandro (Gato) Barbieri
Mario Bauza
Barney Bigard
Dave Brubeck
Hoagy Carmichael
Eddie Condon
Tommy Dorsey
Duke Ellington
Ella Fitzgerald
Stan Getz
João Gilberto
Jean Goldkette
W. C. Handy
Erskine Hawkins
Earl Hines
Milt Jackson
James P. Johnson
Stan Kenton
Jimmie Lunceford
Shelly Manne
Jimmie McPartland
Theolonius Monk
Bennie Moton
Chico O'Farrill
Kid Ory
Oscar Peterson
Perez Prado
Flora Purim
Leon Rappolo
Lucky Roberts
Artie Shaw
Muggsy Spanier
Jack Teagartden
Juan Tizol
Fats Waller
Chick Webb
Lester Young

Lil Hardin Armstrong
Charlie Barnet
Sidney Bechet
Eubie Blake
Ralph Burns
Papa Celestin
Chuck Corea
Eddie Durham
Bill Evans
Aretha Franklin
Gene Gifford
Dizzy Gillespie
Benny Goodman
Lionel Hampton
Woody Herman
Billie Holiday
Harry James
Scott Joplin
Gene Krupa
Machito
William McKinney
Sergio Mendez
Airto M.
Gerry Mulligan
King Joe Oliver
Charlie Palmieri
Oscar Pettiford
Tito Puente
Boyd Raeburn
Don Redman
Jimmy Rushing
George Shearing
Billy Strayhorn
Claude Thornhill
Sarah Vaughn
Dinah Washington
Paul Whiteman

Mildred Bailey
Count Basie
Bix Beiderbecke
Buddy Boldin
Cab Calloway
Ray Charles
Miles Davis
Billy Eckstine
Gil Evans
Errol Garner
Astrud Gilberto
Jimmy Giuffre
Glen Gray
Coleman Hawkins
Fletcher Henderson
Pee Wee Hunt
Blind Lemon Jefferson
Max Kaminsky
Elliot Lawrence
Leadbelly (Huddie Ledbetter)
Glenn Miller
Ferdinand "Jelly Roll" Morton
Sy Oliver
Charkes Parker
Alphonse Picou
Chano Pozo
Gertrude Ma Raines
Buddy Rich
Bolo Sete
Bessie Smith
Art Tatum
Mel Tormé
T-Bone Walker
Ethel Waters
Mary Lou Williams

"SHANGHAI"

Excerpt from

WILLIE AND DWIKE: AN AMERICAN PROFILE

William Zinsser

Willie and Dwike is a fast-moving book about two modern jazz artists, Dwike Mitchell and Willie Ruff, who as visiting artists have brought the pleasures of jazz to school children, college students, men and women in factories, old people's homes, half-way houses, and to the general public all over the United States. They have also been ambassadors of this American art as they played for people in China, Russia, and Europe. Willie Ruff is a professor of music and Afro-American studies at Yale University; Dwike Mitchell teaches piano in New York City; author William Zinsser, also a Yale professor, is one of his students. **Willie and Dwike** tells how these two Southern boys became famous musicians and teachers, how they overcame obstacles, and how blacks and whites helped them on their way.

Jazz came to China for the first time on the afternoon of June 2, 1981, when the American bassist and French-horn player Willie Ruff introduced himself and his partner, the pianist Dwike Mitchell, to several hundred students and professors who were crowded into a large room at the Shanghai Conservatory of Music. The students and the professors were all expectant, without knowing quite what to expect. They only knew that they were about to hear the first American jazz concert ever presented to the Chinese. Probably they were not surprised to find that the two musicians were black, though black Americans are a rarity in the People's Republic. What they undoubtedly didn't expect was that Ruff would talk to them in Chinese, and when he began they murmured with delight.

Ruff is a lithe, dapper man in his early fifties who takes visible pleasure in sharing his enthusiasms, and it was obvious that there was no place he would rather have been than in China's oldest conservatory, bringing the music of his people to still another country deprived of that commodity. In 1959 he and Mitchell—who have played together as the Mitchell-Ruff Duo for almost thirty years—introduced jazz to the Soviet Union, and for that occasion Ruff taught himself Russian, his seventh

---

Chapter 1,"Shanghai," in WILLIE AND DWIKE: AN AMERICAN PROFILE, by William Zinsser, reprinted by permission of the author; copyright © 1984, published by Harper & Row.

© 1985 Tom Victor

Willie Ruff and Dwike Mitchell

language. In 1979 he hit on the idea of making a similar trip to China, and he began taking intensive courses in Chinese at Yale, where he is a professor of music and of Afro-American studies. By the winter of 1981 he felt that he was fluent enough in Mandarin to make the trip.

Now Ruff stood at the front of the room surveying the Chinese faces. He looked somewhat like an Oriental sage himself—or at least like the traditional carving of one; he is the color of old ivory, with a bald head and the beginnings of a Mandarin beard. He was holding several sheets of paper on which he had written, in Chinese characters, what he wanted to tell his listeners about the origins of jazz.

"In the last three hundred and fifty years," he began, "black people in America have created a music that is a rich contribution to Western culture. Of course three hundred and fifty years, compared to the long and distinguished history of Chinese music, seems like only a moment. But please remember that the music of American black people is an amalgam whose roots are deep in African history and also that it has taken many characteristics from the music of Europe."

Ruff has an amiable voice, and as he declaimed the first sentences, relishing the swoops and cadences of his latest adopted language, he had already established contact with the men and women in the room. They were attentive but relaxed—not an audience straining to decipher a foreigner's accent.

"In Africa the drum is the most important musical instrument," Ruff went on. "But to me the intriguing thing is that the people also use their drums to talk. Please imagine that the drum method of speech is so exquisite that Africans can, without recourse to words, recite proverbs, record history and send long messages. The drum is to West African society what the book is to literate society." . . .

"In the seventeenth century," Ruff continued, "when West Africans were captured and brought to America as slaves, they brought their drums with them. But the slave owners were afraid of the drum because it was so potent; it could be used to incite the slaves to revolt. So they outlawed the drum. This very shrewd law had a tremendous effect on the development of black people's music. Our ancestors had to develop a variety of drum substitutes. One of them, for example, was tap dancing—I'm sure you've all heard of that. Now I'd like to show you a drum substitute that you probably don't know about, one that uses the hands and the body to make rhythm. It's called hambone."

There was no translating "hambone" into Mandarin—the odd word hung in the air. But Ruff quickly had an intricate rhythm going, slapping himself with the palms of his hands and smacking his open mouth to create a series of resonating pops. Applause greeted this proof that the body could be its own drum.

"By the time jazz started to develop," Ruff went on, "all African instruments in America had disappeared. So jazz borrowed the instruments of Western music, like the ones we're playing here today." He went over to his own instrument, the bass, and showed how he used it as a percussion instrument by picking the strings with his fingers instead of playing them with a bow. "Only this morning," he said, "I gave a lesson to your distinguished professor of bass, and he is already <u>very good</u>."

Moving from rhythm to terrain that was more familiar to his listeners, he pointed out that jazz took its structural elements from European harmony. "Mr. Mitchell will now give you an example of the music that American slaves found in the Christian churches—Protestant hymns that had been brought from Europe. Slaves were encouraged to embrace Christianity and to use its music. Please listen."

Mitchell played an old Protestant hymn. "The slaves adopted these harmonies and transformed them into their own very emotional spirituals," Ruff said. "Mr. Mitchell and I will sing you a famous Negro spiritual from the days of slavery. It's called 'My Lord, What a Morning.'" With Mitchell playing a joyful accompaniment, the two men sang five or six choruses of the lovely old song, Mitchell carrying the melody in his deep voice, Ruff taking the higher second part. . . .

"Mr. Mitchell will now show you how the piano can be used as a substitute for the instruments of the orchestra," Ruff said. "Please notice that he uses his left hand to play the bass and also to make his rhythm section. Later he will use his right hand to play the main melody and to fill in the harmony. This style is called ragtime." Mitchell struck up a jaunty rag. The students perked up at the playful pattern of the notes. Ruff looked out at his class and beamed. The teacher in him was beginning to slip away; the musician in him was tugging at his sleeve and telling him to start the concert. . . .

When Mitchell finished his ragtime tune the audience clapped--apparently glad to hear some of the converging elements that Ruff had talked about earlier. "Now," Ruff said, "we're going to give you an example of blues." It was another word that didn't lend itself to Mandarin, and it sounded unusually strung out: bloooooze. "One of the fundamental principles of jazz is form," Ruff continued, "and blues are a perfect illustration. Blues almost always have a twelve-bar form. This twelve-bar form never changes. It wouldn't change even if we stayed here and played it all night." He paused to let this sink in. "But you don't have to worry—we aren't going to play it that long." It was his first joke in Chinese, and it went over well. Mitchell then played an easygoing blues—a classic example of what came up the river from New Orleans, with a strong left hand ornamented by graceful runs in the right hand. Ruff joined in on his bass, and they played several twelve-bar choruses.

After that Ruff brought up the matter of improvisation, which he called "the lifeblood of jazz." He said that when he was young he worried because his people hadn't developed from their experience in America a written tradition of opera, like Chinese opera, that chronicled great or romantic events. "But later I stopped worrying because I saw that the master performers of our musical story—Louis Armstrong, Ella Fitzgerald and so many others—have enriched our culture with the beauty of what they created spontaneously. Now please listen one more time to the blues form, and count the measures along with me." He wanted his listeners to count, he said, because the rules of jazz require the improviser, however wild his melodic changes to repeat the harmonic changes that went into the first statement of the theme. "After you count with me a few times through, Mr. Mitchell will begin one of his famous improvisations."

Mitchell played a simple blues theme, emphasizing the chord changes, and Ruff counted the twelve bars aloud in English. Mitchell then restated the theme, embroidering it slightly, and this time Ruff counted in Chinese: _"Yi, er, san, si, wu, liu, qi, ba. . . ."_ This so delighted the students that they forgot to join him. "I can't hear you," Ruff said, teacher fashion, but they kept quiet and enjoyed his climb up the numerical ladder. Mitchell then embarked on a series of improvisations, some constructed of Tatum-like runs, some built on strong chord progressions (he can move immense chord clusters up and down the keyboard with incredible speed). Next, Ruff took a chorus on the bass; then they alternated their improvised flights, moving in twelve-bar segments to an ending that seemed as inevitable as if they had played it a hundred times before.

Changing the mood, Ruff announced that Mitchell would play a song called "Yesterday." Jerome Kern's plaintive melody is hardly the stuff of traditional jazz, nor was Mitchell's rendition of it—a treatment of classical intricacy, closer to Rachmaninoff (one of his heroes) than to any jazz pianist. The students applauded with fervor. Staying in a relatively classical vein, Ruff switched to the French horn and the two men played Billy Strayhorn's "Lush Life" in a mood which was slow and lyrical, almost like a German _lied_, and which perhaps surprised the students with its lack of an obvious rhythm.

The next number was one that I didn't recognize. It moved at a bright tempo and had several engaging themes that were brought back by the piano or the French horn--the usual jazzmen's game of statement and response. Twice, Mitchell briefly introduced a contrapuntal motif that was a deliberate imitation of Bach, and each time it drew a ripple of amusement from the professors and the students. It was the first time they had heard a kind of music that they knew from their own studies.

"That number," Ruff said, "is called 'Shanghai Blues.' We just made it up." The audience buzzed with amazement and pleasure.

I had been watching the professors and the students closely during the concert. Their faces had the look of people watching the slow approach of some great natural force—a tornado or a tidal wave. They had been listening to music that their experience had not prepared them to understand. Two black men were playing long stretches of music without resorting to any printed notes. Yet they obviously hadn't memorized what they were playing; their music took unexpected turns, seemingly at the whim of the musicians, straying all over the keyboard and all over the landscape of Western tonality. Nevertheless there was order. Themes that had been abandoned came back in different clothes. If the key changed, as it frequently did, the two men were always in the same key. Often there was a playfulness between the two instruments, and always there was rapport. But if the two players were exchanging any signals, the message was too quick for the untrained eye.

From the quality of listeners' attention I could tell that the music was holding them in a strong grip. Their minds seemed to be fully engaged. Their bodies, however, were not. Only three pairs of feet in the whole room were tapping—Mitchell's, Ruff's and mine. Perhaps this was a Chinese characteristic, this stillness of listening. But beyond that, the music wasn't easy. It never again approached the overt syncopation of the ragtime that Mitchell had played early in the program; that was where the essential gaiety of jazz had been most accessible. Nor did it have the flat-out gusto that an earlier generation of black musicians might have brought to China--the thumping rhythms and simpler harmonies of a James P. Johnson or a Fats Waller.

It wasn't that Mitchell and Ruff were playing jazz that was pedantic or sedate; on the contrary, I have seldom heard Mitchell play with more exuberant shifts of energy. But the music was full of subtleties--even a Westerner accustomed to jazz would have been charmed by its subtlety and wit. I had to remind myself that the Chinese had heard no Western music of any kind from 1966 to 1976. A twenty-one-year old student in the audience, for instance, would only have begun to listen to composers like Mozart and Brahms within the past five years. The jazz that he was hearing now was not so different as to be a whole new branch of music. Mitchell was clearly grounded in Bach and Chopin; Ruff's French horn had echoes of all the classical works--Debussy's "Reverie," Ravel's "Pavane"--in which that instrument has such uncanny power to move us.

After "Shanghai Blues" Ruff invoked the ancient device of teachers who know they have been presenting too much material too fast. He asked for questions. The serious faces relaxed.

"Where do people go to study jazz in America?" a student wanted to know. "What kind of courses do they take?"

Ruff explained that jazz courses, where they existed at all, would be part of a broad college curriculum that included, say, languages and history and physics. "But, really, jazz isn't learned in universities or conservatories," he said. "It's music that is passed on by older musicians to those of us who are younger."

It was not a helpful answer. What kind of subject doesn't have its own academy? A shyness settled over the room, though the students seemed full of curiosity. Professor Tan got up and stood next to Ruff. "I urge you to ask questions," he said. "I can assure you that jazz has many principles that apply to your studies here. In fact, I have many questions myself."

An old professor stood up. "When you created 'Shanghai Blues' just now," he said, "did you have a form for it, or a logical plan?"

"I just started tapping my foot," Ruff replied, tapping his foot to reconstruct the moment. "And then I started to play the first thought that came into my mind with the horn. And Mitchell heard it. And he answered. And after that we heard and answered, heard and answered, heard and answered."

"But how can you ever play it again?" the old professor said.

"We never can," Ruff replied.

"That is beyond our imagination," the professor said. "Our students here play a piece a hundred times, or two hundred times, to get it exactly right. You play something once—something very beautiful—and then you just throw it away."

Now the questions tumbled out. What was most on the students' minds quickly became clear: it was the mystery of improvisation. (The Chinese don't even have a word for improvisation of this kind; Ruff translated it as "something created during the process of delivery.") All the questions poked at this central riddle—"Could a Chinese person improvise?" and "Could two strangers improvise together?" and "How can you compose at such speed?"—and it was at this point that Ruff took one question and turned it into a moment that stood us all on our ear.

Was it really possible, a student wanted to know, to improvise on any tune at all—even one that the musicians had never heard before?

Ruff's reply was casual. "I would like to invite one of the pianists here to play a short traditional Chinese melody that I'm sure we would not know," he said, "and we will make a new piece based on that."

The room erupted in oohs and cheers. I caught a look on Mitchell's face that said, "This time you've gone too far." The students began to call the name of the young man they wanted to have play. When they found him in the crowd he was so diffident that he got down on the floor to keep from being dragged out. But his friends dragged him out anyway, and, regaining his aplomb, he walked to the piano and sat down with the formality of a concert artist. He was about twenty-two. Mitchell stood at one side, looking grave.

The young man played his melody beautifully and with great feeling. It seemed to be his own composition, unknown to the other people. It began with four chords of distinctively Chinese structure, moved down the scale in a stately progression, paused, turned itself around with a transitional figure of lighter weight, and then started back up, never repeating itself and finally resolving the theme with a suspended chord that was satisfying because it was so unexpected. It was a perfect small piece, about fourteen bars long. The student walked back to his seat and Mitchell went back to the piano. The room got very quiet.

Mitchell's huge hands hovered briefly over the keys, and then the young man's melody came back to him. It was in the same key; it had the same chords, slightly embellished near the end; and, best of all, it had the same mood. Having stated the theme, Mitchell broadened it the second time, giving it a certain majesty, coloring the student's chords with dissonances that were entirely apt; he gave the "Chinese" chords a jazz texture but still preserved their mood. Then Ruff joined him on his bass, and they took the melody through a number of variations, Mitchell giving it a whole series of new lives but never losing its integrity. I listened to his feat with growing excitement. For me it was the climax of years of marveling at his ear and at his sensitivity to the material at hand. The students were equally elated and astonished. For them it was the ultimate proof—because it touched their own heritage—that for a jazz improviser no point of departure is alien.

After that a few more questions were asked, and Mitchell and Ruff concluded with a Gershwin medley from **Porgy and Bess** and a genial rendition of "My Old Flame." Professor Tan thanked the two men and formally ended the concert. Then he went over to Mitchell and took his hands in his own. "You are an artist," he said.

Later I told Mitchell that I thought Ruff had given him an unduly nervous moment when he invited one of the students to supply a melody.

"Well, naturally I was nervous," he said, "because I didn't have any idea what to expect. But, you know, that boy phrased his piece perfectly. The minute he started to play I got his emotions. I understood exactly what he was feeling, and the rest was easy. The notes and the chords just fell into place."

* * *

SENTENCE COMBINING WITH LOGICAL CONNECTIVES

As college students, you sense relationships between thoughts in your sentences and look for words and punctuation to express those relationships. Your more sophisticated ideas demand more sophisticated transportation, sentence-carriers with special punctuation and signal words. The chart entitled "Guide to Sentence Combining" on page 81 gives an overview of the special punctuation and signal words.

CONTRAST

College writing often expresses the relationship of CONTRAST. We see a CONTRAST relationship when a sentence contains both good news and bad news: **Rain had flooded the streets and slowed traffic, but it brought snow to the local mountains, delighting skiers.**

We also see a CONTRAST relationship when a sentence starts out with one thought and then reverses its direction with another: **A job at that fast foods restaurant offers a good starting wage; however, the chances of working enough hours to make a living or of getting promoted are slim.**

William Zinsser's sentence pairs below describe the reaction of the Chinese when they heard Mitchell and Ruff improvise together. There is a contrast between the kind of playing the Chinese are used to and what the performers are doing, between Chinese explanations based on classical music and what they see and hear.

1. Two black men were playing long stretches of music without resorting to any printed notes. 2. Yet they obviously hadn't memorized what they were playing.

(Sentences 1 and 2 contrast the fact that the musicians were playing without sheet music with the fact that they had not memorized what they were playing--the usual explanation of such a feat.)

3. Their music took unexpected turns, seemingly at the whim of the musicians, straying all over the keyboard and all over the landscape of Western tonality.
4. Nevertheless there was order.

(Sentences 3 and 4 contrast the fact that although the music went outside any patterns that the Chinese knew, it still had order.)

5. Often there was playfulness between the two instruments, and always there was rapport. 6. But if the two players were exchanging any signals, the message was too quick for the untrained eye.

(Sentences 5 and 6 contrast the unity between the musicians with the absence of any signals to keep them together.)

Imitation

A simpler version of contrasting ideas is below. The contrast here is between the lack of verbal communication between a husband and wife and their actual closeness.

1. The husband and wife warming themselves by the den fireplace hadn't spoken to each other in the last half hour. 2. Yet they obviously were at peace with one another.

3. They were occupied with different tasks, the husband paying bills and the wife writing a letter. 4. Nevertheless, there was oneness.

5. Often they looked in each other's direction and always there was awareness of the other person. 6. But no spoken words were necessary.

Your Imitation

Experiment with your own contrasting thoughts on a subject in three pairs of sentences. Do this with a partner or on your own.

1. ____

_____________________. 2. Yet ______________________

____

3. ____

____. 4.

Nevertheless, ________________

____.

5. ____

_____________________. 6. But ______________________

____.

Two contrasting sentences can also be combined into one sentence. If you can master the tricky punctuation required, you can write these very effective, sophisticated sentences. Here are your punctuation options:

Option One

You can contrast the thought in sentence A with the thought in sentence B by joining them with a comma and but or yet.

_______Sentence A_______, but _______Sentence B_______
, yet

Sample: This class requires a lot of reading and writing, but the skills I am learning help me in all my other classes.

There are several good protections against temptation, but the surest is cowardice.

—Mark Twain

Option Two

You can join two contrasting sentences with a semicolon (;) and a signal word (a conjunctive adverb) however, instead, still, nevertheless, nonetheless, on the contrary, despite this, etc.

______ Sentence A ______; on the contrary, ______ Sentence B ______

Sample: It wasn't that Mitchell and Ruff were playing jazz that was pedantic or sedate; **on the contrary,** I have seldom heard Mitchell play with more exuberant shifts of energy.

—William Zinsser

Option Three

You can join two contrasting sentences with just a semicolon.

______ Sentence A ______; ______ Sentence B ______

Samples: And so, my fellow Americans, ask not what your country can do for you; ask what you can do for your country.

—John F. Kennedy

The test of our progress is not whether we add more to the abundance of those who have much; it is whether we provide enough for those who have too little.

—Franklin D. Roosevelt

Wit has truth in it; wisecracking is simply calisthenics in words.

—Dorothy Parker

Option Four

A later chapter will show you how to use words like although, though (subordinating conjunctions) to contrast NOT two sentences but one sentence and a dependent clause.

~~~~~~~~~~~~, ______ Sentence A ______

Sample: Although jazz is less popular than rock, there are enough jazz fans to support several jazz programs and stations.
~~~~~~~~~~~~

Non-Options

You cannot join two sentences with just a comma.

__________Sentence A__________, __________Sentence B__________.

Comma Splice Error

You cannot join two sentences without any punctuation.

__________Sentence A____________________Sentence B__________.

Run-on Sentence Error

These non-options produce the dreaded comma splice and run-on errors. These sentence errors are dreaded because they are considered illiteracies in the business and academic worlds and are penalized heavily on exit, proficiency and placement tests.

ADDITION

One sentence or thought is often ADDED to the previous thought. The second thought moves the first idea or action along, adds a related idea to the first, amplifies it or enlarges it by giving more details, or explains it. Look at these samples.

1. Mitchell's huge hands hovered briefly over the keys, and then the young man's melody came back to him.

   (The second thought following ", and then" moves the action along.)

2. He looked like an Oriental sage himself—or at least like the traditional carving of one; he is the color of old ivory, with a bald head and the beginnings of a Mandarin beard.

   (The second thought following the semicolon (;) amplifies the comparison suggested in the first thought by giving specific details.)

3. The slave owners were afraid of the drum because it was so potent; it could be used to incite slaves to revolt.

   (The second thought after the semicolon explains why the drum was powerful and why slave owners feared it.)

You have several options in adding one thought to another. You can keep them as two separate sentences and signal their relationship by beginning the second sentence with a word like "And" or "Moreover," or you can combine them into one

sentence using the options below. (See also the "Guide to Sentence Combining" on page 81.)

Directions:

In the space below the samples in options 1, 2, and 3 write your own sentence.

Option One

You can add the thought of sentence B to the thought of sentence A by joining them with a comma and and.

______Sentence A______, and ______Sentence B______

Mitchell, then seventeen, needed an accompanist, and he gave the newly arrived Ruff, a sixteen-year-old French-horn player, a crash course in playing the bass.

—William Zinsser

Option Two

You can join the two sentences with a semicolon (;) and a signal word like moreover, besides, in addition, furthermore, then, next, etc.

______Sentence A______; moreover, ______Sentence B______

Meteorologists cannot explain the unusual weather we are having; moreover, they are amazed by the number of weather records suddenly being broken.

Option Three

You can add sentence B to sentence A with just a semicolon (;). In doing this be sure you have a complete sentence on either side of the semicolon.

______Sentence A______; ______Sentence B______

A lady's imagination is very rapid; it jumps from admiration to love, from love to matrimony in a minute.

—Jane Austen, **Pride and Prejudice**

The love of chocolate is the root of all my calories; it leads from Almond Joys to See's Candies, from fudge to fat.

Rare Option

When the sentences are very short and are written in parallel style, you can add them to each other with commas.

> Mitchell's harmonies were elegant and stunning, his technique was awesome, his taste was impeccable.
>
> —William Zinsser

> I came, I saw, I conquered.
>
> —Julius Caesar

Non-Options

Never add a sentence beginning with <u>then</u> to the previous sentence with only a comma; use a semicolon.

LIST OF MAJOR CONJUNCTIVE ADVERBS

accordingly	moreover
also	nevertheless
besides	otherwise
consequently	still
furthermore	then
hence	therefore
however	thus

GUIDE TO SENTENCE-COMBINING

NOTE: a straight line indicates an independent clause; a wavy line indicates a dependent clause (a fragment by itself)

Relationship	Words	Punctuation Scheme	Examples
Addition	, and	_____, and _____.	I shall survive, and I may even prevail.
	; also, moreover, furthermore, etc.	_____; moreover, ____.	I shall survive; moreover I shall write a book about my experience.
Contrast	but, yet	_____, but _____.	I shall survive, but it won't be easy. I shall survive, yet victory is not assured.
	; however, still, nevertheless, on the other hand, etc.	_____; nevertheless, _______________.	I shall survive; nevertheless, the situation is grim.
	although, though,	Although ~~~~~~~~, _______________.	Although the situation is grim, I shall survive.
Cause	, for	_____, for _____.	I shall survive, for I eat my King Vitamins every day.
	because, since	Because ~~~~~~~~, _____. _______________.	Because I eat my King Vitamins every day, I shall survive.
Effect, Result Consequence	, so	_____, so _______	I shall survive, so my heirs will just have to wait for their money.
	; therefore, consequently, hence, as a result	_________; therefore, ____________.	I shall survive; therefore, the world will be a more delightful place for us all.

Relationship	Words	Punctuation Scheme	Examples
Condition	If, unless, provided that	If~~~~, ______.	If my paycheck arrives tomorrow, I shall survive. Unless you marry me, I shall not survive. Even if you leave me, I shall survive.
Time sequence	and	_____, and ______.	I shall survive, and I shall return to the island for gold.
	; then, later	_____; then ______.	I shall survive; then I shall return to the island for gold.
	when, whenever, while, as, before, after, until	Until~~~~~, ______ _______________.	Until the rescue ship comes, I shall have difficulty surviving. After I drink my Tigers' Milk, I shall survive.
Alternatives	or; either....or	_____; or _______.	I shall survive, or I shall die trying.
	otherwise	_____, otherwise_____. _______________.	I shall survive; otherwise I shall perish.
Manner Hypothetical condition	as if as though	_____, as if ______.	He acted recklessly, as if his survival were assured.

Note: Some teachers prefer a comma before "so" and "yet," while others prefer a semicolon. Always ask which one to use (, yet / , so / ; yet / ; so)

VOCABULARY

Directions: **Supply the missing forms of the words in the boxes as directed on page 60.**

1. **Sage** (noun) a profoundly wise person

Verbs	Nouns	Adjectives	Adverbs
	sage		a.__________ly
	sagacity	b.__________	c.__________
	sageness		

2. **Amalgam** (noun) mixture or combination
Can you make another noun from the verb amalgamate, meaning to mix or combine? d.____________________

3. **Potent** (adj) powerful, mighty, strong, effective

Verbs	Nouns	Adjectives	Adverbs
	potency	**potent**	
	impotency	e.__________	
	potentate (a powerful ruler)		
	potential (capability of, possibility of power)	f.__________	g.________

4. The Latin roots soni, son, and sono all have to do with sound

Resonate (verb) to resound

Verbs	Nouns	Adjectives	Adverbs
Resonate	**Resonance**	**Resonant**	h.________
	Sonar	**Sonic**	
		Sonorous	
	Dissonance	i.__________	

5. **Fervor** (noun) great warmth and earnestness of feeling
Fervent and fervently come from the same root.

6. **Rapport** (noun) a harmonious or sympathetic relation

7. **Plaintive** (adj) expressing sorrow or melancholy
Related words are plaint (grievance) plaintiff—the person who brings suit, who has a complaint, complaint, complain

8. **Diffident** (adj) shy, timid, not confident, reserved

9. **Aplomb** (noun) poise, assurance

"SONNY'S BLUES"

Excerpt from

GOING TO MEET THE MAN

James Baldwin

James Baldwin (1924-), a minister's son, grew up in Harlem. By the 1950's, Baldwin had become the leading literary spokesman on the issue of racial equality. Among his works are the plays **Amen Corner** and **Blues for Mister Charlie,** the novel **Go Tell It on the Mountain,** a collection of short stories, **Going to Meet the Man,** and essays collections, **Notes of a Native Son** and **Nobody Knows My Name.** Critic Irving Howe rates Baldwin among the two or three greatest essayists this country has produced.

I read about it in the paper, in the subway, on my way to work. I read it, and I couldn't believe it, and I read it again. Then perhaps I just stared at it, at the newsprint spelling out his name, spelling out the story. I stared at it in the swinging lights of the subway car, and in the faces and bodies of the people, and in my own face, trapped in the darkness which roared outside.

It was not to be believed and I kept telling myself that, as I walked from the subway station to the high school. And at the same time I couldn't doubt it. I was scared, scared for Sonny. He became real to me again. A great block of ice got settled in my belly and kept melting there slowly all day long, while I taught my classes algebra. It was a special kind of ice. It kept melting, sending trickles of ice water all up and down my veins, but it never got less. Sometimes it hardened and seemed to expand until I felt my guts were going to come spilling out or that I was going to choke or scream. This would always be at a moment when I was remembering some specific thing Sonny had once said or done.

When he was about as old as the boys in my classes, his face had been bright and open, with a lot of copper in it; and he'd had wonderfully direct brown eyes, and great gentleness and privacy. I wondered what he looked like now. He had been

---

"Sonny's Blues" from Going To Meet The Man by James Baldwin. Copyright (c) 1948, 1951, 1957, 1958, 1969 by James Baldwin. Reprinted by permission of Doubleday and Company, Inc.

picked up, the evening before, in a raid on an apartment downtown, for peddling and using heroin.

I couldn't believe it: but what I mean by that is that I couldn't find any room for it anywhere inside me. I had kept it outside me for a long time. I hadn't wanted to know. I had had suspicions, but I didn't name them. I kept putting them away. I told myself that Sonny was wild, but he wasn't crazy. And he'd always been a boy; he hadn't ever turned hard or evil or disrespectful, the way kids can, so quick, so quick, especially in Harlem. I didn't want to believe that I'd ever see my brother going down, coming to nothing, all that light in his face gone out, in the condition I'd already seen so many others. Yet it had happened and here I was, talking about algebra to a lot of boys who might, every one of them for all I knew, be popping off needles every time they went to the head. Maybe it did more for them than algebra could.

I was sure that the first time Sonny had ever had horse, he couldn't have been much older than these boys were now. These boys, now, were living as we'd been living then: they were growing up with a rush and their heads bumped abruptly against the low ceiling of their actual possibilities. They were filled with rage. All they really knew were two darknesses, the darkness of their lives, which was now closing in on them, and the darkness of the movies, which had blinded them to that other darkness, and in which they now, vindictively, dreamed, at once more together than they were at any other time, and more alone.

When the last bell rang, the last class ended, I let out my breath. It seemed I'd been holding it for all that time. My clothes were wet--I may have looked as though I'd been sitting in a steam bath, all dressed up, all afternoon. I sat alone in the classroom a long time. I listened to the boys outside, downstairs, shouting and cursing and laughing. Their laughter struck me for perhaps the first time. It was not the joyous laughter which--God knows why--one associates with children. It was mocking and insular; its intent was to denigrate. It was disenchanted, and in this, also, lay the authority of their curses. Perhaps I was listening to them because I was thinking about my brother and in them I heard my brother. And myself.

One boy was whistling a tune, at once very complicated and very simple. It seemed to be pouring out of him as though he were a bird, and it sounded very cool and moving through all that harsh, bright air, only just holding its own through all those other sounds.

I stood up and walked over to the window and looked down into the courtyard. It was the beginning of the spring and the sap was rising in the boys. A teacher passed through them every now and again, quickly, as though he or she couldn't wait to get out of that courtyard, to get those boys out of their sight and off their minds. I started collecting my stuff. I thought I'd better get home and talk to Isabel.

The courtyard was almost deserted by the time I got downstairs. I saw this boy standing in the shadow of a doorway, looking just like Sonny. I almost called his name. Then I saw that it wasn't Sonny, but somebody we used to know, a boy from around our block. He'd been Sonny's friend. He'd never been mine, having been too young for me, and, anyway, I'd never liked him. And now, even though he was a grown-up man, he still hung around that block, still spent hours on the street corners, was always high and raggy. I used to run into him from time to time, and he'd often work around to asking me for a quarter or fifty cents. He always had some real good excuse, too, and I always gave it to him. I don't know why.

But now, abruptly, I hated him. I couldn't stand the way he looked at me, partly like a dog, partly like a cunning child. I wanted to ask him what the hell he was doing in the school courtyard.

He sort of shuffled over to me, and he said, "I see you got the papers. So you already know about it."

"You mean about Sonny? Yes, I already know about it. How come they didn't get you?"

He grinned. It made him repulsive and it also brought to mind what he'd looked like as a kid. "I wasn't there. I stay away from them people."

"Good for you." I offered him a cigarette and I watched him through the smoke. "You come all the way down here just to tell me about Sonny?"

"That's right." He was sort of shaking his head and his eyes looked strange, as though they were about to cross. The bright sun deadened his damp dark brown skin and it made his eyes look yellow and showed up the dirt in his conked hair. He smelled funky. I moved a little away from him and I said, "Well, thanks. But I already know about it and I got to get home."

"I'll walk you a little ways," he said. We started walking. There were a couple of kids still loitering in the courtyard and one of them said goodnight to me and looked strangely at the boy beside me.

"What're you going to do?" he asked me. "I mean, about Sonny?"

"Look. I haven't seen Sonny for over a year, I'm not sure I'm going to do anything. Anyway, what the hell **can** I do?"

"That's right," he said quickly, "ain't nothing you can do. Can't much help old Sonny no more, I guess."

It was what I was thinking and so it seemed to me he had no right to say it.

"I'm surprised at Sonny, though," he went on—he had a funny way of talking. He looked straight ahead as though he were talking to himself—"I thought Sonny was a smart boy. I thought he was too smart to get hung."

"I guess he thought so too," I said sharply, "and that's how he got hung. And how about you? You're pretty goddamn smart, I bet."

Then he looked directly at me, just for a minute. "I ain't smart," he said. "If I was smart, I'd have reached for a pistol a long time ago."

"Look. Don't tell *me* your sad story. If it was up to me, I'd give you one." Then I felt guilty—guilty, probably, for never having supposed that the poor bastard **had** a story of his own, much less a sad one, and I asked, quickly, "What's going to happen to him now?"

He didn't answer this. He was off by himself some place. "Funny thing," he said, and from his tone we might have been discussing the quickest way to get to Brooklyn, "when I saw the papers this morning, the first thing I asked myself was if I had anything to do with it. I felt sort of responsible."

I began to listen more carefully. The subway station was on the corner, just before us, and I stopped. He stopped, too. We were in front of a bar and he ducked slightly, peering in, but whoever he was looking for didn't seem to be there. The juke box was blasting away with something black and bouncy and I half watched the barmaid as she danced her way from the juke box to her place behind the bar. And I watched her face as she laughingly responded to something someone said to her, still keeping time to the music. When she smiled one saw the little girl; one sensed the doomed, still-struggling woman beneath the battered face of the semi-whore.

"I never **give** Sonny nothing," the boy said finally, "but a long time ago I come to school high and Sonny asked me how it felt." He paused. I couldn't bear to watch him; I watched the barmaid, and I listened to the music which seemed to be causing the pavement to shake. "I told him it felt great." The music stopped, the barmaid paused and watched the juke box until the music began again. "It did."

All this was carrying me some place I didn't want to go. I certainly didn't want to know how it felt. It filled everything, the people, the houses, the music, the dark, quicksilver barmaid, with menace; and this menace was their reality.

"What's going to happen to him now?" I asked again.

"They'll send him away some place and they'll try to cure him." He shook his head. "Maybe he'll even think he's kicked the habit. Then they'll let him loose"—he gestured, throwing his cigarette into the gutter. "That's all."

"What do you mean, that's **all**?"

But I knew what he meant.

"I **mean,** that's all." He turned his head and looked at me, pulling down the corners of his mouth. "Don't you know what I mean?" he asked, softly.

"How the hell **would** I know what you mean?" I almost whispered, I don't know why.

"That's right," he said to the air, "how would he know what I mean?" He turned toward me again, patient and calm, and yet I somehow felt him shaking, shaking as though he were going to fall apart. I felt that ice in my guts again, the dread I'd felt all afternoon; and again I watched the barmaid, moving about the bar, washing glasses, and singing. "Listen. They'll let him out and then it'll just start all over again. That's what I mean."

"You mean--they'll let him out. And then he'll just start working his way back in again. You mean he'll never kick the habit. Is that what you mean?"

"That's right," he said, cheerfully. "You see what I mean."

"Tell me," I said at last, "why does he want to die? He must want to die; he's killing himself. Why does he want to die?"

He looked at me in surprise. He licked his lips. "He don't want to die. He wants to live. Don't nobody want to die, ever."

Then I wanted to ask him—too many things. He could not have answered, or if he had, I could not have borne the answers. I started walking. "Well, I guess it's none of my business."

"It's going to be rough on old Sonny," he said. We reached the subway station. "This is your station?" he asked. I nodded. I took one step down. "Damn!" he said, suddenly. I looked up at him. He grinned again. "Damn it if I didn't leave all my money home. You ain't got a dollar on you, have you? Just for a couple of days, is all."

All at once something inside gave and threatened to come pouring out of me. I didn't hate him any more. I felt that in another moment I'd start crying like a child.

"Sure," I said. "Don't sweat." I looked in my wallet and didn't have a dollar, I only had a five. "Here," I said. "That hold you?"

He didn't look at it--he didn't want to look at it. A terrible, closed look came over his face, as though he were keeping the number on the bill a secret from him and me. "Thanks," he said, and now he was dying to see me go. "Don't worry about Sonny. Maybe I'll write him or something."

"Sure," I said. "You do that. So long."

"Be seeing you," he said. I went on down the steps.

And I didn't write Sonny or send him anything for a long time. When I finally did, it was just after my little girl died, he wrote me back a letter which made me feel like a bastard.

Here's what he said:

Dear brother,

You don't know how much I needed to hear from you. I wanted to write you many a time but I dug how much I must have hurt you and so I didn't write. But now I feel like a man who's been trying to climb up out of some deep, real deep and funky hole and just saw the sun up there, outside. I got to get outside.

I can't tell you much about how I got here. I mean I don't know how to tell you. I guess I was afraid of something or I was trying to escape from something and you know I have never been very strong in the head (smile). I'm glad Mama and Daddy are dead and can't see what's happened to their son and I swear if I'd known what I was doing I would never have hurt you so, you and a lot of other fine people who were nice to me and who believed in me.

I don't want you to think it had anything to do with me being a musician. It's more than that. Or maybe less than that. I can't get anything straight in my head down here and I try not to think about what's going to happen to me when I get outside again. Sometime I think I'm going to flip and never get outside and sometime I think I'll come straight back. I tell you one thing, though, I'd rather blow my brains out than go through this again. But that's what they all say, so they tell me. If I tell you when I'm coming to New York and if you could meet me, I sure would appreciate it. Give my love to Isabel and the kids and I was sure sorry to hear about little Gracie. I wish I could be like Mama and say the Lord's will be done, but I don't know it seems to me that trouble is the one thing that never does get stopped and I don't know what good it does to blame it on the Lord. But maybe it does some good if you believe it.

Your brother,
Sonny

Then I kept in constant touch with him and I sent him whatever I could and I went to meet him when he came back to New York. When I saw him, many things I thought I had forgotten came flooding back to me. This was because I had begun, finally, to wonder about Sonny, about the life that Sonny lived inside. This life, whatever it was, had made him older and thinner and it had deepened the distant stillness in which he had always moved. He looked very unlike my baby brother. Yet, when he smiled, when we shook hands, the baby brother I'd never known looked out from the depths of his private life, like an animal waiting to be coaxed into the light.

"How you been keeping?" he asked me.

"All right. And you?"

"Just fine." He was smiling all over his face. "It's good to see you again."

"It's good to see you."

The seven years' difference in our ages lay between us like a chasm: I wondered if these years would ever operate between us as a bridge. I was remembering, and it made it hard to catch my breath, that I had been there when he was born; and I had heard the first words he had ever spoken. When he started to walk, he walked from our mother straight to me. I caught him just before he fell when he took the first steps he ever took in this world.

"How's Isabel?"

"Just fine. She's dying to see you."

"And the boys?"

"They're fine, too. They're anxious to see their uncle."

"Oh, come on. You know they don't remember me."

"Are you kidding? Of course they remember you."

He grinned again. We got into a taxi. We had a lot to say to each other, far too much to know how to begin.

As the taxi began to move, I asked, "You still want to go to India?"

He laughed. "You still remember that. Hell, no. This place is Indian enough for me."

"It used to belong to them," I said.

And he laughed again. "They damn sure knew what they were doing when they got rid of it."

Years ago, when he was around fourteen, he'd been all hipped on the idea of going to India. He read books about people sitting on rocks, naked, in all kinds of weather, but mostly bad, naturally, and walking barefoot through hot coals and arriving at wisdom. I used to say that it sounded to me as though they were getting away from wisdom as fast as they could. I think he sort of looked down on me for that.

"Do you mind," he asked, "if we have the driver drive alongside the park? On the west side—I haven't seen the city in so long."

"Of course not," I said. I was afraid that I might sound as though I were humoring him, but I hoped he wouldn't take it that way.

So we drove along, between the green of the park and the stony, lifeless elegance of hotels and apartment buildings, toward the vivid, killing streets of our childhood. These streets hadn't changed, though housing projects jutted up out of them now like rocks in the middle of a boiling sea. Most of the houses in which we had grown up had vanished, as had the stores from which we had stolen, the basements in which we had first tried sex, the rooftops from which we had hurled tin cans and bricks. But houses exactly like the houses of our past yet dominated the landscape, and boys exactly like the boys we once had been found themselves smothering in these houses, came down into the streets for light and air and found themselves encircled by disaster. Some escaped the trap, most didn't. Those who got out always left something of themselves behind, as some animals amputate a leg and leave it in the trap. It might be said, perhaps, that I had escaped, because I was a school teacher; or that Sonny had, because he hadn't lived in Harlem for years. Yet, as the cab moved uptown through streets which seemed, with a rush, to darken with dark people, and as I covertly studied Sonny's face, it came to me that what we both were seeking through our separate cab windows was that part of ourselves which had been left behind. It's always at the hour of trouble and confrontation that the missing member aches.

We hit 110th Street and started rolling up Lenox Avenue. And I'd known this avenue all my life, but it seemed to me again, as it had seemed on the day I'd first heard about Sonny's trouble, filled with a hidden menace which was its very breath of life.

"We almost there," said Sonny.

"Almost." We were both too nervous to say anything more.

We live in a housing project. It hasn't been up long. A few days after it was up it seemed uninhabitably new; now, of course, it's already rundown. It looks like a parody of the good, clean, faceless life—God knows the people who live in it do their best to make it a parody. The beat-looking grass lying around isn't enough to make their lives green, the hedges will never hold out the streets, and they know it. The big windows fool no one; they aren't big enough to make space out of no space. They don't bother with the windows; they watch the TV screen instead. The playground is most popular with the children who don't play at jacks, or skip rope, or roller skate, or swing, and they can be found in it after dark. We moved in partly because it's not too far from where I teach, and partly for the kids; but it's really just like the houses in which Sonny and I grew up. The same things happen; they'll have the same things to remember. The moment Sonny and I started into the house I had the feeling that I was simply bringing him back into the danger he had almost died trying to escape.

Sonny has never been talkative. So I don't know why I was sure he'd be dying to talk to me when supper was over the first night. Everything went fine--the oldest boys remembered him, and the youngest boy liked him, and Sonny had remembered to bring something for each of them; and Isabel, who is really much nicer than I am, more open and giving, had gone to a lot of trouble about dinner and was genuinely glad to see him. And she's always been able to tease Sonny in a way that I haven't. It was nice to see her face so vivid again and to hear her laugh and watch her make Sonny laugh. She wasn't, or, anyway, she didn't seem to be, at all uneasy or embarrassed. She chatted as though there were no subject which had to be avoided and she got Sonny past his first, faint stiffness. And thank God she was there, for I was filled with that icy dread again. Everything I did seemed awkward to me, and everything I said sounded freighted with hidden meaning. I was trying to remember everything I'd heard about dope addiction and I couldn't help watching Sonny for signs. I wasn't doing it out of malice. I was trying to find out something about my brother. I was dying to hear him tell me he was safe.

"Safe!" my father grunted, whenever Mama suggested trying to move to a neighborhood which might be safer for children. "Safe, hell! Ain't no place safe for kids, nor nobody."

He always went on like this, but he wasn't ever, really as bad as he sounded, not even on weekends, when he got drunk. As a matter of fact, he was always on the lookout for "something a little better," but he died before he found it. He died suddenly, during a drunken weekend in the middle of the war, when Sonny was fifteen. He and Sonny hadn't ever got on too well. And this was partly because Sonny was the apple of his father's eye. It was because he loved Sonny so much and was frightened for him, that he was always fighting with him. It doesn't do any good to fight with Sonny. Sonny just moves back, inside himself, where he can't be reached. But the principal reason that they never hit it off is that they were so much alike. Daddy was big and rough and loud-talking, just the opposite of Sonny, but they both had--that same privacy.

Mama tried to tell me something about this, just after Daddy died. I was home on leave from the army.

This was the last time I ever saw my mother alive. Just the same, this picture gets all mixed up in my mind with pictures I had of her when she was younger. The way I always see her is the way she used to be on a Sunday afternoon, say, when the old folks were talking after the big Sunday dinner. I always see her wearing pale blue. She'd be sitting on the sofa. And my father would be sitting in the easy chair, not far from her. And the living room would be full of church folks and relatives. There they sit, in chairs all around the living room, and the night is creeping up outside, but nobody knows it yet. You can see the darkness growing against the windowpanes and you hear the street noises every now and again, or maybe the jangling beat of a tambourine from one of the churches close by, but it's real quiet in the room. For a moment nobody's talking, but every face looks darkening, like the sky outside. And my mother rocks a little from the waist, and my father's eyes are closed. Everyone is looking at something a child can't see. For a minute they've forgotten the children. Maybe a kid is lying on the rug, half asleep. Maybe somebody's got a kid in his lap and is absent-mindedly stroking the kid's head. Maybe there's a kid, quiet and big-eyed, curled up in a big chair in the corner. The silence, the darkness coming, and the darkness in the faces frightens the child obscurely. He hopes that the hand which strokes his forehead will never stop—will never die. He hopes that there will never come a time when the old folks won't be sitting around the living room, talking about where they've come from, and what they've seen, and what's happened to them and their kinfolk.

But something deep and watchful in the child knows that this is bound to end, is already ending. In a moment someone will get up and turn on the light. Then the old folks will remember the children and they won't talk any more that day. And when light fills the room, the child is filled with darkness. He knows that every time this happens he's moved just a little closer to that darkness outside. The darkness outside is what the old folks have been talking about. It's what they've come from. It's what they endure. The child knows that they won't talk any more because if he knows too much about what's happened to them, he'll know too much too soon, about what's going to happen to him.

There Mama sat, in black, by the window. She was humming an old church song, "Lord, you brought me from a long ways off." Sonny was out somewhere. Mama kept watching the streets.

"I don't know," she said, "if I'll ever see you again, after you go off from here. But I hope you'll remember the things I tried to teach you."

"Don't talk like that," I said, and smiled. "You'll be here a long time yet."

She smiled, too, but she said nothing. She was quiet for a long time. And I said, "Mama, don't you worry about nothing. I'll be writing all the time, and you be getting the checks..."

"I want to talk to you about your brother," she said, suddenly. "If anything happens to me, he ain't going to have nobody to look out for him."

"Mama," I said, "ain't nothing going to happen to you **or** Sonny. Sonny's all right. He's a good boy and he's got good sense."

"It ain't a question of his being a good boy," Mama said, "nor of his having good sense. It ain't only the bad ones, nor yet the dumb ones that gets sucked under." She stopped, looking at me. "Your Daddy once had a brother," she said, and she smiled in a way that made me feel she was in pain. "You didn't never know that, did you?"

"No," I said, "I never knew that," and I watched her face.

"Oh, yes," she said, "your Daddy had a brother." She looked out of the window again. "I know you never saw your Daddy cry. But **I** did—many a time, through all these years."

I asked her, "What happened to his brother? How come nobody's ever talked about him?"

This was the first time I ever saw my mother look old.

"His brother got killed," she said, "when he was just a little younger than you are now. I knew him. He was a fine boy. He was maybe a little full of the devil, but he didn't mean nobody no harm."

Then she stopped and the room was silent, exactly as it had sometimes been on those Sunday afternoons. Mama kept looking out into the streets.

"He used to have a job in the mill," she said, "and, like all young folks, he just liked to perform on Saturday nights. Saturday nights, him and your father would drift around to different places, go to dances and things like that, or just sit around with people they knew, and your father's brother would sing, he had a fine voice, and play along with himself on his guitar. Well, this particular Saturday night, him and your father was coming home from some place, and they were both a little drunk and there was a moon that night. It was bright like day. Your father's brother was feeling kind of good, and he was whistling to himself, and he had his guitar slung over his shoulder. They was coming down a hill and beneath them was a road that turned off from the highway. Well, your father's brother, being always kind of frisky, decided to run down this hill, and he did, with that guitar banging and clanging behind him, and he ran across the road, and he was making water behind a tree. And your father was sort of amused at him and he was still coming down the hill, kind of slow. Then he heard a car motor and that same minute his brother stepped from behind the tree, into the road, in the moonlight. And he started to cross the road. And your father started to run down the hill; he says he don't know why. This car was full of white men. They was all drunk, and when they seen your father's brother they let out a great whoop and holler and they aimed the car straight at him. They was having fun. They just wanted to scare him, the way they do sometimes, you know. But they was drunk. And I guess the boy, being drunk, too, and scared, kind of lost his head. By the time he jumped it was too late. Your father says he heard his brother scream when the car rolled over him, and he heard the wood of that guitar when it give, and he heard them strings go flying, and he heard them white men shouting, and the car kept on a-going and it ain't stopped till this day. And, time your father got down the hill, his brother weren't nothing but blood and pulp."

Tears were gleaming on my mother's face. There wasn't anything I could say.

"He never mentioned it," she said, "because I never let him mention it before you children. Your Daddy was like a crazy man that night and for many a night thereafter. He says he never in his life seen anything as dark as that road after the lights of that car had gone away. Weren't nothing, weren't nobody on that road, just your Daddy and his brother and that busted guitar. Oh, yes. Your Daddy never did really get right again. Till the day he died he weren't sure but that every white man he saw was the man that killed his brother."

She stopped and took out her handkerchief and dried her eyes and looked at me.

"I ain't telling you all this," she said, "to make you scared or bitter or to make you hate nobody. I'm telling you this because you got a brother. And the world ain't changed."

I guess I didn't want to believe this. I guess she saw this in my face. She turned away from me, toward the window again, searching those streets.

"But I praise my Redeemer," she said at last, "that He called your Daddy home before me. I ain't saying it to throw no flowers at myself, but, I declare, it keeps me from feeling too cast down to know I helped your father get safely through this world. Your father always acted like he was the roughest, strongest man on earth. And everybody took him to be like that. But if he hadn't had **me** there—to see his tears!"

She was crying again. Still, I couldn't move. I said, "Lord, Lord, Mama, I didn't know it was like that."

"Oh, honey," she said, "there's a lot that you don't know. But you are going to find it out." She stood up from the window and came over to me. "You got to hold on to your brother," she said, "and don't let him fall, no matter what it looks like is happening to him and no matter how evil you gets with him. You going to be evil with him many a time. But don't you forget what I told you, you hear?"

"I won't forget," I said. "Don't you worry. I won't forget. I won't let nothing happen to Sonny."

My mother smiled as though she were amused at something she saw in my face. Then, "You may not be able to stop nothing from happening. But you got to let him know you's *there*."

Two days later I was married, and then I was gone. And I had a lot of things on my mind and I pretty well forgot my promise to Mama until I got shipped home on a special furlough for her funeral.

And, after the funeral, with just Sonny and me alone in the empty kitchen, I tried to find out something about him.

"What do you want to do?" I asked him.

"I'm going to be a musician," he said.

For he had graduated, in the time I had been away, from dancing to the juke box to finding out who was playing what, and what they were doing with it, and he had bought himself a set of drums.

"You mean, you want to be a drummer?" I somehow had the feeling that being a drummer might be all right for other people but not for my brother Sonny.

"I don't think," he said, looking at me very gravely, "that I'll ever be a good drummer. But I think I can play a piano."

I frowned. I'd never played the role of the older brother quite so seriously before, had scarcely ever, in fact, *asked* Sonny a damn thing. I sensed myself in the presence of something I didn't really know how to handle, didn't understand. So I made my frown a little deeper as I asked: "What kind of musician do you want to be?"

He grinned. "How many kinds do you think there are?"

"Be *serious*," I said.

He laughed, throwing his head back, and then looked at me. "I *am* serious."

"Well, then, for Christ's sake, stop kidding around and answer a serious question. I mean, do you want to be a concert pianist, you want to play classical music and all that, or—or what?" Long before I finished he was laughing again. "For Christ's sake, Sonny!"

He sobered, but with difficulty. "I'm sorry. But you sound so—*scared!*" and he was off again.

"Well, you may think it's funny now, baby, but it's not going to be so funny when you have to make your living at it. Let me tell you that." I was furious because I knew he was laughing at me and I didn't know why.

"No," he said, very sober now, and afraid, perhaps, that he'd hurt me, "I don't want to be a classical pianist. That isn't what interests me. I mean"—he paused, looking hard at me, as though his eyes would help me to understand, and then gestured helplessly, as though perhaps his hand would help—"I mean, I'll have a lot of studying to do, and I'll have to study *everything*, but, I mean, I want to play with—jazz musicians." He stopped. "I want to play jazz," he said.

Well, the word had never before sounded as heavy, as real, as it sounded that afternoon in Sonny's mouth. I just looked at him and I was probably frowning a real frown by this time. I simply couldn't see why on earth he'd want to spend his time hanging around nightclubs, clowning around on bandstands, while people pushed each other around a dance floor. It seemed—beneath him, somehow. I had never thought about it before, had never been forced to, but I suppose I had always put jazz musicians in a class with what Daddy called "good-time people."

"Are you *serious*?"

"Hell, *yes*, I'm serious."

He looked more helpless than ever, and annoyed, and deeply hurt.

I suggested, helpfully: "You mean—like Louis Armstrong?"

His face closed as though I'd struck him. "No. I'm not talking about none of that old-time, down home crap."

"Well, look, Sonny, I'm sorry. Don't get mad. I just don't altogether get it, that's all. Name somebody—you know, a jazz musician you admire."

"Bird."

"Who?"

"Bird! Charlie Parker! Don't they teach you nothing in the goddamn army?"

I lit a cigarette. I was surprised and then a little amused to discover that I was trembling. "I've been out of touch," I said. "You'll have to be patient with me. Now. Who's this Parker character?"

"He's just one of the greatest jazz musicians alive," said Sonny, sullenly, his hands in his pockets, his back to me. "Maybe the greatest," he added, bitterly, "that's probably why *you* never heard of him."

"All right," I said, "I'm ignorant. I'm sorry. I'll go out and buy all the cat's records right away, all right?"

"It don't," said Sonny, with dignity, "make any difference to me. I don't care what you listen to. Don't do me no favors."

I was beginning to realize that I'd never seen him so upset before. With another part of my mind I was thinking that this would probably turn out to be one of those things kids go through and that I shouldn't make it seem important by pushing it too hard. Still, I didn't think it would do any harm to ask: "Doesn't all this take a lot of time? Can you make a living at it?"

He turned back to me and half leaned, half sat, on the kitchen table. "Everything takes time," he said, "and—well, yes, sure, I can make a living at it. But what I don't seem to be able to make you understand is that it's the only thing I want to do."

"Well, Sonny," I said, gently, "you know people can't always do exactly what they want to do—"

"No, I don't know that," said Sonny, surprising me. "I think people *ought* to do what they want to do. What else are they alive for?"

"You getting to be a big boy," I said desperately, "it's time you started thinking about your future."

"I'm thinking about my future," said Sonny, grimly. "I think about it all the time."

I gave up. I decided, if he didn't change his mind, that we could always talk about it later. "In the meantime," I said, "you got to finish school." We had already decided that he'd have to move in with Isabel and her folks. I knew this wasn't the ideal arrangement because Isabel's folks are inclined to be dicty and they hadn't especially wanted Isabel to marry me. But I didn't know what else to do. "And we have to get you fixed up at Isabel's."

There was a long silence. He moved from the kitchen table to the window. "That's a terrible idea. You know it yourself."

"Do you have a _better_ idea?"

He just walked up and down the kitchen for a minute. He was as tall as I was. He had started to shave. I suddenly had the feeling that I didn't know him at all.

He stopped at the kitchen table and picked up my cigarettes. Looking at me with a kind of mocking, amused defiance, he put one between his lips. "You mind?"

"You smoking already?"

He lit the cigarette and nodded, watching me through the smoke. "I just wanted to see if I'd have the courage to smoke in front of you." He grinned and blew a great cloud of smoke to the ceiling. "It was easy." He looked at my face. "Come on, now. I bet you was smoking at my age. Tell the truth."

I didn't say anything but the truth was on my face, and he laughed. But now there was something very strained in his laugh. "Sure. And I bet that ain't all you was doing."

He was frightening me a little. "Cut the crap," I said. "We already decided that you was going to go and live at Isabel's. Now what's got into you all of a sudden?"

"_You_ decided it," he pointed out. "_I_ didn't decide nothing." He stopped in front of me, leaning against the stove, arms loosely folded. "Look, brother. I don't want to stay in Harlem no more. I really don't." He was very earnest. He looked at me, then over toward the kitchen window. There was something in his eyes I'd never seen before, some thoughtfulness, some worry all his own. He rubbed the muscle of one arm. "It's time I was getting out of here."

"Where do you want to go, Sonny?"

"I want to join the army. Or the navy, I don't care. If I say I'm old enough, they'll believe me."

Then I got mad. It was because I was so scared. "You must be crazy. You goddamn fool, what the hell do you want to go and join the army for?"

"I just told you. To get out of Harlem."

"Sonny, you haven't even finished school. And if you really want to be a musician, how do you expect to study if you're in the army?"

He looked at me, trapped, and in anguish. "There's ways. I might be able to work out some kind of deal. Anyway, I'll have the G.I. Bill when I come out."

"If you come out." We stared at each other. "Sonny, please. Be reasonable. I know the setup is far from perfect. But we got to do the best we can."

"I ain't learning nothing in school," he said. "Even when I go." He turned away from me and opened the window and threw his cigarette out into the narrow alley. I watched his back. "At least, I ain't learning nothing you'd want me to learn." He slammed the window so hard I thought the glass would fly out, and turned back to me. "And I'm sick of the stink of these garbage cans!"

"Sonny," I said, "I know how you feel. But if you don't finish school now, you're going to be sorry later that you didn't." I grabbed him by the shoulders. "And you only got another year. It ain't so bad. And I'll come back and I swear I'll help you do whatever you want to do. Just try to put up with it till I come back. Will you please do that? For me?"

He didn't answer and he wouldn't look at me.

"Sonny. You hear me?"

He pulled away. "I hear you. But you never hear anything I say."

I didn't know what to say to that. He looked out of the window and then back at me. "Okay," he said, and sighed, "I'll try."

Then I said, trying to cheer him up a little, "They got a piano at Isabel's. You can practice on it."

And as a matter of fact, it did cheer him up for a minute. "That's right," he said to himself. "I forgot that." His face relaxed a little. But the worry, the thoughtfulness, played on it still, the way shadows play on a face which is staring into the fire.

But I thought I'd never hear the end of that piano. At first, Isabel would write me, saying how nice it was that Sonny was so serious about his music and how, as soon as he came in from school, or wherever he had been when he was supposed to be at school, he went straight to that piano and stayed there until suppertime. And, after supper, he went back to that piano and stayed there until everybody went to bed. He was at the piano all day Saturday and all day Sunday. Then he bought a record player and started playing records. He'd play one record over and over again, all day long sometimes, and he'd improvise along with it on the piano. Or he'd play one section of the record, one chord, one change, one progression; then he'd do it on the piano. Then back to the record. Then back to the piano.

Well, I really don't know how they stood it. Isabel finally confessed that it wasn't like living with a person at all; it was like living with sound. And the sound didn't make any sense to her, didn't make any sense to any of them—naturally. They began, in a way, to be afflicted by this presence that was living in their home. It was as though Sonny were some sort of god, or monster. He moved in an atmosphere which wasn't like theirs at all. They fed him and he ate, he washed himself, he walked in and out of their door; he certainly wasn't nasty or unpleasant or rude. Sonny isn't any of those things; but it was as though he were all wrapped up in some cloud, some fire, some vision all his own; and there wasn't any way to reach him.

At the same time, he wasn't really a man yet. He was still a child, and they had to watch out for him in all kinds of ways. They certainly couldn't throw him out. Neither did they dare to make a great scene about that piano because even they dimly sensed, as I sensed, from so many thousands of miles away, that Sonny was at that piano playing for his life.

But he hadn't been going to school. One day a letter came from the school board and Isabel's mother got it—there had, apparently, been other letters but Sonny had torn them up. This day, when Sonny came in, Isabel's mother showed him the letter and asked where he'd been spending his time. And she finally got it out of him that he'd been down in Greenwich Village, with musicians and other characters, in a white girl's apartment. And this scared her and she started to scream at him and what came up, once she began—though she denies it to this day—was what sacrifices they were making to give Sonny a decent home and how little he appreciated it.

Sonny didn't play the piano that day. By evening, Isabel's mother had calmed down but then there was the old man to deal with, and Isabel herself. Isabel says she did her best to be calm but she broke down and started crying. She says she just watched Sonny's face. She could tell, by watching him, what was happening with him. And what was happening was that they penetrated his cloud; they had reached him. Even if their fingers had been a thousand times more gentle than human fingers ever are, he could hardly help feeling that they had stripped him naked and were spitting on that nakedness. For he also had to see that his presence, that music, which was life or death to him, had been torture for them and that they had endured it, not at all for his sake, but only for mine. And Sonny couldn't take that. He can take it a little better today than he could then but he's still not very good at it and, frankly, I don't know anybody who is.

The silence of the next few days must have been louder than the sound of all the music ever played since time began. One morning, before she went to work, Isabel was in his room for something and she suddenly realized that all of his records were gone. And she knew for certain that he was gone. And he was. He went as far as the navy would carry him. He finally sent me a postcard from some place in Greece and that was the first I knew that Sonny was still alive. I didn't see him any more until we were both back in New York and the war had long been over.

He was a man by then, of course, but I wasn't willing to see it. He came by the house from time to time, but we fought almost every time we met. I didn't like the way he carried himself, loose and dreamlike all the time, and I didn't like his friends, and his music seemed to be merely an excuse for the life he led. It sounded just that weird and disordered.

Then we had a fight, a pretty awful fight, and I didn't see him for months. By and by I looked him up, where he was living, in a furnished room in the Village, and I tried to make it up. But there were lots of other people in the room and Sonny just lay on his bed, and he wouldn't come downstairs with me, and he treated these other people as though they were his family and I weren't. So I got mad and then he got mad, and then I told him that he might just as well be dead as live the way he was living. Then he stood up and he told me not to worry about him any more in life, that he _was_ dead as far as I was concerned. Then he pushed me to the door, and the other people looked on as though nothing were happening, and he slammed the door behind me. I stood in the hallway, staring at the door. I heard somebody laugh in the room and then the tears came to my eyes. I started down the steps, whistling to keep from crying. I kept whistling to myself, "_You going to need me, baby, one of these cold, rainy days._"

I read about Sonny's trouble in the spring. Little Grace died in the fall. She was a beautiful little girl. But she only lived a little over two years. She died of polio and she suffered. She had a slight fever for a couple of days, but it didn't seem like anything and we just kept her in bed. And we would certainly have called the doctor, but the fever dropped. She seemed to be all right. So we thought it had just been a cold. Then, one day, she was up, playing, Isabel was in the kitchen fixing lunch for the two boys when they'd come in from school, and she heard Grace fall down in the living room. When you have a lot of children you don't always start running when one of them falls, unless they start screaming or something. And, this time, Grace was quiet. Yet, Isabel says that when she heard that _thump_ and then that silence, something happened in her to make her afraid. And she ran to the living room and there was little Grace on the floor, all twisted up, and the reason she hadn't screamed was that she couldn't get her breath. And when she did scream, it was the worst sound, Isabel says, that she'd ever heard in all her life, and she still hears it sometimes in her dreams. Isabel will sometimes wake me up with a low, moaning, strangled sound, and I have to be quick to awaken her and hold her to me and where Isabel is weeping against me seems a mortal wound.

I think I may have written Sonny the very day that little Grace was buried. I was sitting in the living room in the dark, by myself, and I suddenly thought of Sonny. My trouble made his real.

One Sunday afternoon, when Sonny had been living with us, or anyway, been in our house, for nearly two weeks, I found myself wandering aimlessly about the living room, drinking from a can of beer, and trying to work up the courage to search Sonny's room. He was out, as he usually was whenever I was home, and Isabel had taken the children to see their grandparents. Suddenly I was standing still in front of the living room window, watching Seventh Avenue. The idea of searching Sonny's room made me still. I scarcely dared to admit to myself what I'd be searching for. I didn't know what I'd do if I found it. Or if I didn't.

On the sidewalk across from me, near the entrance to a barbecue joint, some people were holding an old-fashioned revival meeting. The barbecue cook, wearing a dirty white apron, his conked hair reddish and metallic in the pale sun, and a cigarette between his lips, stood in the doorway, watching them. Kids and older people paused in the errands and stood there, along with some older men and a couple of very tough-looking women who watched everything that happened on the avenue as though they owned it, or were maybe owned by it. Well, they were watching this, too. The revival was being carried on by three sisters in black, and a brother. All they had were their voices and their Bibles and a tambourine. The brother was testifying and while he testified two of the sisters stood together, seeming to say, amen, and the third sister walked around with the tambourine outstretched and a couple of people dropped coins into it. Then the brother's testimony ended and the sister who had been taking up the collection dumped the coins into her palm and transferred them to the pocket of her long black robe. Then she raised both hands, striking the tambourine against the air, and then against one hand, and she started to sing. And the two other sisters and the brother joined in.

It was strange, suddenly, to watch, though I had been seeing these street meetings all my life. So, of course, had everybody else down there. Yet, they paused and watched and listened and I stood still at the window. "*Tis the old ship of Zion,*" they sang, and the sister with the tambourine kept a steady, jangling beat, "*it has rescued many a thousand!*" Not a soul under the sound of their voices was hearing this song for the first time; not one of them had been rescued. Nor had they seen much in the way of rescue work being done around them. Neither did they especially believe in the holiness of the three sisters and the brother. They knew too much about them, knew where they lived, and how. The woman with the tambourine, whose voice dominated the air, whose face was bright with joy, was divided by very little from the woman who stood watching her, a cigarette between her heavy, chapped lips, her hair a cuckoo's nest, her face scarred and swollen from many beatings, and her black eyes glittering like coal. Perhaps they both knew this, which was why, when, as rarely, they addressed each other, they addressed each other as Sister. As the singing filled the air the watching, listening faces underwent a change, the eyes focusing on something within; the music seemed to soothe a poison out of them; and time seemed, nearly, to fall away from the sullen, belligerent, battered faces, as though they were fleeing back to their first condition, while dreaming of their last. The barbecue cook half shook his head and smiled, and dropped his cigarette and disappeared into his joint. A man fumbled in his pockets for change and stood holding it in his hand impatiently, as though he had just remembered a pressing appointment further up the avenue. He looked furious. Then I saw Sonny, standing on the edge of the crowd. He was carrying a wide, flat notebook with a green cover, and it made him look, from where I was standing, almost like a schoolboy. The coppery sun brought out the copper in his skin. He was very faintly smiling, standing very still. Then the singing stopped, and the tambourine turned into a collection plate again. The furious man dropped in his coins and vanished, so did a couple of the women, and Sonny dropped some change in the plate, looking directly at the woman with a little smile. He started across the avenue, toward the house. He has a slow, loping walk, something like the way Harlem hipsters walk, only he's imposed on this his own half-beat. I had never really noticed it before.

I stayed at the window, both relieved and apprehensive. As Sonny disappeared from my sight, they began singing again. And they were still singing when his key turned in the lock.

"Hey," he said.

"Hey, yourself. You want some beer?"

"No. Well, maybe." But he came up to the window and stood beside me, looking out. "What a warm voice," he said.

They were singing "If I could only hear my mother pray again!"

"Yes," I said, "and she can sure beat that tambourine."

"But what a terrible song," he said, and laughed. He dropped his notebook on the sofa and disappeared into the kitchen. "Where's Isabel and the kids?"

"I think they went to see their grandparents. You hungry?"

"No." He came back into the living room with his can of beer. "You want to come some place with me tonight?"

I sensed, I don't know how, that I couldn't possibly say no. "Sure. Where?"

He sat down on the sofa and picked up his notebook and started leafing through it. "I'm going to sit in with some fellows in a joint in the Village."

"You mean, you're going to play, tonight?"

"That's right." He took a swallow of his beer and moved back to the window. He gave me a sidelong look. "If you can stand it."

"I'll try," I said.

He smiled to himself and we both watched as the meeting across the way broke up. The three sisters and the brother, heads bowed, were singing "God be with you till we meet again." The faces around them were very quiet. Then the song ended. The small crowd dispersed. We watched the three women and the lone man walk slowly up the avenue.

"When she was singing before," said Sonny, abruptly, "her voice reminded me for a minute of what heroin feels like sometimes--when it's in your veins. It makes you feel sort of warm and cool at the same time. And distant. And—and sure." He sipped his beer, very deliberately not looking at me. I watched his face. "It makes you feel—in control. Sometimes you've got to have that feeling."

"Do you?" I sat down slowly in the easy chair.

"Sometimes." He went to the sofa and picked up his notebook again. "Some people do."

"In order," I asked, "to play?" And my voice was very ugly, full of contempt and anger.

"Well"—he looked at me with great, troubled eyes, as though, in fact, he hoped his eyes would tell me things he could never otherwise say—"they think so. And if they think so—!"

"And what do you think?" I asked.

He sat on the sofa and put his can of beer on the floor. "I don't know," he said, and I couldn't be sure if he were answering my question or pursuing his thoughts. His face didn't tell me. "It's not so much to play. It's to stand it, to be able to make it at all. On any level." He frowned and smiled: "In order to keep from shaking to pieces."

"But these friends of yours," I said, "they seem to shake themselves to pieces pretty goddamn fast."

"Maybe." He played with the notebook. And something told me that I should curb my tongue, that Sonny was doing his best to talk, and I should listen. "But of course you only know the ones that've gone to pieces. Some don't—or at least they haven't yet and that's just about all any of us can say." He paused. "And then there are some who just live, really, in hell, and they know it and they see what's happening and they go right on. I don't know." He sighed, dropped the notebook, folded his arms. "Some guys, you can tell from the way they play, they on something all the time. And you can see that, well, it makes something real for them. But of course," he picked up his beer from the floor and sipped it and put the can down again, "they want to, too, you've got to see that. Even some of them that say they don't--some, not all."

"And what about you?" I asked--I couldn't help it. "What about you? Do you want to?"

He stood up and walked to the window and remained silent for a long time. Then he sighed. "Me," he said. Then: "While I was downstairs before, on my way here, listening to that woman sing, it struck me all of a sudden how much suffering she must have had to go through--to sing like that. It's repulsive to think you have to suffer that much."

I said: "But there's no way not to suffer--is there, Sonny?"

"I believe not," he said and smiled, "but that's never stopped anyone from trying." He looked at me. "Has it?" I realized, with this mocking look, that there stood between us, forever, beyond the power of time or forgiveness, the fact that I had held silence--so long!--when he had needed human speech to help him. He turned back to the window. "No, there's no way not to suffer. But you try all kinds of ways to keep from drowning in it, to keep on top of it, and to make it seem--well, like you. Like you did something, all right, and now you're suffering for it. You know?" I said nothing. "Well you know," he said, impatiently, "why do people suffer? Maybe it's better to do something to give it a reason, any reason."

"But we just agreed," I said, "that there's no way not to suffer. Isn't it better, then, just to--take it?"

"But nobody just takes it," Sonny cried, "that's what I'm telling you! Everybody tries not to. You're just hung up on the way some people try--it's not your way!"

The hair on my face began to itch; my face felt wet. "That's not true," I said, "that's not true. I don't give a damn what other people do. I don't even care how they suffer. I just care how <u>you</u> suffer." And he looked at me. "Please believe me," I said, "I don't want to see you--die--trying not to suffer."

"I won't," he said, flatly, "die trying not to suffer. At least, not any faster than anybody else."

"But there's no need," I said, trying to laugh, "is there, in killing yourself?"

I wanted to say more, but I couldn't. I wanted to talk about will power and how life could be--well, beautiful. I wanted to say that it was all within; but was it? Or, rather, wasn't that exactly the trouble? And I wanted to promise that I would never fail him again. But it would all have sounded--empty words and lies.

So I made the promise to myself and prayed that I would keep it.

"It's terrible sometimes, inside," he said, "that's what's the trouble. You walk these streets, black and funky and cold, and there's not really a living ass to talk to, and there's nothing shaking, and there's no way of getting it out--that storm inside. You can't talk it and you can't make love with it, and when you finally try to get with it and play it, you realize <u>nobody's</u> listening. So <u>you've</u> got to listen. You got to find a way to listen."

And then he walked away from the window and sat on the sofa again, as though all the wind had suddenly been knocked out of him. "Sometimes you'll do <u>anything</u> to play, even cut your mother's throat." He laughed and looked at me. "Or your brother's." Then he sobered. "Or your own." Then: "Don't worry. I'm all right now and I think I'll <u>be</u> all right. But I can't forget--where I've been. I don't mean just the physical place I've been; I mean where I've <u>been</u>. And <u>what</u> I've been."

"What have you been, Sonny?" I asked.

He smiled--but sat sideways on the sofa, his elbow resting on the back, his fingers playing with his mouth and chin, not looking at me. "I've been something I didn't recognize, didn't know I could be. Didn't know anybody could be." He stopped, looking inward, looking helplessly young, looking old. "I'm not talking about it now because I feel <u>guilty</u> or anything like that--maybe it would be better if I did. I don't know. Anyway, I can't really talk about it. Not to you, not to anybody." And now he turned and faced me. "Sometimes, you know, and it was actually when I was most <u>out</u> of the world, I felt that I was in it, that I was <u>with</u> it, really, and I could play or I didn't really have to <u>play</u>. Just came out of me. It was there. And I don't know how I played. Thinking about it now, but I know I did awful things, those times, sometimes, to people. Or it wasn't that I did anything to them—it was that they weren't real." He picked up the beer can; it was empty; he rolled it between his palms: "And other times—well, I needed a fix. I needed to find a place to lean; I needed to clear a space to listen—and I couldn't find it, and I—went crazy. I did terrible things to me, I was terrible for me." He began pressing the beer can between his hands. I watched the metal begin to give. It glittered, as he played with it, like a knife, and I was afraid he would cut himself, but I said nothing. "Oh, well. I can never tell you. I was all by myself at the bottom of something, stinking and sweating and crying and shaking, and I smelled it, you know? My stink, and I thought I'd die if I couldn't get away from it and yet, all the same, I knew that everything I was doing was just locking me in with it. And I didn't know," he paused, still flattening the beer can, "I didn't know, I still don't know. Something kept telling me that maybe it was good to smell your own stink, but I didn't think that that was what I'd been trying to do—and—who can stand it?" and he abruptly dropped the ruined beer can, looking at me with a small, still smile, and then rose, walking to the window as though it were the lodestone rock. I watched his face; he watched the avenue. "I couldn't tell you when Mama died--but the reason I wanted to leave Harlem so bad was to get away from drugs. And then, when I ran away, that's what I was running from—really. When I came back, nothing had changed. I hadn't changed, I was just—older." And he stopped, drumming with his fingers on the windowpane. The sun had vanished, soon darkness would fall. I watched his face. "It can come again," he said, almost as though speaking to himself. Then he turned to me. "It can come again," he repeated. "I just want you to know that."

"All right," I said, at last. "So it can come again. All right."

He smiled, but the smile was sorrowful. "I had to try to tell you," he said.

"Yes," I said. "I understand that."

"You're my brother," he said, looking straight at me, and not smiling at all.

"Yes," I repeated, "yes. I understand that."

He turned back to the window, looking out. "All that hatred down there," he said, "all that hatred and misery and love. It's a wonder it doesn't blow the avenue apart."

We went to the only nightclub on a short, dark street, downtown. We squeezed through the narrow, chattering, jam-packed bar to the entrance of the big room, where the bandstand was. And we stood there for a moment, for the lights were very dim in this room and we couldn't see. Then, "Hello, boy," said a voice and an enormous black man, much older than Sonny or myself, erupted out of all that atmospheric lighting and put an arm around Sonny's shoulder. "I been sitting right here," he said, "waiting for you."

He had a big voice, too, and heads in the darkness turned toward us.

Sonny grinned and pulled a little away, and said, "Creole, this is my brother. I told you about him."

Creole shook my hand. "I'm glad to meet you, son," he said, and it was clear that he was glad to meet me *there*, for Sonny's sake. And he smiled, "You got a real musician in *your* family," and he took his arm from Sonny's shoulder and slapped him, lightly, affectionately, with the back of his hand.

"Well. Now I've heard it all," said a voice behind us. This was another musician, and a friend of Sonny's, a coal-black, cheerful-looking man, built close to the ground. He immediately began confiding to me, at the top of his lungs, the most terrible things about Sonny, his teeth gleaming like a lighthouse and his laugh coming up out of him like the beginning of an earthquake. And it turned out that everyone at the bar knew Sonny, or almost everyone; some were musicians, working there, or nearby, or not working, some were simply hangers-on, and some were there to hear Sonny play. I was introduced to all of them and they were all very polite to me. Yet, it was clear that, for them, I was only Sonny's brother. Here, I was in Sonny's world. Or, rather: his kingdom. Here, it was not even a question that his veins bore royal blood.

They were going to play soon and Creole installed me, by myself, at a table in a dark corner. Then I watched them, Creole, and the little black man, and Sonny, and the others, while they horsed around, standing just below the bandstand. The light from the bandstand spilled just a little short of them and, watching them laughing and gesturing and moving about, I had the feeling that they, nevertheless, were being most careful not to step into that circle of light too suddenly: that if they moved into the light too suddenly, without thinking, they would perish in flame. Then, while I watched, one of them, the small, black man, moved into the light and crossed the bandstand and started fooling around with his drums. Then—being funny and being, also, extremely ceremonious—Creole took Sonny by the arm and led him to the piano. A woman's voice called Sonny's name and a few hands started clapping. And

Sonny, also being funny and being ceremonious, and so touched, I think, that he could have cried, but neither hiding it nor showing it, riding it like a man, grinned, and put both hands to his heart and bowed from the waist.

Creole then went to the bass fiddle and a lean, very bright-skinned brown man jumped up on the bandstand and picked up his horn. So there they were, and the atmosphere on the bandstand and in the room began to change and tighten. Someone stepped up to the microphone and announced them. Then there were all kinds of murmurs. Some people at the bar shushed others. The waitress ran around, frantically getting in the last orders, guys and chicks got closer to each other, and the lights on the bandstand, on the quartet, turned to a kind of indigo. Then they all looked different there. Creole looked about him for the last time, as though he were making certain that all his chickens were in the coop, and then he—jumped and struck the fiddle. And there they were.

All I know about music is that not many people ever really hear it. And even then, on the rare occasions when something opens within, and the music enters, what we mainly hear, or hear corroborated, are personal, private, vanishing evocations. But the man who creates the music is hearing something else, is dealing with the roar rising from the void and imposing order on it as it hits the air. What is evoked in him, then, is of another order, more terrible because it has no words, and triumphant, too, for that same reason. And his triumph, when he triumphs, is ours. I just watched Sonny's face. His face was troubled, he was working hard, but he wasn't with it. And I had the feeling that, in a way, everyone on the bandstand was waiting for him, both waiting for him and pushing him along. But as I began to watch Creole, I realized that it was Creole who held them all back. He had them on a short rein. Up there, keeping the beat with his whole body, wailing on the fiddle, with his eyes half closed, he was listening to everything, but he was listening to Sonny. He was having a dialogue with Sonny. He wanted Sonny to leave the shoreline and strike out for the deep water. He was Sonny's witness that deep water and drowning were not the same thing—he had been there, and he knew. And he wanted Sonny to know. He was waiting for Sonny to do the things on the keys which would let Creole know that Sonny was in the water.

And, while Creole listened, Sonny moved, deep within, exactly like someone in torment. I had never before thought of how awful the relationship must be between the musician and his instrument. He has to fill it, this instrument, with the breath of life, his own. He has to make it do what he wants it to do. And a piano is just a piano. It's made out of so much wood and wires and little hammers and big ones, and ivory. While there's only so much you can do with it, the only way to find this out is to try—to try and make it do everything.

And Sonny hadn't been near a piano for over a year. And he wasn't on much better terms with his life, not the life that stretched before him now. He and the piano stammered, started one way, got scared, stopped; started another way, panicked, marked time, started again; then seemed to have found a direction, panicked again, got stuck. And the face I saw on Sonny I'd never seen before. Everything had been burned out of it, and, at the same time, things usually hidden were being burned in, by the fire and fury of the battle which was occurring in him up there.

Yet, watching Creole's face as they neared the end of the first set, I had the feeling that something had happened, something I hadn't heard. Then they finished, there was scattered applause, and then, without an instant's warning, Creole started into something else. It was almost sardonic; it was Am I Blue. And, as though he commanded, Sonny began to play. Something began to happen. And Creole let out the reins. The dry, low, black man said something awful on the drums, Creole answered, and the drums talked back. Then the horn insisted, sweet and high, slightly detached perhaps, and Creole listened, commenting now and then, dry, and driving, beautiful and calm and old. Then they all came together again, and Sonny was part of the family again. I could tell this from his face. He seemed to have found, right there beneath his fingers, a damn brand-new piano. It seemed that he couldn't get over it. Then, for awhile, just being happy with Sonny, they seemed to be agreeing with him that brand-new pianos certainly were a gas.

Then Creole stepped forward to remind them that what they were playing was the blues. He hit something in all of them; he hit something in me, myself; and the music tightened and deepened. Apprehension began to beat the air. Creole began to tell us what the blues were all about. They were not about anything very new. He and his boys up there were keeping it new, at the risk of ruin, destruction, madness, and death, in order to find new ways to make us listen. For, while the tale of how we suffer, and how we are delighted, and how we may triumph is never new, it always must be heard. There isn't any other tale to tell; it's the only light we've got in all this darkness.

And this tale, according to that face, that body, those strong hands on those strings, has another aspect in every country, and a new depth in every generation. Listen, Creole seemed to be saying, listen. Now these are Sonny's blues. He made the little black man on the drums know it, and the bright, brown man on the horn. Creole wasn't trying any longer to get Sonny in the water. He was wishing him Godspeed. Then he stepped back, very slowly, filling the air with the immense suggestion that Sonny speak for himself.

Then they all gathered around Sonny and Sonny played. Every now and again one of them seemed to say, Amen. Sonny's fingers filled the air with life, his life. But that life contained so many others. And Sonny went all the way back. He really began with the spare, flat statement of the opening phrase of the song. Then he began to make it his. It was very beautiful because it wasn't hurried and it was no longer a lament. I seemed to hear with what burning he had made it his, with what burning we had yet to make it ours, how we could cease lamenting. Freedom lurked around us and I understood, at last, that he could help us to be free if we would listen, that he would never be free until we did. Yet, there was no battle in his face now. I heard what he had gone through, and would continue to go through until he came to rest in earth. He had made it his: that long line, of which we knew only Mama and Daddy. And he was giving it back, as everything must be given back, so that passing through death, it can live forever. I saw my mother's face again, and felt, for the first time, how the stones of the road she had walked on must have bruised her feet. I saw the moonlit road where my father's brother died. And it brought something else back to me, and carried me past it. I saw my little girl again and felt Isabel's tears again, and I felt my own tears begin to rise. And I was yet aware that this was only a moment, that the world waited outside, as hungry as a tiger, and that trouble stretched above us, longer than the sky.

Then it was over. Creole and Sonny let out their breath, both soaking wet, and grinning. There was a lot of applause and some of it was real. In the dark, the girl came by and I asked her to take drinks to the bandstand. There was a long pause, while they talked up there in the indigo light and after a while I saw the girl put a Scotch and milk on top of the piano for Sonny. He didn't seem to notice it, but just before they started playing again, he sipped from it and looked toward me, and nodded. Then he put it back on top of the piano. For me, then, as they began to play again, it glowed and shook above my brother's head like the very cup of trembling.

SENTENCE-COMBINING EXERCISE
FOR BALDWIN'S "SONNY'S BLUES"

Each of the short sentences below supports the idea about "Sonny's Blues" given in the topic sentence. By combining the short sentences into longer sentences, you are developing the topic sentence into a unified paragraph. After you are satisfied with your combinations, write sentences one through thirteen in paragraph form.

1. TOPIC SENTENCE: The main action in "Sonny's Blues" is the narrator's progress in understanding and being reconciled with his brother Sonny.

2. At the beginning of the story, the narrator and Sonny are estranged.

3. They haven't seen each other for a year.
   They haven't seen each other since a terrible quarrel.
   The quarrel was triggered by the narrator's fears concerning Sonny's life-style.

4. There are several reasons that communication between the brothers has been poor.
   There is a seven-year age difference.
   Sonny is a very private person.
   The older brother has been too caught up in his own life to really listen to Sonny.

5. For example,
   The narrator did not understand Sonny's urgent desire to leave Harlem.
   He did not understand Sonny's need to escape the availability of drugs.

6. Nor did he understand Sonny's longing to be a jazz musician.

7. The narrator wrote Sonny in prison.
   This was the narrator's first step toward understanding.

8. He, himself, experienced suffering through the death of his baby girl.
   Then he was able to understand Sonny's suffering.

9. More understanding comes during Sonny's stay with his brother's family after his release from prison.

10. Sonny tries to explain to his brother why he used heroin in the past.
Heroin gave him a feeling of control.
Using heroin was an attempt not to suffer.

11. The narrator does not approve of drugs.
He understands that Sonny might use them again.

12. Finally, he understands what a great musical gift Sonny has.
He understands how important it is for him to express himself through music.

13. Hearing Sonny play, his brother understands how Sonny can take his personal pain, his family's sufferings, the anguish of the community, and through music lift these blues to momentary freedom, hope and meaning.

VOCABULARY

Directions: **Supply the missing forms of the words in the boxes as directed on page 60.**

1. **Parody** (verb) to imitate for the purposes of humor, ridicule or satire

   Parody (noun) a poor or feeble imitation as <u>His acting was a parody of his past greatness.</u>

2. **Obscurely** (adv) not clearly or plainly; indistinctly, dimly, darkly

Verbs	Nouns	Adjectives	Adverbs
	a.__________ity	b.__________	**obscurely**

3. **Belligerent** (adj) warlike, hostile

Verbs	Nouns	Adjectives	Adverbs
	c.__________ence	**belligerent**	d.__________

4. **Lope** (verb) to move with a long, easy stride

5. **Lament** (verb) to feel or express sorrow or regret for

6. The Latin root voc, vok means to call. A vocation for instance can be a calling to a special work in life or one's ordinary occupation, business or profession. Look at the list of verbs and their meanings and then complete the chart below.

Evoke	to call forth, to evoke a memory, smile, comment, protest
Convoke	to call or summon to assemble
Invoke	to call for in earnest desire, to call on in prayer, as to invoke God's mercy
Provoke	to call forth anger, annoyance, to stir up, excite, rouse
Revoke	to call back, cancel, annul as The Department of Motor Vehicles revoked his driver's license.

Verbs	Nouns	Adjectives	Adverbs
Evoke	**Evocation**	**Evocative**	**Evocatively**
Convoke	e.__________		
Invoke	f.__________		
Provoke	g.__________	h.__________	i.__________
Revoke	j.__________		

MAJOR WRITING ASSIGNMENT

Blues have been described in each of the readings about jazz. This assignment asks you to pull ideas from all three readings and to look at blues in a special way; it asks you to describe the connections between blues and American blacks.

To do this you do **not** have to summarize the three readings or use all their ideas on blues. Instead, you draw on the ideas you like from each reading.

Write one or two pages on the connections between blues and American blacks touching on **at least two** of the following connections or some of your own.

1. The origin of blues--how they were invented by American blacks
2. Some of the topics in blues songs
3. Improvisation as an important feature of blues
4. Blues as an expression of suffering that lifts the musician and listeners out of suffering
5. The attitude toward suffering expressed in blues
6. The form of the blues

Guidelines

After you have decided which two connections you want to write about, reread the sections on the blues:

pages 52 through in "Jazz: A Study in Black and White"

pages 69 through 74 in "Shanghai"

pages 113 through 114 in "Sonny's Blues"

As you read, take notes on the ideas you want to use. Then group your notes according to the connections and start writing.

CHAPTER 3

FAIRY TALES:
A PREPARATION FOR REALITY?

by

Marianne Boretz

Contributor:

Jo An Simmons

OVERVIEW

The major article in this section is the first chapter in **The Uses of Enchantment** by Bruno Bettelheim, an important modern thinker and writer. In his book, he is examining a kind of literature that most of us have forgotten about—the fairy tales that we heard or read when we were children.

Many modern parents worry about the effect of TV and books upon their children. When is it safe for a child to learn about complex realities like aging, death, violence, and sex? Some parents disapprove of fairy tales as too violent for small children. But Bettelheim feels quite differently.

This excerpt from Bettelheim's book is challenging; the ideas concerning psychological theory are more abstract than the ideas in earlier chapters concerning reading or musical theory. Furthermore, in presenting his ideas, Bettelheim uses background knowledge unfamiliar to most of us. To help you meet this challenge, we've included some guides:

1. Some advice from a well-known writer, Mortimer J. Adler, called "How to Mark a Book," and

2. A brief sketch of the chief assumptions behind Bettelheim's reasoning.

WHAT TO LOOK FOR

Since the major writing assignment asks you to apply Bettelheim's ideas to a specific fairy tale, you will want to look for Bettelheim's reasons for believing that fairy tales can help a child's mental health, and specific fairy tale characteristics that can be therapeutic to a child.

CHAPTER PLAN

GRAPHIC ORGANIZER

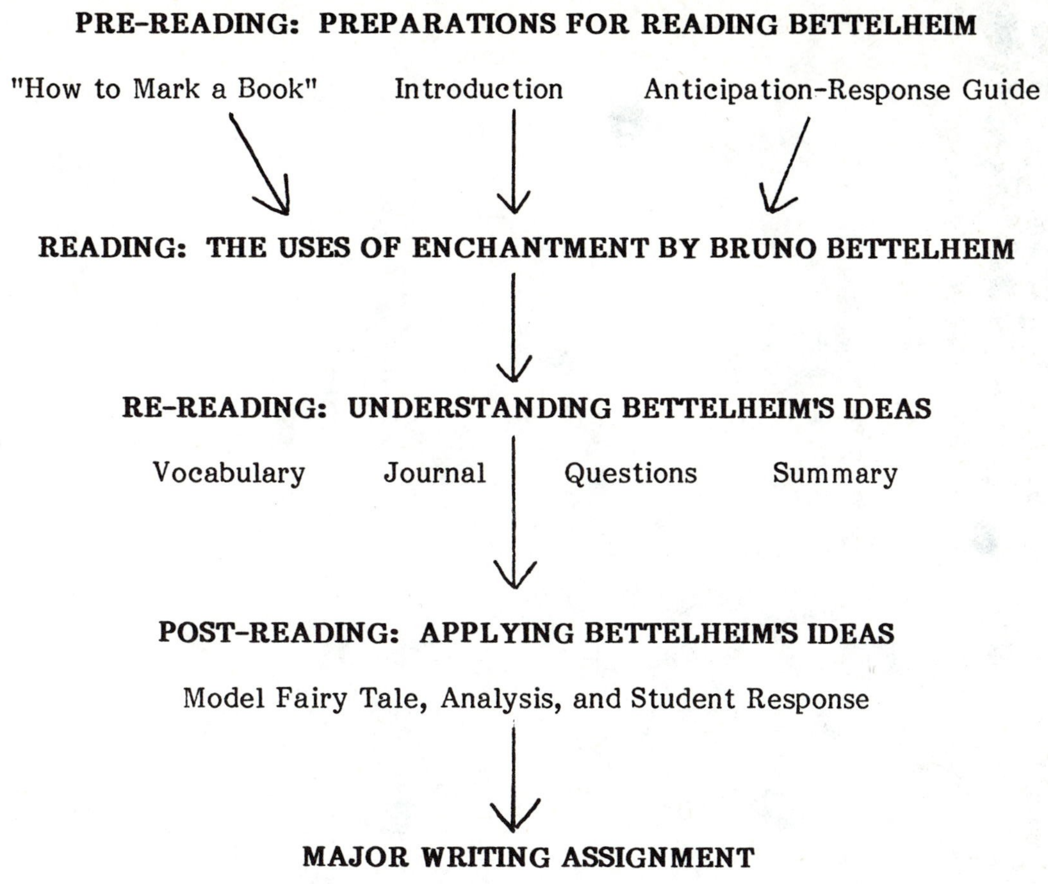

PRE-READING: PREPARATIONS FOR READING BETTELHEIM

"How to Mark a Book" Introduction Anticipation-Response Guide

↓

READING: THE USES OF ENCHANTMENT BY BRUNO BETTELHEIM

↓

RE-READING: UNDERSTANDING BETTELHEIM'S IDEAS

Vocabulary Journal Questions Summary

↓

POST-READING: APPLYING BETTELHEIM'S IDEAS

Model Fairy Tale, Analysis, and Student Response

↓

MAJOR WRITING ASSIGNMENT

From the MGM release "The Wizard of Oz," © 1939 Loew's Inc.
Renewed 1966, Metro-Goldwyn-Mayer Inc.

Mortimer J. Adler, chairman of the board of editors of **Encyclopaedia Britannica,** is is a prolific writer, philosopher, editor, and teacher. A member of the board since its inception in 1947, Dr. Adler devoted 15 years to planning and developing the 15th edition of **Britannica.** Dr. Adler is also the director of the Institute for Philosophical Research in Chicago, which was founded in 1952 for the study of ideas.

Dr. Adler's books include **The Conditions of Philosophy, The Time of Our Lives, Aristotle for Everybody, How to Think about God,** and **The Paideia Proposal. Six Great Ideas** was televised by Bill Moyers in 1982.

In "How to Mark a Book," Dr. Adler has some very specific advice on how to understand a writer as challenging as Bruno Bettelheim. Certain terms have been updated by the editors.

HOW TO MARK A BOOK

Mortimer J. Adler (1902-)

You know you have to read "between the lines" to get the most out of anything. I want to persuade you to do something equally important in the course of your reading. I want to persuade you to "write between the lines." Unless you do, you are not likely to do the most efficient kind of reading. I contend, quite bluntly, that marking up a book is not an act of mutilation, but of love.

You shouldn't mark up a book which isn't yours. Librarians (or your friends) who lend you books expect you to keep them clean, and you should. If you decide that I am right about the usefulness of marking books, you will have to buy them. Most of the world's great books are available today, in reprint editions, at less than five dollars.

WHEN NOT TO MARK

There are two ways in which one can own a book. The first is the property right you establish by paying for it, just as you pay for

---

Mortimer J. Adler, "How to Mark a Book," Saturday Review of Literature, July 6, 1940. Copyright (c) 1940 by Mortimer J. Adler. Copyright (c) renewed 1967 by Mortimer J. Adler. Reprinted by permission of the author.

clothes and furniture. But this act of purchase is only the prelude to possession. Full ownership comes only when you have made it a part of yourself, and the best way to make yourself a part of it is by writing in it. An illustration may make the point clear. You buy a beefsteak and transfer it from the butcher's refrigerator to your own. But you do not own the beefsteak in the most important sense until you consume it and get it into your bloodstream. I am arguing that books, too, must be absorbed in your bloodstream to do you any good.

DEGREES OF OWNERSHIP

Confusion about what it means to own a book leads people to a false reverence for paper, binding, and type--a respect for the physical thing--the craft of the printer rather than the genius of the author. They forget that it is possible for a man to acquire the idea, to possess the beauty, which a great book contains, without staking his claim by pasting his bookplate inside the cover. Having a fine library doesn't prove that its owner has a mind enriched by books; it proves nothing more than that he, his father, or his wife, was rich enough to buy them.

Better to own the book's ideas, than the book itself

There are three kinds of book owners. The first has all the standard sets and best-sellers--unread, untouched. (This deluded individual owns woodpulp and ink, not books.) The second has a great many books--a few of them read through, most of them dipped into, but all of them as clean and shiny as the day they were bought. (This person would probably like to make books his own, but is restrained by a false respect for their physical appearance.) The third has a few books or many--every one of them dog-eared and dilapidated, shaken and loosened by continual use, marked and scribbled in from front to back. (This man owns books.)

For example, people who have decorators order so many yards of books in red leather

Is it false respect, you may ask, to preserve intact and unblemished a beautifully printed book, an elegantly bound edition? Of course not. I'd no more scribble all over a first edition of *Paradise Lost* than I'd give my baby a set of crayons and an original Rembrandt! I wouldn't mark up a painting or a statue. Its soul, so to speak, is inseparable from its body. And the beauty of a rare edition

Adler not talking about rare books or special editions

or of a richly manufactured volume is like that of a painting or a statue.

But the soul of a book can be separated from its body. A book is more like the score of a piece of music than it is like a painting. No great musician confuses a symphony with the printed sheets of music. Arturo Toscanini reveres Brahms, but Toscanini's score of the C-minor Symphony is so thoroughly marked up that no one but the maestro himself can read it. The reason why a great conductor makes notations on his musical scores--marks them up again and again each time he returns to study them—is the reason why you should mark your books. If your respect for magnificent binding or typography gets in the way, buy yourself a cheap edition and pay your respects to the author. (by understanding his ideas through writing)

Can separate ideas (soul) from the body (physical text)

Comparison with music

Marked musical score → Notes

Marked book → Ideas

Why is marking up a book indispensable to reading? First, it keeps you awake. (And I don't mean merely conscious; I mean wide awake.) In the second place, reading, if it is active, is thinking, and thinking tends to express itself in words spoken or written. The marked book is usually the thought-through book. Finally, writing helps you remember the thoughts you had, or the thoughts the author expressed. Let me develop these three points.

SUPPORT FOR ADLER'S RECOMMENDATION

You have to think about an idea in order to mark it.

(1) If reading is to accomplish more than passing time, it must be active. You can't let your eyes glide across the lines of a book and come up with an understanding of what you have read. Now an ordinary piece of light fiction, like say, Gone With the Wind, doesn't require the most active kind of reading. The books you read for pleasure can be read in a state of relaxation, and nothing is lost. But a great book, rich in ideas and beauty, a book that raises and tries to answer great fundamental questions, demands the most active reading of which you are capable. You don't absorb the ideas of Bruno Bettelheim the way you absorb the crooning of Johnny Mathis. You have to reach for them. That you cannot do while you're asleep.

ELABORATION OF SUPPORT POINTS

Not necessary for novels, but for books about ideas

← Definition of a great book

(2) If, when you've finished reading a book, the pages are filled with your notes, you know that you read actively. The most famous active reader of great books I know is President Hutchins, of the University of Chicago. He also has the hardest schedule of business activities of any man I know. He invariably reads with a pencil, and sometimes, when he picks up a book and pencil in the evening, he finds himself, instead of making intelligent notes, drawing what he calls "caviar factories" on the margins. When that happens, he puts the book down. He knows he's too tired to read, and he's just wasting time.

example

But, you may ask, why is writing necessary? Well, the physical act of writing, with your own hand, brings words and sentences more sharply before your mind and preserves them better in your memory. To set down your reaction to important words and sentences you have read, and the questions they have raised in your mind, is to preserve those reactions and sharpen those questions.

Writing re-inforces learning and aids memory

Even if you wrote on a scratch pad, and threw the paper away when you had finished writing, your grasp of the book would be surer. But you don't have to throw the paper away. The margins (top and bottom, as well as side), the end-papers, the very space between the lines, are all available. They aren't sacred. And, best of all, your marks and notes become an integral part of the book and stay there forever. You can pick up the book the following week or year, and there are all your points of agreement, disagreement, doubt, and inquiry. It's like resuming an interrupted conversation with the advantage of being able to pick up where you left off.

Writing provides a record

And that is exactly what reading a book should be: a conversation between you and the author. Presumably he knows more about the subject than you do; naturally, you'll have the proper humility as you approach him. But don't let anybody tell you that a reader is supposed to be solely on the receiving end. Understanding is a two-way operation; learning doesn't consist in being an empty receptacle. The learner has to question himself and question the teacher. He even has to argue with the teacher, once he understands what the teacher is saying. And marking a book is

Important to react to ideas, rather than accept them without question

literally an expression of your differences, or agreements of opinion, with the author.

There are all kinds of devices for marking a book intelligently and fruitfully. Here's the way I do it: HOW TO MARK

1. Underlining: of major points, of important or forceful statements.
2. Vertical lines at the margin: to emphasize a statement already underlined.
3. Star, asterisk, or other doo-dad at the margin: to be used sparingly, to emphasize the ten or twenty most important statements in the book. (You may want to fold the bottom corner of each page on which you use such marks. It won't hurt the sturdy paper on which most modern books are printed, and you will be able to take the book off the shelf at any time and, by opening it at the folded-corner page, refresh your recollection of the book.)
4. Numbers in the margin: to indicate the sequence of points the author makes in developing a single argument.
5. Numbers of other pages in the margin: to indicate where else in the book the author made points relevant to the point marked; to tie up the ideas in a book, which, though they may be separated by many pages, belong together.
6. Circling of key words or phrases.
7. Writing in the margin, or at the top or bottom of the page, for the sake of: recording questions (and perhaps answers) which a passage raised in your mind; reducing a complicated discussion to a simple statement; recording the sequence of major points right through the books. I use the end-papers at the back of the book to make a personal index of the author's points in the order of their appearance.

WHERE TO MARK

The front end-papers are, to me, the most important. Some people reserve them for a fancy bookplate. I reserve them for fancy thinking. After I have finished reading the book and making my personal index on the back end-papers, I turn to the front and try to outline the book, not page by page, or point by point (I've already done that at the back), but as an integrated structure, with a basic unity and an order of parts. This outline is, to me, the measure of my understanding of the work.

OVERCOMES OBJECTIONS TO MARKING A BOOK

NOT ENOUGH SPACE OBJECTION

If you're a die-hard anti-book-marker, you may object that the margins, the space between the lines, and the end-papers don't give you room enough. All right. How about using a scratch pad slightly smaller than the page-size of the book—so that the edges of the sheets won't protrude? Make your index, outlines, and even your notes on the pad, and then insert these sheets permanently inside the front and back covers of the book.

SLOW PROCESS OBJECTION

Or, you may say that this business of marking books is going to slow up your reading. It probably will. That's one of the reasons for doing it. Most of us have been taken in by the notion that speed of reading is a measure of our intelligence. There is no such thing as the right speed for intelligent reading. Some things should be read quickly and effortlessly, and some should be read slowly and even laboriously. The sign of intelligence in reading is the ability to read different things differently according to their worth. In the case of good books, the point is not to see how many of them you can get through, but rather how many can get through you—how many you can make your own. A few friends are better than a thousand acquaintances. If this be your aim, as it should be, you will not be impatient if it takes more time and effort to read a great book than it does a newspaper.

CAN'T LEND OBJECTION

You may have one final objection to marking books. You can't lend them to your friends because nobody else can read them without being distracted by your notes. Furthermore, you won't want to lend them because a marked copy is a kind of intellectual diary, and lending it is almost like giving your mind away.

If your friend wishes to read your Plutarch's Lives, Shakespeare, or The Federalist Papers, tell him gently but firmly to buy a copy. You will lend him your car or your coat—but your books are as much a part of you as your head or your heart.

* * *

QUESTIONS FOR DISCUSSION AND WRITING

The following questions can be used for class discussion, for individual or group writing assignments, and for entries in a reading journal. Follow your teacher's instructions.

1. Would highlighting every other word with a yellow marker achieve what Adler is recommending? Why not? Is it the marking itself or the thought that goes into selecting what is important and into commenting that is valuable?

2. Marking is inappropriate or unnecessary for what kinds of books?

3. In Adler's opinion, do you fully own a book that you've paid for but whose ideas you haven't thought through?

4. What reasons does Adler give to support his thesis that writing about what you're reading empowers you to better understand the reading?

   a.

   b.

   c.

5. Do you generally accept the ideas you learn in class without thinking about them? In which classes do you find yourself questioning, arguing with, or trying to come to terms with the ideas presented?

6. If Richard Rodriguez had had Mortimer Adler as his teacher, what changes would Rodriguez have made in his reading program?

INTRODUCTION

Existentialism

Like many (but by no means all) serious thinkers today (and unlike those of previous centuries), Bruno Bettelheim believes that human life has no meaning in itself; meaning must be created by each individual. Each person must face basic "existential dilemmas"—problems that are a basic and inescapable part of existing, problems such as the necessity of separating from parents, aging, losing love, dying. These problems can tempt each of us to a sense of meaninglessness or despair. But each one of us has the responsibility to face these painful realities and decide what our life means: each one of us must make our own individual life mean something. It is this basic idea that Bettelheim is referring to when he mentions mental activities like "giving structure to daydreams" or "wringing meaning out of existence."

Psychoanalysis

To Bettelheim and many other serious thinkers, human existence is difficult not only because of the presence of unpleasant and inescapable realities but also because of the nature of the human mind itself. Psychoanalysts divide the mind into two parts: (1) consciousness, everything that we are aware of about ourselves and our world, and (2) the unconscious, consisting of strong feelings and impulses, often frightening or socially unacceptable, that have been repressed or pushed "down" below the level of awareness. Psychoanalysts and psychologists believe (and Bettelheim mentions this in his first few paragraphs) that these feelings must be allowed an outlet. If not, they may force themselves into consciousness. The person at the mercy of these feelings may lose control over them and commit acts that cause great unhappiness or even violence to himself or others. On the other hand, if these feelings are totally denied or repressed, a person may become afraid of all emotion. But mental health practitioners know that emotion is necessary for a rich, complete human life. If too many emotions are repressed, people can become rigid, stifled, only half alive. So the trick is to find a healthy way to deal with these strong feelings, neither bottling them up nor letting them dominate.

Now you are more prepared to read the excerpt from Bettelheim's book. To focus your attention, ask yourself what you think about the following statements:

ANTICIPATION-RESPONSE GUIDE

Agree	Disagree	
_____	_____	1. Modern psychologists do not approve of fairy tales as suitable stories for children.
_____	_____	2. Fairy tales present an unreal world in which evil doesn't exist.
_____	_____	3. Daydreams and fantasies are a necessary part of a child's growth as a person.
_____	_____	4. Children should not read stories dealing with death and violence.
_____	_____	5. The fear of losing one or both parents is a common childhood fear.
_____	_____	6. The fairy tale ending "they lived happily ever after" is senseless wish fulfillment and will not help a child grow up.
_____	_____	7. Fairy tales encourage children to take on the struggles of life.
_____	_____	8. Fairy tales are less important for modern children than they were for children of older times.

Now read Bettelheim to see what his views are. Follow Mortimer Adler's advice in "How to Mark a Book": Read Bettelheim with pencil or pen in hand and keep your attention focused on what you are reading by writing in the margin as you read: summarize main points, ask yourself questions, argue, and so on. I've included my notes on the first 13 paragraphs. You can add to these if you like, but then you're on your own: write down in the margin whatever notes will help you follow Bettelheim's argument and make his ideas important for you.

THE USES OF ENCHANTMENT

Bruno Bettelheim

Bruno Bettelheim, a distinguished psychologist and educator, was born in 1903 in Vienna. He was naturalized as a U.S. citizen in 1939 and has served as a professor of psychology at Rockford College and the University of Chicago. Bettelheim has been awarded the honor of Fellow by several prestigious professional associations. He is a prolific writer and has contributed articles to numerous popular and professional publications. His list of books includes **Love Is Not Enough—The Treatment of Emotionally Disturbed Children, The Informed Heart, Surviving,** and **The Uses of Enchantment.**

1 In order to master the psychological problems of growing up, a child needs to understand what is going on within his conscious self so that he can also cope with that which goes on in his unconscious. He can achieve this understanding, and with it the ability to cope, not through rational comprehension of the nature and content of his unconscious, but by becoming familiar with it through spinning out daydreams--ruminating, rearranging, and fantasizing about suitable story elements in response to unconscious pressures. By doing this, the child fits unconscious content into conscious fantasies, which then enable him to deal with that

conscious self? unconscious?

Excerpt from The Uses of Enchantment: The Meaning and Importance of Fairy Tales. Copyright (c) 1975, 1976 by Bruno Bettelheim. Reprinted by permission of Alfred A. Knopf, Inc.

content. It is here that fairy tales have unequalled value, because they offer new dimensions to the child's imagination which would be impossible for him to discover as truly on his own. Even more important, the form and structure of fairy tales suggest images to the child by which he can structure his daydreams and with them give better direction to his life.

2 In child or adult, the unconscious is a powerful determinant of behavior. When the unconscious is repressed and its content denied entrance into awareness, then eventually the person's conscious mind will be partially overwhelmed by derivatives of these unconscious elements, or else he is forced to keep such rigid, compulsive control over them that his personality may become severely crippled. But when unconscious material is to some degree permitted to come to awareness and worked through in imagination, its potential for causing harm—to ourselves or others—is much reduced; some of its forces can then be made to serve positive purposes. However, the prevalent parental belief is that a child must be diverted from what troubles him most: his formless, nameless anxieties, and his chaotic, angry, and even violent fantasies. Many parents believe that only conscious reality or pleasant and wish-fulfilling images should be presented to the child—that he should be exposed only to the sunny side of things. But such one-sided fare nourishes the mind only in a one-sided way, and real life is not all sunny.

Children should not repress unconscious!

Can be over-whelmed or become rigid. (examples?)

Modern parents shield children from anxieties and violence.

3 There is a widespread refusal to let children know that the source of much that goes wrong in life is due to our very own natures--the propensity of all men for acting aggressively, asocially, selfishly, out of anger and anxiety. Instead, we want our children to believe that, inherently, all men are good. But children know that they are not always good; and often, even when they are, they would prefer not to be. This contradicts what they are told by their parents, and therefore makes the child a monster in his own eyes.

We want children to believe all men are good. They know this isn't true. guilt!

4 The dominant culture wishes to pretend, particularly where children are concerned, that the dark side of man does not exist, and professes a belief in an optimistic meliorism. Psycho-

analysis itself is viewed as having the purpose of making life easy—but this is not what its founder intended. Psychoanalysis was created to enable man to accept the problematic nature of life without being defeated by it, or giving in to escapism. Freud's prescription is that only by struggling courageously against what seem like overwhelming odds can man succeed in wringing meaning out of his existence.

5 This is exactly the message that fairy tales get across to the child in manifold form: that a struggle against severe difficulties in life is unavoidable, is an intrinsic part of human existence—but that if one does not shy away, but steadfastly meets unexpected and often unjust hardships, one masters all obstacles and at the end emerges victorious.

6 Modern stories written for young children mainly avoid these existential problems, although they are crucial issues for all of us. The child needs most particularly to be given suggestions in symbolic form about how he may deal with these issues and grow safely into maturity. "Safe" stories mention neither death nor aging, the limits to our existence, nor the wish for eternal life. The fairy tale, by contrast, confronts the child squarely with the basic human predicaments.

7 For example, many fairy stories begin with the death of a mother or father; in these tales the death of the parent creates the most agonizing problems, as it (or the fear of it) does in real life. Other stories tell about an aging parent who decides that the time has come to let the new generation take over. But before this can happen, the successor has to prove himself capable and worthy. The Brothers Grimm's story "The Three Feathers" begins: "There was once upon a time a king who had three sons. . . . When the king had become old and weak, and was thinking of his end, he did not know which of his sons should inherit the kingdom after him." In order to decide, the king sets all his sons a difficult task; the son who meets it best "shall be king after my death."

8 It is characteristic of fairy tales to state an existential dilemma briefly and pointedly. This permits the child to come to

grips with the problem in its most essential form, where a more complex plot would confuse matters for him. The fairy tale simplifies all situations. Its figures are clearly drawn; and details, unless very important, are eliminated. All characters are typical rather than unique.

9 Contrary to what takes place in many modern children's stories, in fairy tales evil is as omnipresent as virtue. In practically every fairy tale good and evil are given body in the form of some figures and their actions, as good and evil are omnipresent in life and the propensities for both are present in every man. It is this duality which poses the moral problem, and requires the struggle to solve it.

10 Evil is not without its attractions--symbolized by the mighty giant or dragon, the power of the witch, the cunning queen in "Snow White"--and often it is temporarily in the ascendancy. In many fairy tales a usurper succeeds for a time in seizing the place which rightfully belongs to the hero--as the wicked sisters do in "Cinderella." It is not that the evildoer is punished at the story's end which makes immersing oneself in fairy stories an experience in moral education, although this is part of it. In fairy tales, as in life, punishment or fear of it is only a limited deterrent to crime. The conviction that crime does not pay is a much more effective deterrent, and that is why in fairy tales the bad person always loses out. It is not the fact that virtue wins out at the end which promotes morality, but that the hero is most attractive to the child, who identifies with the hero in all his struggles. Because of this identification the child imagines that he suffers with the hero his trials and tribulations, and triumphs with him as virtue is victorious. The child makes such identifications all on his own, and the inner and outer struggles of the hero imprint morality on him.

11 The figures in fairy tales are not ambivalent--not good and bad at the same time, as we all are in reality. But since polarization dominates the child's mind, it also dominates fairy tales. A person is either good or bad, nothing in between. One brother is stupid, the other is clever. One sister is virtuous and

industrious, the others are vile and lazy. One is beautiful, the others are ugly. One parent is all good, the other evil. The juxtaposition of opposite characters is not for the purpose of stressing right behavior, as would be true for cautionary tales. (There are some amoral fairy tales where goodness or badness, beauty or ugliness play no role at all.) Presenting the polarities of character permits the child to comprehend easily the difference between the two, which he could not do as readily were the figures drawn more true to life, with all the complexities that characterize real people. Ambiguities must wait until a relatively firm personality has been established on the basis of positive identifications. Then the child has a basis for understanding that there are great differences between people, and that therefore one has to make choices about who one wants to be. This basic decision, on which all later personality development will build, is facilitated by the polarizations of the fairy tale.

Characters either good or bad

Children aren't ready for complexities—must decide who they want to be

12 Furthermore, a child's choices are based, not so much on right versus wrong, as on who arouses his sympathy and who his antipathy. The more simple and straightforward a good character, the easier it is for a child to identify with it and to reject the bad other. The child identifies with the good hero not because of his goodness, but because the hero's condition makes a deep positive appeal to him. The question for the child is not "Do I want to be good?" but "Who do I want to be like?" The child decides this on the basis of projecting himself wholeheartedly into one character. If this fairy-tale figure is a very good person, then the child decides that he wants to be good, too.

Decide on basis of sympathy, not morality

13 Amoral fairy tales show no polarization or juxtaposition of good and bad persons; that is because these amoral stories serve an entirely different purpose. Such tales or type figures as "Puss in Boots," who arranges for the hero's success through trickery, and Jack, who steals the giant's treasure, build character not by promoting choices between good and bad, but by giving the child the hope that even the meekest can succeed in life. After all, what's the use of choosing to become a good person when one feels so

another kind of F.T. hero not good or bad—clever

Can succeed even if meek

insignificant that he fears he will never amount to anything? Morality is not the isssue in these tales, but rather, assurance that one can succeed. Whether one meets life with a belief in the possibility of mastering its difficulties or with the expectation of defeat is also a very important existential problem.

14 The deep inner conflicts originating in our primitive drives and our violent emotions are all denied in much of modern children's literature, and so the child is not helped in coping with them. But the child is subject to desperate feelings of loneliness and isolation, and he often experiences mortal anxiety. More often than not, he is unable to express these feelings in words, or he can do so only by indirection: fear of the dark, of some animal, anxiety about his body. Since it creates discomfort in a parent to recognize these emotions in his child, the parent tends to overlook them, or he belittles these spoken fears out of his own anxiety, believing this will cover over the child's fears.

15 The fairy tale, by contrast, takes these existential anxieties and dilemmas very seriously and addresses itself directly to them: the need to be loved and the fear that one is thought worthless; the love of life, and the fear of death. Further, the fairy tale offers solutions in ways that the child can grasp on his level of understanding. For example, fairy tales pose the dilemma of wishing to live eternally by occasionally concluding: "If they have not died, they are still alive." The other ending--"And they lived happily ever after"--does not for a moment fool the child that eternal life is possible. But it does indicate that which alone can take the sting out of the narrow limits of our time on this earth: forming a truly satisfying bond to another. The tales teach that when one has done this, one has reached the ultimate in emotional security of existence and permanence of relation available to man; and this alone can dissipate the fear of death. If one has found true adult love, the fairy story also tells, one doesn't need to wish for eternal life. This is suggested by another ending found in fairy tales: "They lived for a long time afterward, happy and in pleasure."

16 An uninformed view of the fairy tale sees in this type of ending an unrealistic wish-fulfillment, missing completely the important message it conveys to the child. These tales tell him that by forming a true interpersonal relation, one escapes the separation anxiety which haunts him (and which sets the stage for many fairy tales, but is always resolved at the story's ending). Furthermore, the story tells, this ending is not made possible, as the child wishes and believes, by holding on to his mother eternally. If we try to escape separation anxiety and death anxiety by desperately keeping our grasp on our parents, we will only be cruelly forced out, like Hansel and Gretel.

17 Only by going out into the world can the fairy-tale hero (child) find himself there; and as he does, he will also find the other with whom he will be able to live happily ever after; that is, without ever again having to experience separation anxiety. The fairy tale is future-oriented and guides the child--in terms he can understand in both his conscious and his unconscious mind—to relinquish his infantile dependency wishes and achieve a more satisfying independent existence.

18 Today children no longer grow up within the security of an extended family, or of a well-integrated community. Therefore, even more than at the times fairy tales were invented, it is important to provide the modern child with images of heroes who have to go out into the world all by themselves and who, although originally ignorant of the ultimate things, find secure places in the world by following their right way with deep inner confidence.

19 The fairy-tale hero proceeds for a time in isolation, as the modern child often feels isolated. The hero is helped by being in touch with primitive things—a tree, an animal, nature—as the child feels more in touch with those things than most adults do. The fate of these heroes convinces the child that, like them, he may feel outcast and abandoned in the world, groping in the dark, but, like them, in the course of his life he will be guided step by step, and given help when it is needed. Today, even more than in past times, the child needs the reassurance offered by the image of the isolated

man who nevertheless is capable of achieving meaningful and rewarding relations with the world around him.

* * *

VOCABULARY

Directions: **Supply the missing forms of the words in the boxes as directed on page 60.**

1. **Ruminate** (verb) to think about something for a long time, to ponder. (This word originally meant "to chew cud," the food cows and similar animals, ruminants, bring up from their stomachs into their mouths and chew again for a long time. The expression "to chew your cud" also has the additional meaning of "to ponder.")

2. **Repress** (verb) to hold back, restrain, to force memories, ideas, or fears into the unconscious mind

Related Words

Verbs	Nouns	Adjectives	Adverbs
repress	a.________ **repressiveness**	**repressed** b.__________	**repressively**

3. **Chaotic** (adj) totally disordered and confused, e.g., the chaotic jumble of papers, unpaid bills, books and mail on my desk

Verbs	Nouns	Adjectives	Adverbs
	c.________	**chaotic**	d.__________

4. **Asocial** (adj) inconsiderate of others, self-centered (the prefix a means "without," "not," or "opposite to")

5. **Amoral** (adj) without moral quality, neither moral nor immoral; having no moral standards, restraints or principles, as a completely amoral person

6. **Inherent** (adj) existing as a permanent and inseparable element, quality, or attribute, e.g., Two-year olds have an inherent sense of ownership toward all toys, their own and other children's.

7. **Intrinsic** (adj) — belonging to a thing by its very nature, built-in. Whether the committee accepts your idea or not, it has intrinsic 8erit.

8. **Symbol** (noun) — something that represents something else by association, resemblance, or convention, especially a material object used to represent something abstract or invisible such as the flag or Uncle Sam as symbols of the U.S., a cross or star as religious symbols.

Verbs	Nouns	Adjectives	Adverbs
e.________	**symbol**	f.________	symbolically

9. **Duality** (noun) — the quality of having two parts. (Dualism is the concept that there are two basic principles like body and mind or that the world or the mind is ruled by antagonistic or opposite forces: good and evil, mind and body, physical and spiritual, etc.)

10. **Optimistic** (adj) — expecting a favorable outcome

Verbs	Nouns	Adjectives	Adverbs
	g.________	**optimistic**	h.________

11. **Facilitate** (verb) — to make easier, assist, aid; to free from difficulties

Verbs	Nouns	Adjectives	Adverbs
	facility (ease)	i. ________	
facilitate	j. ________		
	k. ________ or (a person who makes processes easier)		

12. **Propensity** (noun) — tendency or leaning. Americans have a propensity to take the part of the underdog.

The prefix **ambi,** means both

An ambidexterous person can use both hands easily, is both right-handed and left-handed.

13. An **ambivalent** attitude or feeling takes in both sides, for example, love and hate, at the same time. What is the noun that goes with the adjective?

l. ____________________

14. **Ambiguity** is having two or more meanings, being understood in more than one way; uncertainty of meaning, significance, position.

Mona Lisa is famous for her ambiguous smile.

15. **to pose the problem:** to state what the problem is.

16. **Deterrent:** fear of dangerous, difficult or unpleasant consequences, as the death penalty is a deterrent to crime.

17. The root word **pole** refers to each of the extremities of the axis of the earth or of any spherical body or to one of two opposite principles. From this root word we get polar, which means characterized by opposite extremes and the verb polarize which means to break into opposing factions or groupings.

Verbs	Nouns	Adjectives	Adverbs
	Pole	**Polar**	
	Polarity		
m.__________	**Polarization**	**Polarized, Polarizing**	

18. **Relinquish** (verb): to give up, let go.

DISCUSSION

Look at the Anticipation-Response Guide. What does Bettelheim think about each of the eight points? Have his arguments made you want to change any of your original responses or not?

SAMPLE STUDENT JOURNAL ENTRIES

I don't remember many fairy tales—just movies. One was about a guy who could turn himself invisible. His name was Lucifer. There was this scene where he was going to shoot this guy and was invisible and pointing the gun (which WAS visible) at him...and the victim kept backing up and screaming as the gun got closer and closer. Then just Lucifer's head appeared...just his evil looking head. Then BANGG!!!! Fade out!!

I used to wake up in the dark convinced Lucifer was in the room—I was about five—I lay there just waiting for the gun to materialize and was convinced I could almost see the outlines of Lucifer's head there in the dark...

Well...this wasn't a fairy tale. Maybe that was the problem...It taught me there was evil in the world but evil was so powerful I wouldn't have stood a chance...Even though I guess Lucifer was defeated, that didn't do the dead man much good...

In fact, I remember how we used to play we were Lucifer, us kids, and had the power to be invisible...Not good!

Of course I don't have fantasies like that anymore—but I'm still a little scared of the dark. Maybe it's wise to be afraid of the dark, especially in LA.

The article really made me think but there was at least one thing I didn't understand: Bettelheim says that the fear of punishment is not as powerful a deterrent as the "conviction that crime does not pay." But what's the difference between fear of being punished and being convinced that crime doesn't pay? Let's see—I'll try to answer my own question...Hold on...I'm thinking...Well, I guess fear of punishment is kind of negative...Knowing that crime doesn't pay is more positive? It doesn't PAY—you don't <u>get</u> anywhere with it...you don't <u>succeed</u>...It's not so much that you are punished...You just aren't <u>rewarded</u>...It doesn't work out.

One thing really bothered me! B. writes that the fairytale ending "they lived happily ever after" is not simple escapism or wish fulfillment, but teaches the child that it is possible to leave his parents and form a "satisfying bond with another." What century was he living in! No couple lives happily ever after anymore—I wonder if they ever did—or at least no one I know...I think it's unrealistic and maybe even dangerous to expect to be "happy ever after." Maybe it <u>is</u> reassuring for a <u>really</u> little kid to hear or else they might think they can't survive without mommy and daddy...But they're in deep trouble if they hold on to an idea like that for too long. In my case, I think I may be still waiting for the prince to come and find me and make everything all right. Maybe they need some fairytales for adolescents about how to face NOT living happily ever after...

QUESTIONS FOR DISCUSSION AND WRITING

The following questions can be used for class discussion, for individual or group writing assignments, and for entries in a reading journal. Follow your teacher's instructions. Reread Bettelheim before you answer the following questions.

1. Think back to your own childhood. What were your experiences with fairy tales or any other stories? Movies? TV shows?

2. Can you remember being frightened or shocked by any stories that were read to you or that you read or saw?

3. What's your opinion about Bettelheim's main point—do you think fairy tales are good or bad for children? Why?

4. How will you handle the difficult problem of what to let your children read and see?

SUMMARIZING

Much of your college writing will be about what you read. Essay tests and research papers all require you to "digest" a lot of reading and to show on paper that you have understood it. Naturally, you cannot just copy down the words of an author. This shows nothing: no teacher can tell from this if you have understood the material. Additionally, you hardly ever have time to repeat (even in your own words) every single detail that you have read. Thus, summarizing is an important writing/reading skill to develop.

HOW TO SUMMARIZE COLLEGE READING

1. **Read the article once through quickly; try to get an overeview of it. Don't linger over words you don't know or sentences you don't understand.**

2. **Read it a second time very carefully. Mark your book. Write in the margins. Try to identify the main point the author is making (this may or may not be stated in a single sentence). Note where the author supports his main point: what are the principal sub-points of his argument or explanation? Notice the conclusion—is it different from the rest of the article or simply a restatement? Does the author "expand" his idea further into new areas or does he simply restate what he said before?**

3. **If the article has been difficult, read it a third time, or a fourth or fifth. Now is the time to look up words that you don't know. Reread difficult passages. Perhaps you can write about these in your journal. Write also about your reactions to what you have read.**

4. **When you start to write your summary,* refer to the notes you have written in the margin. Try to restate each paragraph with one or two sentences. Give equal space to the different portions of the article—not just the parts that interest you. Be sure that you have stated the author's main point, explained his supporting evidence and summarized his conclusion. That's all! Do not, in a formal summary, include your own opinion unless you are specifically asked.**

---

*Begin a discussion of an article or book by naming the title or author:

> In The Uses of Enchantment by Bruno Bettelheim, the author says . .
> In ____(title)____, ____(author)____ explains . . .

Watch sentence structure: not

> In ____(title)____, by ____(author)____, it says . . .

Give the full name of the author with your first reference to him. For all other references use the author's last name only.

MODEL SUMMARY AND PRACTICE SUMMARY

Here's a summary of part of the excerpt from Bettelheim's The Uses of Enchantment. It ends at paragraph 14. Read it carefully.

I wrote my summary following my own directions—approximately one sentence per paragraph (I included the paragraph number in the margin so that you could see which paragraph corresponds to which sentence).

Model Summary

1 In an excerpt from **The Uses of Enchantment**, Bruno Bettelheim says that fairy tales help children grow up. All children need fairy tales so they can fit their unconscious impulses into conscious life. More importantly, Bettelheim believes that fairy tales help the child by suggesting ways in which he can give meaning to his life.

2 Bettelheim maintains that children should not be forced to repress
unconscious contents, for this can stunt their growth. He is troubled that
many modern parents think a child should be shielded from his anxieties and
3 his tendencies toward violence. But, according to Bettelheim, if children
4 aren't allowed to learn that no one is always good, they feel that something
is wrong with them. Psychoanalysts know that people must fight against

5 difficult circumstances in order to survive and that it is only through this
kind of struggle that people can find meaning to life.

6 Bettelheim finds that while modern children's stories avoid unpleasant-
7 ness, children need to know that realities like death and aging exist. Fairy
tales often present these unpleasant realities, depicting basic life
8 problems in simple form. Both good and evil are present in these stories as
they are in life. Even though evil can be attractive in fairy tales, it never
9 wins out, and this is also important to the "moral education" of the child.
But even more important than the idea that "crime doesn't pay" is the fact
10 that the child identifies with the fairy tale hero. It is from this
identification that he learns morality.

11 Many fairy tales present people as either good or evil, not as a
mixture of both (as they are in real life). This is appropriate for children, as
12 they aren't ready yet for this ambivalent mixture. Children readily identify
with the hero not because he is good but because he is more attractive and
they want to be like him.

13 Some fairy tales don't make any moral judgments. In these "amoral
fairy tales" the hero succeeds not because he is good but because he is
clever. From this circumstance a child learns that even if he feels weak or
oppressed, he can succeed: he develops a positive attitude toward life.

Practice Summary:

Following the steps for summary writing on page 143, complete the summary of Bettelheim. (Paragraph 14 to the end of the article.)

MANAGING SENTENCES WITH LOGICAL CONNECTIVES— CAUSE AND EFFECT

Another important relationship between ideas besides that of **contrast** and **addition** (see Chapter Two) is that of **cause and effect.** In this case, when one event is the cause or result of another, we can use certain connectives to illustrate the relationship—either in the same sentence or in separate sentences.

Here are some sentences I've taken or adapted from Bettelheim that show these relationships:

Cause

1. Fairy tales have unequaled value <u>because</u> they offer new dimensions to the child's imagination.

2. <u>Because</u> the child identifies with the hero, he imagines that he suffers with the hero and triumphs with him.

3. The child identifies with the hero, for the hero's condition makes a deep positive appeal to him.

4. Since it creates discomfort in a parent to recognize these emotions in a child, the parent tends to overlook them.

Effect or Result

1. We want our children to believe that all men are good, but children know that they are not always good. This contradicts what they are told by their parents and therefore makes the child a monster in his own eyes. (The result of the contradiction between the child's experience and what his parents say is that the child thinks of himself as a monster.)

2. There are great differences between people; therefore, one has to make choices about who one wants to be.

3. The deep inner conflicts originating in our primitive drives and our violent emotions are all denied in modern children's literature, and so the child is not helped in coping with them.

4. Today children no longer grow up within the security of an extended family. Therefore, it is important to provide the child with images of heroes who have to go out into the world all by themselves.

As in relations of contrast and addition, you can express cause or effect either in separate sentences or within the same sentence. Number 4 above is an example of a cause and effect relationship expressed in two sentences.

COMBINING CAUSE AND EFFECT IN ONE SENTENCE

Option One

Cause: You can express the causal relationship between sentence A and sentence B by joining them with a comma and for. (In this use, for means because)

______Sentence A______, for ______Sentence B______

Sample: Parents tend to overlook violent feelings in a child, for these emotions can make parents uncomfortable.

Effect: You can show that the thought in one sentence is the effect or result of the thought in the other sentence by joining them with a comma and so.

______Sentence A______, so ______Sentence B______

Sample: Violent emotions can make parents uncomfortable, so they often overlook these feelings in their children.

Option Two

You join two sentences expressing cause-effect with a semicolon (;) and a signal word or phrase like therefore, as a result, because of this, consequently, or hence.

Sentence A ; therefore, Sentence B .

Sample: Violent emotions can make parents uncomfortable; therefore, they often overlook violent feelings in their own children.

Option Three

You may use words like because or since to show the relation of cause and effect in one sentence. (A later chapter will explain this kind of sentence in more detail.) The joining word can come at the beginning or in the middle of the sentence:

Because feelings of violence or anxiety make parents uncomfortable, they often overlook them in their children.

Parents often overlook feelings of violence or anxiety in their children because these feelings make them uncomfortable.

Non-options

1. You cannot join two sentences with just a comma.

2. **If you use because or since, your sentence must have two parts. You cannot write: "Because violent emotions can make parents uncomfortable." This is not a complete sentence. If you punctuated it as such, you would have written a fragment, an error as serious as the comma splice and run on sentence described in the previous chapter.**

Sentence Combining

As a warm-up for your major writing assignment, do the following: Use options 1, 2, or 3 to combine the sentences below in effective sentences which express cause and effect:

1. Fairy tales have value.

   Fairy tales offer new dimensions to the child's imagination.

2. The child identifies with the hero.
The child imagines that he suffers and triumphs with the hero.

3. It creates discomfort in a parent to recognize strong emotion in a child.
Parents overlook a child's anxiety about the dark.

4. Bettelheim believes that each person must confront painful realities in order to create meaning in his life.

Bettelheim believes that imaginative mental activities enable people to wring "meaning out of existence."

5. Strong feelings and impulses often reside in our unconscious.
Bettelheim proposes various mentally healthful ways to deal with these urges.

6. Figures in fairy tales are clearly polarized--either good or bad.
Polarization allows the child to easily understand the difference between good and evil.

Pick two of the model cause and effect sentences from Bettelheim and combine them using options 1, 2, and 3. You may change the wording, shorten the sentence, or paraphrase it. But you must end up with sentences expressing the cause-effect relationships that Bettelheim had in mind. Pay careful attention to punctuation. Pay attention to meaning too; make sure that what you write makes sense. Avoid a sentence like the following which expresses the wrong relationship:

> Strong emotions can make parents uncomfortable because parents often overlook these emotions in their children.

Parents aren't uncomfortable because they overlook their children's emotion; it's the other way around. They ignore their children's emotions because the emotions make them uncomfortable.

APPLYING IDEAS: ANALYSIS

In college papers and essay examinations you will often be asked to apply what you have read to specific situations. Applying ideas is a difficult mental process. First, of course, you have to have a thorough understanding of what you've read. Since we've studied Bruno Bettelheim so thoroughly, see if you can apply his ideas to a specific "case." What would he say about the fairy tale I've summarized below?

The Prince, The Ring, and the Dragon

A good old king dies. His evil prime minister takes over and exiles the king's young son. As the son is preparing to leave, his fairy godmother appears to him and gives him a magic ring which will make him invisible whenever he puts it on.

He spends a year traveling all over the world and has many terrifying adventures. In each case, just as he is about to lose his life, he remembers the magic ring and puts it on. In this way he is able to escape and survive.

His last and worst adventure is an attempt to rescue a beautiful princess who has been imprisoned for years by a large, fierce, very nasty, fire-breathing dragon. The prince isn't doing too well in the fight. Suddenly once again he remembers the magic ring and slips it on his finger.

Unfortunately the dragon too has magical powers and can see the prince through his invisible shield. It now looks very bad for the prince until he remembers that dragons are particularly sensitive to having sand thrown in their eyes. He tries this, the dragon, kills him, rescues the princess, returns to his homeland, kills the evil minister, marries the princess, and rules the kingdom. They live happily ever after.

SAMPLE ANALYSIS ASSIGNMENT

If you were reading Bettelheim for a psychology class or a course in children's literature, you might well be asked a question like the following:

> **Analyze "The Prince, the Ring, and the Dragon" according to Bruno Bettelheim's ideas: Would he find this fairy tale valuable to children?**

Put simply, this assignment asks you what Bettelheim would think about the fairy tale. To answer this question, look back at the excerpt from Bettelheim's book. Look for places where Bettelheim's specific descriptions of fairy tale characteristics would fit the details of the tale:

paragraph 6:	Is the child in this tale confronted with basic human problems? Which ones?
paragraph 9:	Are good and evil both present?
paragraph 10:	Would the child "identify with the hero in his struggles"?
paragraph 13:	Does the hero succeed because he is good or because he is clever?
paragraph 15:	Does the ending suggest that the child can overcome "separation anxiety" and form "a satisfying bond with another"?
paragraph 18:	Is this tale suitable for a modern child? Does it contain a hero who goes out into life isolated but who is helped by others and finally succeeds through his own resources?

Below is a fairly good student response to this assignment. Read it carefully.

Student Response

Bruno Bettelheim would find "The Prince, the Ring, and the Dragon" very helpful for children, particularly a modern child. It presents the reality of evil, gives the child a clever hero to identify with, and shows him the possibility of overcoming "separation anxiety" and forming a "satisfactory bond" with another. It is particularly helpful to a modern child because it helps him overcome his isolation and teaches him to rely on his own resources.

In the tale, two characters are definitely evil—the prime minister and the dragon. There is no ambivalence here. The child would be able to visualize which type of person he wants to identify with, the hero or the villains. At first, evil seems attractive, but although the prime minister's evil schemes seem to succeed, he meets defeat in the end.

The hero here is somewhat of a victim. He does nothing wrong—and so it is possible to say that he is "good." He succeeds finally, though, because he has the intelligence to outwit the destructive dragon. From this a child would learn that even if the cards seem to be stacked against him, he can win out if he uses his wits and perseveres. The child would certainly identify with the hero rather than with either the prime minister or the dragon. He would be able to visualize himself as an outcast alone and afraid at first but one who learns to overcome each difficulty and finally succeeds. Through this he would learn to cope with the real world.

The ending of the story would show the child that the hero's determination pays off. He is able to return to his home and conquer his original enemy. Moreover, he wins the princess and lives "happily ever after." Here he has been able to successfully separate from his parents. He has faced the fact of death and learned that "life is not always sunny." He has formed what Bettelheim calls "a truly satisfying bond with another." He has become an independent adult. His separation anxiety and fear of death have been significantly lessened.

Bettelheim would find this tale especially helpful for a modern child. Modern families are small nuclear families consisting of only two generations—parents and children, unlike the older extended families which contained many generations under one roof. Because of this and because of the modern child's relative isolation from any sense of community, the modern child needs a hero such as the prince who goes out into the world alone and is able to succeed. It is true that the prince is helped at first by his magic ring—a gift from his heritage, his fairy godmother--but in the end the ring doesn't help him. He must, like most of us, rely on his own intelligence. He is able to remember an important fact about dragons--their sensitivity to sand—and it is this reliance on his own intelligence that saves him. So while his heritage is important for a while, self-reliance helps him win out. Only then can he unite with the princess and return to defeat the evil prime minister who caused his isolation.

* * *

Discussion Questions

1. How is this essay organized?

2. Is the relationship between Bettelheim's ideas and the details of the tale a clear one or do we need to hear more about Bettelheim's ideas?

3. Are quotations handled well? Could they be improved?

MAJOR WRITING ASSIGNMENT: ANALYZING A FAIRY TALE

Choose one of the following fairy tales and analyze it according to Bettelheim's ideas. Would Bettelheim find this fairy tale valuable for children? You may use the questions following the analysis assignment (p. 150) as a guide. Cover all six points.

The Story of the Three Little Pigs

(Traditional)

Once upon a time there was an old sow with three little pigs, and as she had not enough to keep them, she sent them out to seek their fortune. The first that went off met a man with a bundle of straw, and said to him:

"Please, man, give me that straw to build a house."

Which the man did, and the little pig built a house with it. Presently along came a wolf, and knocked at the door, and said:

"Little pig, little pig, let me come in."

To which the pig answered:

"No, no, by the hair of my chinny chin chin."

The wolf then answered to that:

"Then I'll huff, and I'll puff, and I'll blow your house in."

So he huffed, and he puffed, and he blew his house in, and ate up the little pig.

The second little pig met a man with a bundle of furze and said:

"Please, man, give me that furze to build a house."

Which the man did, and the pig built his house. Then along came the wolf, and said:

"Little pig, little pig, let me come in."

"No, no, by the hair of my chinny chin chin."

"Then I'll puff, and I'll huff, and I'll blow your house in."

So he huffed, and he puffed, and he puffed, and he huffed, and at last he blew the house down, and he ate up the little pig.

The third little pig met a man with a load of bricks, and said:

"Please, man, give me those bricks to build a house with."

So the man gave him the bricks, and he built his house with them. So the wolf came, as he did to the other little pigs, and said:

"Little pig, little pig, let me come in."

"No, no, by the hair on my chinny chin chin."

"Then I'll huff, and I'll puff, and I'll blow your house in."

Well, he huffed, and he puffed, and he huffed and he puffed, and he puffed and huffed; but he could **not** get the house down. When he found that he could not, with all his huffing and puffing, blow the house down, he said:

"Little pig, I know where there is a nice field of turnips."

"Where?" said the little pig.

"Oh, in Mr. Smith's Home-field, and if you will be ready tomorrow morning I will call for you, and we will go together and get some for dinner."

"Very well," said the little pig. "I will be ready. What time do you mean to go?"

"Oh, at six o'clock."

Well, the little pig got up at five and got the turnips before the wolf came (which he did about six), who said:

"Little pig, are you ready?"

The little pig said: "Ready! I have been and come back again, and got a nice potful for dinner."

The wolf felt very angry at this, but thought that he would be **up to** the little pig somehow or other, so he said:

"Little pig, I know where there is a nice apple-tree."

"Where?" said the pig.

"Down at Merry-garden," replied the wolf, "and if you will not deceive me I will come for you at five o'clock tomorrow and we will go together and get some apples."

Well, the little pig bustled up the next morning at four o'clock and went off for the apples, hoping to get back before the wolf came; but he had farther to go and had to climb the tree, so that just as he was coming down from it, he saw the wolf coming, which, as you may suppose, frightened him very much. When the wolf came up he said:

"Little pig, what! Are you here before me? Are they nice apples?"

"Yes, very," said the little pig. "I will throw you down one."

And he threw it so far that, while the wolf was gone to pick it up, the little pig jumped down and ran home. The next day the wolf came again and said to the little pig:

"Little pig, there is a fair at Shanklin this afternoon. Will you go?"

"Oh, yes," said the pig, "I will go. What time shall you be ready?"

"At three," said the wolf. So the little pig went off before the time as usual, and got to the fair and bought a butter-churn, which he was going home with, when he saw the wolf coming. Then he could not tell what to do. So he got into the churn to hide, and by so doing turned it round, and it rolled down the hill with the pig in it, which frightened the wolf so much that he ran home without going to the fair. He went to the little pig's house and told him how frightened he had been by a great round thing which came down the hill past him. Then the little pig said:

"Hah, I frightened you, then. I had been to the fair and bought a butter-churn, and when I saw you, I got into it and rolled down the hill."

Then the wolf was very angry indeed, and declared he **would** eat up the little pig and that he would get down the chimney after him. When the little pig saw what he was about, he hung on the pot full of water and made a blazing fire, and, just as the wolf was coming down, took off the cover, and in fell the wolf; so the little pig put on the cover again in an instant, boiled him up, and ate him for supper, and lived happily ever afterwards.

Hansel and Gretel

Close to a large forest there lived a woodcutter with his wife and his two children. The boy was called Hansel and the girl Gretel. They were always very poor and had very little to live on. And at one time when there was famine in the land, he could no longer procure daily bread.

One night when he lay in bed worrying over his troubles, he sighed and said to his wife, "What is to become of us? How are we to feed our poor children when we have nothing for ourselves?"

"I'll tell you what, husband," answered the woman. "Tomorrow morning we will take the children out quite early into the thickest part of the forest. We will light a fire and give each of them a piece of bread. Then we will go to our work and leave them alone. They won't be able to find their way back, and so we shall be rid of them."

"Nay, wife," said the man, "we won't do that. I could never find it in my heart to leave my children alone in the forest. Wild animals would soon tear them to pieces."

"What a fool you are!" she said. "Then we must all four die of hunger. You may as well plane the boards for our coffins at once."

She gave him no peace till he consented. "But I grieve over the poor children all the same," said the man.

The two children could not go to sleep for hunger either, and they heard what their stepmother said to their father.

Gretel wept bitterly and said, "All is over with us now."

"Be quiet, Gretel," said Hansel. "Don't cry! I will find some way out of it."

When the old people had gone to sleep, he got up, put on his little coat, opened the door, and slipped out. The moon was shining brightly and the white pebbles round the house shone like newly minted coins. Hansel stooped down and put as many into his pockets as they would hold.

Then he went back to Gretel and said, "Take comfort, little sister, and go to sleep. God won't forsake us." And then he went to bed again.

At daybreak, before the sun had risen, the woman came and said, "Get up, you lazybones! We are going into the forest to fetch wood."

Then she gave them each a piece of bread and said, "Here is something for your dinner, but don't eat it before then, for you'll get no more."

Gretel put the bread under her apron, for Hansel had the stones in his pockets. Then they all started for the forest. When they had gone a little way, Hansel stopped and looked back at the cottage, and he did the same thing again and again.

His father said, "Hansel, what are you stopping to look back at? Take care and put your best foot foremost."

"Oh, father," said Hansel, "I am looking at my white cat. It is sitting on the roof, wanting to say good-by to me."

"Little fool, that's no cat! It's the morning sun shining on the chimney," said the mother.

But Hansel had not been looking at the cat. He had dropped a pebble on the ground each time he stopped.

When they reached the middle of the forest, their father said, "Now, children, pick up some wood. I want to make a fire to warm you."

Hansel and Gretel gathered the twigs together and soon made a huge pile. Then the pile was lighted, and when it blazed up the woman said, "Now lie down by the fire and rest yourselves while we go and cut wood. When we have finished we will come back to fetch you."

Hansel and Gretel sat by the fire, and when dinnertime came they each ate their little bit of bread, and they thought their father was quite near because they could hear the sound of an ax. It was no ax, however, but a branch which the man had tied to a dead tree, and which blew backwards and forwards against it. They sat there so long a time that they got tired. Then their eyes began to close and they were soon fast asleep.

When they woke it was dark night. Gretel began to cry, "How shall we ever get out of the wood?"

But Hansel comforted her and said, "Wait a little while till the moon rises, and then we will find our way."

When the full moon rose, Hansel took his little sister's hand and they walked on, guided by the pebbles, which glittered like newly coined money. They walked the whole night, and at daybreak they found themselves back at their father's cottage.

They knocked at the door, and when the woman opened it and saw Hansel and Gretel she said, "You bad children, why did you sleep so long in the wood? We thought you did not mean to come back any more."

But their father was delighted, for it had gone to his heart to leave them behind alone.

Not long afterwards they were again in great destitution, and the children heard the woman at night in bed say to their father, "We have eaten up everything again but half a loaf, and then we will be at the end of everything. The children must go away! We will take them farther into the forest so that they won't be able to find their way back. There is nothing else to be done."

The man took it much to heart and said, "We had better share our last crust with the children."

But the woman would not listen to a word he said. She only scolded and reproached him. Anyone who once says A must also say B, and as the father had given in the first time he had to do so the second. The children were again wide awake and heard what was said.

When the old people went to sleep Hansel again got up, meaning to go out and get some more pebbles, but the woman had locked the door and he couldn't get out. But he consoled his little sister and said, "Don't cry, Gretel. Go to sleep. God will help us."

In the early morning the woman made the children get up and gave them each a piece of bread, but it was smaller than the last. On the way to the forest Hansel crumbled it up in his pocket, and stopped every now and then to throw a crumb onto the ground.

"Hansel, what are you stopping to look about you for?" asked his father.

"I am looking at my dove which is sitting on the roof and wants to say good-by to me," answered Hansel.

"Little fool," said the woman, "that is no dove! It is the morning sun shining on the chimney."

Nevertheless, Hansel strewed the crumbs from time to time on the ground. The woman led the children far into the forest, where they had never been before.

Again they made a big fire, and the woman said, "Stay where you are, children, and when you are tired you may go to sleep for a while. We are going further on to cut wood, and in the evening when we have finished we will come back and fetch you."

At dinnertime Gretel shared her bread with Hansel, for he had crumbled his upon the road. Then they went to sleep and the evening passed, but no one came to fetch the poor children.

It was quite dark when they woke up, and Hansel cheered his little sister. He said, "Wait a bit, Gretel, till the moon rises, and then we can see the bread crumbs which I scattered to show us the way home."

When the moon rose they started, but they found no bread crumbs, for all the thousands of birds in the forest had picked them up and eaten them.

Hansel said to Gretel, "We shall soon find the way." But they could not find it. They walked the whole night and all the next day from morning till night, but they could not get out of the wood.

They were very hungry, for they had nothing to eat but a few berries which they found. They were so tired that their legs would not carry them any farther, and they lay down under a tree and went to sleep.

When they woke in the morning, it was the third day since they had left their father's cottage. They started to walk again, but they only got deeper and deeper into the wood, and if no help came they must perish.

At midday they saw a beautiful snow-white bird sitting on a tree. It sang so beautifully that they stood still to listen to it. When it stopped, it fluttered its wings and flew around them. They followed it till they came to a little cottage, on the roof of which it settled down.

When they got quite near, they saw that the little house was made of bread and roofed with cake. The windows were transparent sugar.

"Here is something for us," said Hansel. "We will have a good meal. I will have a piece of the roof, Gretel, and you can have a bit of the window. It will be nice and sweet."

Hansel reached up and broke off a piece of the roof to see what it tasted like. A gentle voice called out from within:

"Nibbling, nibbling like a mouse,
Who's nibbling at my little house?"

The children answered:

"The wind, the wind doth blow
From heaven to earth below."

And they went on eating without disturbing themselves. Hansel, who found the roof very good, broke off a large piece for himself, and Gretel pushed a whole round pane out of the window and sat down on the ground to enjoy it.

All at once the door opened and an old, old woman, supporting herself on a crutch, came hobbling out. Hansel and Gretel were so frightened that they dropped what they held in their hands.

But the old woman only shook her head and said, "Ah, dear children, who brought you here? Come in and stay with me. You will come to no harm."

She took them by the hand and led them into the little house. A nice dinner was set before them: pancakes and sugar, milk, apples, and nuts. After this she showed them two little white beds into which they crept, and they felt as if they were in heaven.

Although the old woman appeared to be so friendly, she was really a wicked old witch who was on the watch for children, and she had built the bread house on purpose to lure them to her. Whenever she could get a child into her clutches she cooked it and ate it, and considered it a grand feast. Witches have red eyes and can't see very far, but they have keen noses like animals and can scent the approach of human beings.

When Hansel and Gretel came near her, she laughed wickedly to herself and said scornfully, "Now that I have them, they shan't escape me."

She got up early in the morning before the children were awake, and when she saw them sleeping, with their beautiful rosy cheeks, she murmured to herself, "They will be dainty morsels."

She seized Hansel with her bony hand and carried him off to a little stable, where she locked him up behind a barred door. He might shriek as loud as he liked, she took no notice of him.

Then she went to Gretel and shook her till she woke, and cried, "Get up, little lazybones! Fetch some water and cook something nice for your brother. He is in the stable and has to be fattened. When he is nice and fat, I will eat him."

Gretel began to cry bitterly, but it was no use; she had to obey the witch's orders. The best food was cooked for poor Hansel, but Gretel had only the shells of crayfish.

The old woman hobbled to the stable every morning and cried, "Hansel, put your finger out for me to feel how fat you are."

Hansel put out a knucklebone, and the old woman, whose eyes were too dim to see, thought it was his finger. And she was much astonished that he did not get fat.

When four weeks had passed and Hansel still kept thin, she became impatient and would wait no longer.

"Now then, Gretel," she cried, "bustle along and fetch the water. Fat or thin, I will kill Hansel and eat him."

Oh, how his poor little sister grieved! As she carried the water, the tears streamed down her cheeks. "Dear God, help us!" she cried. "If only the wild animals in the forest had eaten us, we should at least have died together."

You may spare your lamentations! They will do you no good," said the old woman.

Early in the morning Gretel had to go out to fill the kettle with water, and then she had to kindle a fire and hang the kettle over it.

"We will bake first," said the old witch. "I have heated the oven and kneaded the dough."

She pushed poor Gretel towards the oven and said, "Creep in and see if it is properly heated, and then we will put the bread in."

She meant, when Gretel had gone in, to shut the door and roast her, but Gretel saw her intention and said, "I don't know how to get in. How am I to manage it?"

"Stupid goose!" cried the witch. "The opening is big enough. You can see that I could get into it myself."

She hobbled up and stuck her head into the oven. But Gretel gave her a push which sent the witch right in, and then she banged the door and bolted it.

"Oh! oh!" the witch began to howl horribly. But Gretel ran away and left the wicked witch to perish miserably.

Gretel ran as fast as she could to the stable. She opened the door and cried, "Hansel, we are saved! The old witch is dead."

Hansel sprang out, like a bird out of a cage when the door is set open. How delighted they were. They fell upon each other's necks and kissed each other and danced about for joy.

As they had nothing more to fear, they went into the witch's house, and in every corner they found chests full of pearls and precious stones.

"These are better than pebbles," said Hansel, as he filled his pockets.

Gretel said, "I must take something home with me too." And she filled her apron.

"But now we must go," said Hansel, "so that we may get out of this enchanted wood."

Before they had gone very far, they came to a great piece of water.

"We can't get across it," said Hansel. "I see no stepping stones and no bridge."

"And there are no boats either," answered Gretel, "but there is a duck swimming. It will help us over if we ask it."

So she cried:

"Little duck that cries quack, quack,
Here Gretel and here Hansel stand.
Quickly take us on your back,
No path nor bridge is there at hand!"

The duck came swimming towards them, and Hansel got on its back and told his sister to sit on his knee.

"No," answered Gretel, "it will be too heavy for the duck. It must take us over one after the other."

The good creature did this, and when they had got safely over and walked for a while the wood seemed to grow more and more familiar to them, and at last they saw their father's cottage in the distance. They began to run, and rushed inside, where they threw their arms around their father's neck. The man had not had a single happy moment since he deserted his children in the wood, and in the meantime his wife had died.

Gretel shook her apron and scattered the pearls and precious stones all over the floor, and Hansel added handful after handful out of his pockets.

So all their troubles came to an end, and they lived together as happily as possible.

* * *

The Twelve Wild Geese

Patrick Kennedy

There was once a King and Queen that lived very happily together, and they had twelve sons and not a single daughter. We are always wishing for what we haven't, and don't care for what we have, and so it was with the Queen. One day in winter, when the bawn (barn) was covered with snow, she was looking out of the parlor window, and saw there a calf that was just killed by the butcher and a raven standing near it. "Oh," says she, "if I had only a daughter with her skin as white as that snow, her cheeks as red as that blood, and her hair as black as that raven, I'd give away every one of my twelve sons for her." The moment she said the word, she got a great fright, and a shiver went through her, and in an instant after, a severe-looking old woman stood before her. "That was a wicked wish you made," said she, "and to punish you it will be granted. You will have such a daughter as you desire, but the very day of her birth you will lose your other children." She vanished the moment she said the words.

And that very way it turned out. When she expected her delivery, she had her children all in a large room of the palace, with guards all round it, but the very hour her daughter came into the world, the guards inside and outside heard a great whirling

---

Reprinted with permission of Macmillan Publishing Co. From Fairy and Folk Tales of Ireland, edited by W.B. Yeats. Copyright (c) 1973 by Colin Smythe Ltd.

and whistling, and the twelve princes were seen flying one after another out through the open window, and away like so many arrows over the woods. Well, the king was in great grief for the loss of his sons, and he would be very enraged with his wife if he only knew that she was to blame for it.

Everyone called the little princess Snow-white-and-Rose-red on account of her beautiful complexion. She was the most loving and lovable child that could be seen anywhere. When she was twelve years old she began to be very sad and lonely, and to torment her mother, asking her about her brothers that she thought were dead, for no one up to that time ever told her the exact thing that happened to them. The secret was weighing very heavy on the Queen's conscience, and as the little girl persevered in her questions, at last she told her. "Well, mother," said she, "it was on my account my poor brothers were changed into wild geese, and are now suffering all sorts of hardship; before the world is a day older, I'll be off to seek them, and try to restore them to their own shapes."

The King and Queen had her well watched, but all was no use. Next night she was getting through the woods that surrounded the palace, and she went on and on that night, and till the evening of next day. She had a few cakes with her, and she got nuts, and mugoreens (fruit of the sweet briar), and some sweet crabs, as she went along. At last she came to a nice wooden house just at sunset. There was a fine garden round it, full of the handsomest flowers, and a gate in the hedge. She went in, and saw a table laid out with twelve plates, and twelve knives and forks, and twelve spoons, and there were cakes, and cold wild fowl, and fruit along with the plates, and there was a good fire, and in another long room there were twelve beds. Well, while she was looking about her she heard the gate opening, and footsteps along the walk, and in came twelve young men, and there was great grief and surprise on all their faces when they laid eyes on her. "Oh, what misfortune sent you here?" said the eldest. "For the sake of a girl we were obliged to leave our father's court, and be in the shape of wild geese all day. That's twelve years ago, and we took a solemn oath that we would kill the first young girl that came into our hands. It's a pity to put such an innocent and handsome girl as you are out of the world, but we must keep our oath." "But," said she, "I'm your only sister, that never knew anything about this till yesterday; and I stole away from our father's and mother's palace last night to find you out and relieve you if I can." Every one of them clasped his hands, and looked down on the floor, and you could hear a pin fall till the eldest cried out, "A curse light on our oath! What shall we do?" "I'll tell you what," said an old woman that appeared at the instant your wicked oath, which no one should keep. If you attempted to lay an uncivil finger on her I'd change you into twelve booliaun buis (stalks of ragweed), but I wish well to you as well as to her. She is appointed to be your deliverer in this way. She must spin and knit twelve shirts for you out of bog-down, to be gathered by her own hands on the moor just outside of the wood. It will take her five years to do it, and if she once speaks, or laughs, or cries the whole time, you will have to remain wild geese by day till you're called out of the world. So take care of your sister; it is worth your while." The fairy then vanished, and it was only a strife with the brothers to see who would be first to kiss and hug their sister.

So for three long years the poor young princess was occupied pulling bog-down, spinning it, and knitting it into shirts, and at the end of the three years she had eight made. During all that time, she never spoke a word, nor laughed, nor cried: the last was the hardest to refrain from. One fine day she was sitting in the garden spinning, when in sprung a fine grayhound and bounded up to her, and laid his paws on her shoulder, and licked her forehead and her hair. The next minute a beautiful young prince rode up to the little garden gate, took off his hat, and asked for leave to come in. She gave him a little nod, and in he walked. He made ever so many apologies for intruding, and asked her ever so many questions, but not a word could he get out of her. He loved her so much from the first moment, that he could not leave her till he told her he was king of a country just bordering on the forest, and he begged her to come home with him, and be his wife. She couldn't help loving him as much as he did her, and though she shook her head very often, and was very sorry to leave her brothers, at last she nodded her head, and put her hand in his. She knew well enough that the good fairy and her brothers would be able to find her out. Before she went she brought out a basket holding all her bog-down, and another holding the eight shirts. The attendants took charge of these, and the prince placed her before him on his horse. The only thing that disturbed him while riding along was the displeasure his stepmother would feel at what he had done. However, he was full master at home, and as soon as he arrived he sent for the bishop, got his bride nicely dressed, and the marriage was celebrated, the bride answering by signs. He knew by her manner she was of high birth, and no two could be fonder of each other.

The wicked stepmother did all she could to make mischief, saying she was sure she was only a woodman's daughter; but nothing could disturb the young king's opinion of his wife. In good time the young queen was delivered of a beautiful boy, and the king was so glad he hardly knew what to do for joy. All the grandeur of the christening and the happiness of the parents tormented the bad woman more than I can tell you, and she determined to put a stop to all their comfort. She got a sleeping posset given to the young mother, and while she was thinking and thinking how she could best make away with the child, she saw a wicked-looking wolf in the garden, looking up at her, and licking his chops. She lost no time, but snatched the child from the arms of the sleeping woman, and pitched it out. The beast caught it in his mouth, and was over the garden fence in a minute. The wicked woman then pricked her own fingers, and dabbed the blood round the mouth of the sleeping mother.

Well, the young king was just then coming into the big bawn from hunting, and as soon as he entered the house, she beckoned to him, shed a few crocodile tears, began to cry and wring her hands and hurried him along the passage to the bedchamber.

Oh, wasn't the poor king frightened when he saw the queen's mouth bloody, and missed his child? It would take two hours to tell you the devilment of the old queen, the confusion and fright, and grief of the young king and queen, the bad opinion he began to feel of his wife, and the struggle she had to keep down her bitter sorrow, and not give way to it by speaking or lamenting. The young king would not allow any one to be called, and ordered his stepmother to give out that the child fell from the mother's arms at the window, and that a wild beast ran off with it. The wicked woman pretended to do so, but she told underhand to everybody she spoke to what the king and herself saw in the bed-chamber.

The young queen was the most unhappy woman in the three kingdoms for a long time, between sorrow for her child, and her husband's bad opinion; still she neither spoke nor cried, and she gathered bog-down and went on with the shirts. Often the twelve wild geese would be seen lighting on the trees in the park or on the smooth sod, and looking in at her windows. So she worked on to get the shirts finished, but another was at an end, and she had the twelfth shirt finished, except one arm, when she was obliged to take to her bed, and a beautiful girl was born.

Now the king was on his guard, and he would not let the mother and child be left alone for a minute; but the wicked woman bribed some of the attendants, set others asleep, gave the sleepy posset to the queen, and had a person watching to snatch the child away, and kill it. But what should she see but the same wolf in the garden looking up, and licking his chops again? Out went the child, and away with it flew the wolf, and she smeared the sleeping mother's mouth and face with blood, and then roared, and bawled, and cried out to the king and to everybody she met, and the room was filled, and everyone was sure the young queen had just devoured her own babe.

The poor mother thought now her life would leave her. She was in such a state she could neither think nor pray, but she sat like a stone, and worked away at the arm of the twelfth shirt.

The king was for taking her to the house in the wood where he found her, but the stepmother, and the lords of the court, and the judges would not hear of it, and she was condemned to be burned in the big bawn at three o'clock the same day. When the hour drew near, the king went to the farthest part of his palace, and there was no more unhappy man in his kingdom at that hour.

When the executioners came and led her off, she took the pile of shirts in her arms. There was still a few stitches wanted, and while they were tying her to the stake she still worked on. At the last stitch she seemed overcome and dropped a tear on her work, but the moment after she sprang up, and shouted out, "I am innocent; call my husband!" The executioners stayed their hands, except one wicked-disposed creature, who set fire to the faggot next him, and while all were struck in amaze, there was a rushing of wings, and in a moment the twelve wild geese were standing around the pile. Before you could count twelve, she flung a shirt over each bird, and there in the twinkling of a eye were twelve of the finest young men that could be collected out of a thousand. While some were untying their sister, the eldest, taking a strong stake in his hand, struck the busy executioner such a blow that he never needed another.

While they were comforting the young queen, and the king was hurrying to the spot, a fine-looking woman appeared among them holding the babe on one arm and the little prince by the hand. There was nothing but crying for joy, and laughing for joy, and hugging and kissing, and when any one had time to thank the good fairy, who in the shape of a wolf, carried the child away, she was not be to found. Never was such happiness enjoyed in any palace that ever was built, and if the wicked queen and her helpers were not torn by wild horses, they richly deserved it.

CHAPTER 4

ADDICTION:
ITS NATURE AND FORMS

by

Jo An Simmons

Contributors:

James Frisby

Lloyd Thomas

OVERVIEW

The readings in this chapter examine the nature of addiction. The first reading defines addiction; the second and third take opposing views on addiction; and the short story, "Sonny's Blues," dramatizes the plight of the the drug user and his relatives.

One **purpose** of this chapter is to give you **the experience of taking a position on an issue and backing it up with reasons or evidence.** Advanced writing classes often concentrate on argumentative writing; such classes make a detailed study of kinds of arguments, evidence, authority, logic, etc. That is not our purpose. Instead, **this introductory lesson exposes you to a number of viewpoints on addiction and asks you to (1) take a position on the subject and (2) back it up with reasons provided by the reading selections.**

WHAT TO LOOK FOR

Read the articles to discover what the various writers are saying about addiction and to see which view you yourself can support. As a preview, fill out the **Anticipation and Response Guide** now.

Anticipation-Response Guide

	Agree	Disagree
1. The use of drugs and other mood-altering substances is a matter of personal choice; since such use affects only the user, it is really no one else's business.	______	______
2. It is possible for a former addict to live a normal life once he or she gives up the the addictive substance.	______	______
3. The main attraction of mood-altering chemicals is their being "forbidden."	______	______
4. If one is very good to a chemical abuser, keeps peace in the house and avoids confrontations, the chemical abuser is likely to stop his or her destructive habit.	______	______

	Agree	Disagree
5. It is the right of a democratic society both to protect people from themselves when they become addicted to chemicals and to protect the rest of society from their antisocial behavior.	______	______
6. If you love a person who is dependent on some chemical, you will cover up for him or her and keep this person's problem a secret.	______	______
7. In general, addicts are not in a position to judge their condition realistically or accurately.	______	______
8. In the long run, it is not helpful to try to control a person's drinking problem by hiding or destroying bottles of alcohol.	______	______
9. Drugs are only temporarily effective as a way to escape suffering.	______	______

After reading the articles, see if any of your ideas have changed.

CHAPTER PLAN

"Television Addiction," excerpt from **The Plug-In Drug,** by Marie Winn

"Addiction is a Family Disease," by Nick Cavnar

"Drugs," by Gore Vidal, from **Homage to Daniel Shays**

"Sonny's Blues," excerpt from **Going to Meet the Man** by James Baldwin (see Chapter Two, pages 84-114).

Major Writing Assignments

"TELEVISION ADDICTION"

Excerpt from

THE PLUG-IN DRUG

Marie Winn

Marie Winn was born in Czechoslovakia, and emigrated with her family to the United States, where she attended the New York City schools. She was graduated from Radcliffe College and also attended Columbia University. Winn has written eleven books, all of them about children, and been a frequent contributor to the **New York Times** and various other newspapers and periodicals.

"Television Addiction" is the title of a chapter in Marie Winn's highly regarded book **The Plug-In Drug** (1977), and our selection is an excerpt from that chapter. It will be seen that a careful definition of the term "addiction," and a careful application of it to TV viewing, particularly by the young, is of utmost importance to the author's main point, as indicated by the book's title.

1 The word "addiction" is often used loosely and wryly in conversation. People will refer to themselves as "mystery book addicts" or "cookie addicts." E. B. White writes of his annual surge of interest in gardening: "We are hooked and are making an attempt to kick the habit." Yet nobody really believes that reading mysteries or ordering seeds by catalogue is serious enough to be compared with addictions to heroin or alcohol. The word "addiction" is here used jokingly to denote a tendency to overindulge in some pleasurable activity.

2 People often refer to being "hooked on TV." Does this, too, fall into the lighthearted category of cookie eating and other pleasures that people pursue with unusual intensity, or is there a kind of television viewing that falls into the more serious category of destructive addiction?

3 When we think about addiction to drugs or alcohol, we frequently focus on negative aspects, ignoring the pleasures that accompany drinking or drug-taking.

From THE PLUG-IN DRUG by Marie Winn. Copyright © 1977 by Marie Winn Miller. Reprinted by permission of Viking Penguin Inc.

And yet the essence of any serious addiction is a pursuit of pleasure, a search for a "high" that normal life does not supply. It is only the inability to function without the addictive substances that is dismaying, the dependence of the organism upon a certain experience and an increasing inability to function normally without it. Thus a person will take two or three drinks at the end of the day not merely for the pleasure drinking provides, but also because he "doesn't feel normal" without them.

4 An addict does not merely pursue a pleasurable experience and need to experience it in order to function normally. He needs to **repeat** it again and again. Something about that particular experience makes life without it less than complete. Other potentially pleasurable experiences are no longer possible, for under the spell of the addictive experience, his life is peculiarly distorted. The addict craves an experience and yet he is never really satisfied. The organism may be temporarily sated, but soon it begins to crave again.

5 Finally a serious addiction is distinguished from a harmless pursuit of pleasure by its distinctly destructive elements. A heroin addict, for instance, leads a damaged life: his increasing need for heroin in increasing doses prevents him from working, from maintaining relationships, from developing in human ways. Similarly an alcoholic's life is narrowed and dehumanized by his dependence on alcohol.

6 Let us consider television viewing in the light of the conditions that define serious addictions.

7 Not unlike drugs or alcohol, the television experience allows the participant to blot out the real world and enter into a pleasurable and passive mental state. The worries and anxieties of reality are as effectively deferred by becoming absorbed in a television program as by going on a "trip" induced by drugs or alcohol. And just as alcoholics are only inchoately aware of their addiction, feeling that they control their drinking more than they really do ("I can cut it out any time I want—I just like to have three or four drinks before dinner"), people similarly overestimate their control over television watching. Even as they put off other activities to spend hour after hour watching television, they feel they could easily resume living in a different, less passive style. But somehow or other while the television set is present in their homes, the click doesn't sound. With television pleasures available, those other experiences seem less attractive, more difficult somehow.

8 A heavy viewer (a college English instructor) observes:

9 "I find television almost irresistible. When the set is on, I cannot ignore it. I can't turn it off. I feel sapped, will-less, enervated. As I reach out to turn off the set, the strength goes out of my arms. So I sit there for hours and hours."

10 The self-confessed television addict often feels he "ought" to do other things--but the fact that he doesn't read and doesn't plant his garden or sew or crochet or play games or have conversations means that those activities are no longer as desirable as television viewing. In a way a heavy viewer's life is as imbalanced by his television "habit" as a drug addict's or an alcoholic's. He is living in a holding pattern, as it were, passing up the activities that lead to growth or development or a sense of accomplishment. This is one reason people talk about their television viewing so ruefully, so apologetically. They are aware that it is an unproductive experience, that almost any other endeavor is more worthwhile by any human measure.

11 Finally it is the adverse effect of television viewing on the lives of so many people that defines it as a serious addiction. The television habit distorts the sense of time. It renders other experiences vague and curiously unreal while taking on a greater reality for itself. It weakens relationships by reducing and sometimes eliminating normal opportunities for talking, for communicating.

12 And yet television does not satisfy, else why would the viewer continue to watch hour after hour, day after day? "The measure of health," writes Lawrence Kubie, "is flexibility . . . and especially the freedom to cease when sated" (Lawrence Kubie, **Neurotic Distortion and the Creative Process** (Lawrence: University of Kansas Press, 1958)). But the television viewer can never be sated with his television experiences--they do not provide the true nourishment that satiation requires--and thus he finds that he cannot stop watching.

* * *

VOCABULARY

Directions: **Fill in the blanks beside the letters with the appropriate form of the words. See explanation and example on page 60.**

1. **Addict** (verb) — The verb, pronounced ad-dict′, is from a Latin root meaning to surrender, to give oneself over to a habit or pursuit

2. **Addiction** (noun) — the state of being given up to a habit or practice or to a substance that is habit-forming, as a narcotic, to such an extent that not using it causes severe trauma; a surrender

Verbs	Nouns	Adjectives	Adverbs
	Addiction	**Addicted**	
Addict	a._________ (person who is addicted)	b.________ive	

3. **Wry** — twisted or distorted, lopsided like a **wry grin**; away from the expected direction

Adjectives	Adverbs
Wry	c.________________

If one's plans go **awry**, are they contrary to or in line with one's expectations? d.__________________

4. **Distort** (verb) — to twist awry or out of shape, e.g., Arthritis had distorted his fingers; to twist out of true meaning, e.g., He supported the lie with distorted facts; to twist mentally or morally, e.g., She has a distorted sense of honor. (There are also special meanings for electronics and optics.)

Verbs	Nouns	Adjectives	Adverbs
Distort	e.________________		

5. **Energetic** and **Enervate**—These two words with a common root have opposite meanings:

Energetic (adj) vigorous, forceful, powerful in action or effect

Enervate (verb) to deprive of nerve, force or strength; to enfeeble

Outdoor exercise makes me feel f.______________,

but working for more than an hour under the hot sun

makes me feel g.______________ed.

6. **Defer** (verb) to delay or postpone; to exempt temporarily from induction into military service; to yield in judgment or opinion to someone, often out of respect or courtesy

Verbs	Nouns	Adjectives	Adverbs
Defer	h.__________	i.__________ed	
	j.__________ence	k.__________	

7. The Latin root **vert, verse** means to **turn** and appears in many words: **convert, conversion** (to turn round or into); **pervert, perversion, perverse** (turned away from what is right, good, or proper); **introvert** (turned inward); **extrovert** (turned outward); **versus** (turned to face something opposite as in UCLA versus USC).

Adverse (adj) turned against; hostile, unfriendly; unfavorable, unlucky, unfortunate; contrary; disastrous; opposing one's interests or desires.

Verbs	Nouns	Adjectives	Adverbs
	l.__________ity	**Adverse**	
	m.__________ary		

As directed by your teacher, discuss the meanings and forms of the following words:

Reverse

Subvert

Controvert

Divert

Invert

Vertigo

8. The words **satisfy** and **sate** come from the same root but have slightly different meanings.

Satisfy (verb)	to fulfill the desires, expectations, needs, or demands of someone or something
Sate (verb)	to satisfy fully; to oversupply, glut
Satiate (verb)	to satisfy to the full; to supply with anything to excess, so as to disgust or weary

Verbs	Nouns	Adjectives	Adverbs
Satiate	**Satiation**	**Satiable** **Insatiable**	

If one has an **insatiable** appetite for something, is one ever satisfied?____________________

QUESTIONS FOR DISCUSSION

1. In Marie Winn's opinion, what is the essence of any serious addiction?

2. What dismaying characteristics of addiction does she mention in paragraphs (3) and (4)?

3. What dividing line does she give in paragraph (5) to distinguish serious addiction from harmless pursuit of pleasure? What examples does she give?

4. What do television addicts and drug addicts have in common, according to Winn?

   a.

   b.

   c.

   d.

5. Do you agree with Marie Winn that a person can be a television addict? Why or why not?

6. Suppose that, as a class, you're designing a questionnaire which could be used to identify a television addict. What questions might you add to this list?

   a. Do you arrange your daily schedule around certain television programs?

   b. Do some television characters seem more real to you than actual people?

   c. How much time do you spend each day listening to or talking to members of your household?

   d.

   e.

   f.

   g.

   h.

   i.

Part of a person's college education is exposure to a variety of viewpoints. Like the Bruno Bettelheim selection in another chapter, this selection presents a particular view of the world. The article below is from a Catholic charismatic journal, New Covenant, and reflects certain Christian assumptions: (1) that there is a God who heals both in response to prayer and through medical and psychological therapy, and (2) that although abuse of one's body is immoral, a person heavily dependent on chemicals no longer has the free use of his or her will and thus is not fully responsible for his or her use of chemicals.

ADDICTION IS A FAMILY DISEASE

Nick Cavnar

The producer of a popular Catholic television program points to the stacks of mail in his office.

"We get letters from thousands of people who watch our program," he says. "And do you know the single problem they mention most often? Drugs. A son or mother or husband or someone else in the family is an alcoholic or on drugs, and it's tearing these people up. Drugs are creating incredible havoc in this country—not just for the people using them but for their families."

What my producer friend is learning from his mail is a truth that people who work with alcoholics and other drug abusers have long recognized: Drug dependency has a lasting, damaging impact on the whole family. Most therapists and counselors now speak of drug dependency as a "family disease," one that can harm the non-users in a family every bit as much as it harms the dependent person himself. And with chemical abuse of all kinds reaching epidemic proportions across the United States, millions of families are hurting.

Christian families are by no means immune to the problem. Many Christians themselves are caught in some type of chemical dependency. Even larger numbers know the pain of having a chemically dependent spouse or child or parent or sibling.

Originally published in New Covenant, P.O. Box 7009, Ann Arbor, MI 48107.
All Rights Reserved. Reprinted with permission.

© Jane Scherr/Jeroboam, Inc.

Two people who have helped many drug abusers and their families escape the devastation of dependency are Drs. Robert and Mary McAuliffe. This husband-and-wife team of psychologists are founders of the American Chemical Dependency Foundation in Minneapolis, Minnesota, where they operate a clinic treating various types of dependency. The McAuliffes also belong to the board of directors of the Association of Christian Therapists.

Understanding Chemical Dependency

"One of the major problems we face in treating chemical dependency is to convince people that we are dealing with a sickness," says Bob McAuliffe. "It is very common, especially among Christians, to look at chemical dependency primarily as a moral problem, a sin. And, objectively, the behavior of the person who abuses chemicals **is** morally reprehensible. But what must be understood is that the chemical dependent no longer has the personal integrity required for sin. He is acting by compulsion, not by reason or choice."

The idea that chemical dependency is a disease rather than a moral problem dates back only 50 years, to the beginnings of Alcoholics Anonymous in the early 1930's. The key insight reached by the founders of A.A. was that they were powerless over alcohol: They could not control their drinking no matter how hard they tried. To condemn themselves for this powerlessness only made their condition worse. But when they learned to see it as a disease, as something essentially outside their control or moral responsibility, they were able to surrender the problem to a "Higher Power" and discover the road to recovery.

A.A.'s approach has won wide acceptance for the simple reason that it works. Yet many people remain unclear on just what **kind** of disease chemical dependency is. Is it a physical illness or a mental one? Is it an inherited condition or a sign of underlying emotional problems? Or is it simply caused by the addictive quality of the chemicals themselves?

Chemical dependency can actually involve all these factors. Yet the McAuliffes believe that to understand the disease of dependency we have to go beyond the usual concepts of physical or mental or emotional illness and think in terms of a **relational** sickness.

"We define chemical dependency essentially as a sick or pathological love relationship between a person and a mood-altering chemical," says Bob McAuliffe. "Think of all the relationships we have with people and with things. Some are casual; they come and go without making any great difference to us. Others are firm and deep and mean a great deal. The difference is that in some cases we make a commitment to the person or thing that is the object of our relationship, and in other cases we do not.

"With mood-altering chemicals, as with other things, we may have only a casual relationship. Or we may make a commitment that sets up a deep and lasting bond with them. That is essentially what happens in chemical dependency: An individual makes a personal commitment to drugs for the sake of the rewards—the highs or euphoria—he or she expects to get from taking them."

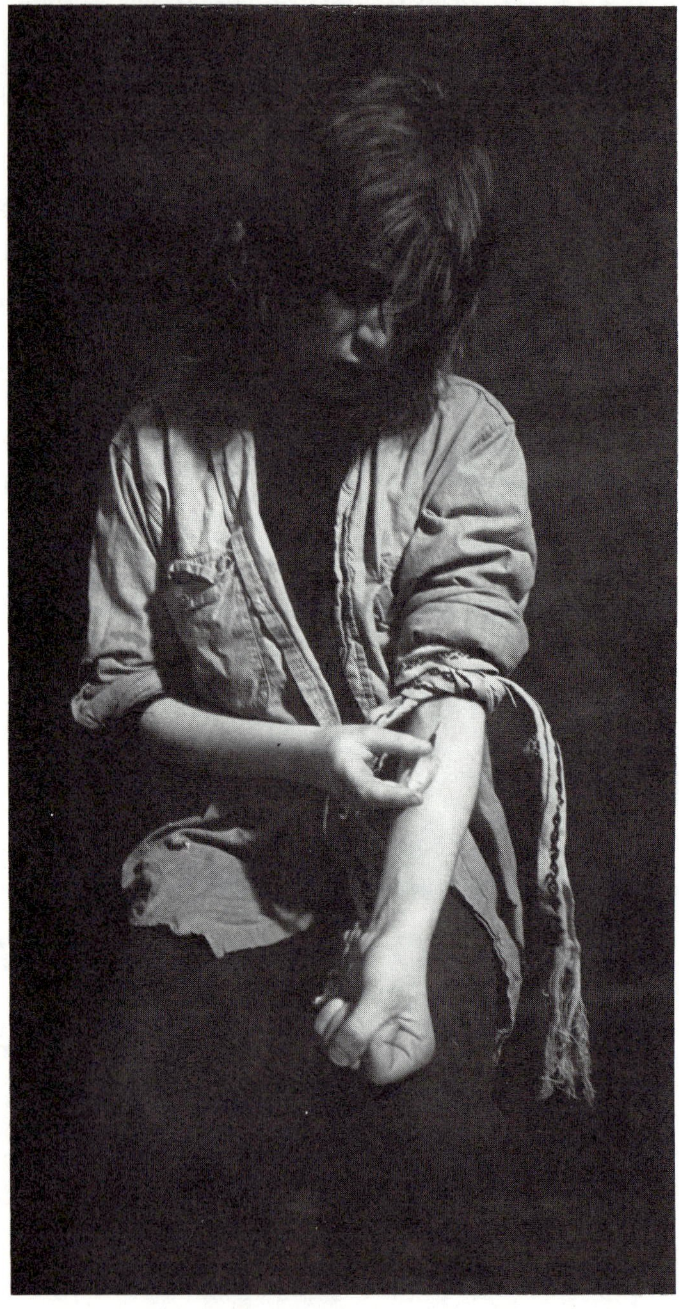

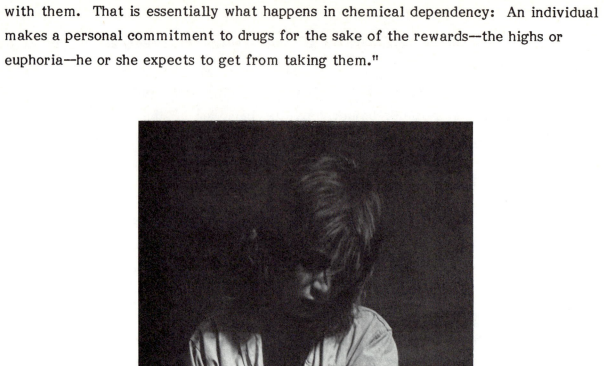

© Michael Weisbrot and Family

The Dependency Grows

A love affair with a mood-altering chemical is a deadly thing. Such chemicals —alcohol, narcotics, tranquilizers, marijuana, and the rest—are extremely powerful. They can produce intensely pleasurable highs; they can also distort a person's thinking and grasp of reality. Some have beneficial uses in moderate, controlled amounts. But when used to the point of intoxication they are all basically poison. A person who abuses one of these chemicals more and more frequently actually comes to enjoy it less. His body adjusts to the toxic effects of the chemical, and it no longer produces so high a high. But the lows that follow plummet lower and last longer.

For one thing, the body needs the chemical now and no longer functions well without it. Perhaps even more uncomfortable is the heavy load of negative emotions that builds up around the drug use. Deep within, the person knows something is out of control in his relationship with drugs, and he feels ashamed and guilty. Soon he is turning to the chemical not so much because he enjoys it as to blot out the misery and self-loathing he feels when he is sober.

If a person were able to be honest at this point, he could see that drugs are causing the pain rather than relieving it. But already his commitment to the drug has become so strong and so important that he cannot admit this, even to himself. He tells himself that the chemical is really no problem; he can give it up whenever he wants. Something else is causing his misery—his job or his family or a run of bad luck.

A chemical dependent does not consciously deceive himself; he truly believes these things. Under the powerful influence of the drug, he has lost almost all touch with reality. Unless something is able to break through his delusions and make him realize his true condition, he will remain locked in a deadly embrace with this drug until it destroys him.

Involving the Family

Understanding chemical dependency as a sick love relationship helps explain why it has such an impact on the family of the dependent. From the outset, even before the drug use has become an obvious problem, family members are competing with another commitment, another love, in this person's life. Because they do not recognize the dependency or understand how it works, they often interpret what is happening as a personal rejection.

"In the earlier stages," says Mary McAuliffe, "family members often get the sense that they are playing second fiddle to something more important, but they don't tend to see the alcohol or drugs as the problem. All they see is that the person isn't really interested in them anymore. Very naturally they tend to look at themselves and wonder, 'What am I not doing right here? Am I holding up my end of the relationship?' "

The uncertainty and guilt the family feels play very neatly into an emerging pattern of denial and dishonesty.

"The dependent person begins very early to project blame onto the rest of the family," Mary McAuliffe explains. "It's part of the whole defense system that develops, a way to account for one's own unacceptable behavior by projecting the fault on somebody else. And it is very difficult for the other family members to resist taking that blame. There's always a grain of truth in every accusation, so they think, 'Well, maybe he's right. Perhaps I am the problem.' "

Soon the people around the chemical dependent are caught in the same web of guilt and negative feelings and deception that has ensnared him. "They truly love this person. They want the relationship to work. Their focus becomes more and more fixed on the dependent person—trying to make the relationship more satisfying for him or for her, trying to be the kind of husband or wife or parent or child that person wants.

"What they do not understand is the nature of the dependency itself. They do not realize that this person is operating under the influence of an illness. And so they end up relating to the person in ways that are just as sick and dysfunctional and harmful as the person's relationship to chemicals."

The most harmful, and yet most typical, way families try to deal with chemical dependency is to attempt in one way or another to control the problem.

Some try forcibly to keep the person from using drugs. They hide bottles or empty them down the drain; they search out the pills and flush them away; they try to keep the person away from people or places that offer temptation. Others try to go along with the person and keep him happy. They make every effort to prevent anything that might upset him or give him an excuse to get stoned.

Perhaps the most common way families try to control the problem is simply to deny that a problem exists.

"Silence is one of their best defenses," says Mary McAuliffe. "Not to talk about the problem, not to admit it to anyone. Somehow, they think, if they can just rise above the behavior, it will go away. Family members get into a lot of their own dishonesty, as they create alibis in order to cover up for the dependent individual and hide the problem from others."

Whatever form the family's attempts to control their problem takes, the net result is that they adjust their lives more and more to the behavior of the substance abuser. Rather than helping him in any way, the whole family becomes locked into his illness.

Tell the Truth

If the family cannot control the problem what **can** they do?

"If all else has failed, start telling the truth," says Bob McAuliffe. "Stop covering up; stop hiding the problem. Say what you see going on.

"There is so much cover-up in families affected by dependency," he explains. "And actually it leaves the person who is chemically dependent even more helpless. It means that all his defenses and delusions are working. Until someone tells the truth, the delusion is never even touched."

Mary McAuliffe points out that honesty has to begin with yourself.

"Family members need to focus on themselves," she explains. "They need to focus on their own response to the chemical dependent, their own anger and hostile feelings, and begin to get some appropriate professional help for that. As they begin to change they can let go of the control, the caretaking, trying to please this person, and getting sick with the person all the time. They begin to make a life for themselves, moving ahead in areas of growth and recovery.

"Oftentimes family members don't want to hear that," she adds. "They have come to us so we can tell them what to do about the person with the chemical dependency. But I tell them that getting help for themselves is the best thing they can do for the other person. As the rest of the family becomes healthier the sickness of the person with the problem stands out more clearly. It puts him in closer touch with the seriousness of his condition."

As family members begin to recover they must learn to maintain a "holy detachment" toward the dependent person and his illness.

"You must allow the dependent person to experience the consequences of his or her own behavior," says Bob McAuliffe. "That doesn't mean you totally abandon the person, but it does mean that you say, 'I'm not going to enable anymore. I won't tell the lies. If you fail in school this semester, you have to suffer the consequences of that. If you're too drunk or hung over to go to work, you have to take the consequences of that.'

"Whatever the consequences we allow them to experience, we need to make a hookup between the behavior and the disease, so that they are confronted with the truth about what their drinking or drug use is doing to them. Allowing the person to experience these consequences brings reality in, so that an attitude of honesty can develop and healing can begin."

Where is God?

A Christian who struggles with chemical dependency, either personally or in another family member, often has one other cause for pain and confusion: Why is God letting this problem continue? He has the power to heal. Why doesn't He intervene?

"I find a lot of anger against God among the committed Christians who come to us," says Mary McAuliffe. "They have been striving so diligently to serve God and be loyal to God, and they say, 'Look what he's doing to me.' There's a great fear to express it, but often that anger is there, locked in."

Dr. McAuliffe believes that such anger reflects a fundamental misunderstanding of how God heals.

"Many Christians see God as a kind of **deus ex machina**," she explains, "a God from out there who is somehow going to come and touch me and take away all my pain. They want to pray for a miracle rather than get involved in the process of healing. Some have told us outright that they don't want to hear anything 'natural'—anything based on science or on the natural process of healing. They just want to know it's from God."

The McAuliffes have no doubts about the power of prayer and the need for prayer in dealing with chemical dependency. A group of volunteers intercedes daily for all the clients of their clinic, and they have seen many breakthroughs come in connection with prayer. But they also believe that God is present in the natural process of therapy.

"I happen to believe that God works very powerfully **through** our program," says Mary McAuliffe. "He works through the other people in it, through our staff. He is working through family members as they come together in love and get honest with one another and work toward reconciliation. It is in the stuff of illness, the stuff of therapy, that God works in our human condition, day in and day out."

The Hope of Healing

The point is sometimes emphasized that alcoholics and drug addicts never really recover or get cured; at best they are "recovering." To many people this sounds somewhat discouraging. Is there really no hope for a full healing from chemical dependency?

"If you mean, Can a recovered dependent ever safely invest in chemicals again? I would say no, absolutely," answers Bob McAufliffe. "It never happens that people can safely and comfortably resume what made them sick in the first place.

"But other than that, I see that chemical dependency truly is a sickness, and, with treatment, healing or recovery can be as complete as it is with other illnesses. The obsession with chemicals does resolve, and the compulsion to use them is removed. The low self-image produced by the relationship--that goes. I see people getting weller than well."

The hope of recovery does exist then, but the road that leads there is not easy for either the chemical dependent or the family. It demands a painful honesty and a steadfast commitment to change and grow. It demands too the prayers, understanding, and support of the whole Christian community.

* * *

VOCABULARY

Directions: Supply the missing forms of the words in the boxes as directed on page 60.

1. **Havoc** (noun) — ruinous devastation

2. **Sibling** (noun) — brother or sister

3. **Compel** (verb) — to force or drive; to have a powerful, irresistible effect. The rising floodwaters compel us to seek higher ground.

   Compelling (adj) — means both driving as in compelling motives and commanding admiration, attention, respect

   Compulsion (noun) — general meaning—the state of being driven
   psychological meaning—a strong, usually irresistible impulse to perform an act contrary to one's will

Verbs	Nouns	Adjectives	Adverbs
	Compulsion	a.________ive c.________ry	b.________

4. **Toxin** (noun) — a poisonous compound

Verbs	Nouns	Adjectives	Adverbs
	Toxin, Antitoxin, Toxicity	d.____________	

The related word **Intoxication** means drunkenness, alcohol poisoning.

5. **Projection** (noun) — general meaning—something thrown forward
   psychological meaning—the tendency to assign to another person feelings, thoughts, or attitudes present in oneself

6. **Affect** (verb) — to influence, e.g., Our hidden angers can affect our health.

   Effect (noun) — the result, e.g., One effect of hidden angers is a tension headache.

7. **Obsess** (verb) to dominate the thoughts, feelings, and desires of a person; to trouble a person abnormally

Verbs	Nouns	Adjectives	Adverbs
Obsess	e.__________	f.__________	g.__________

QUESTIONS FOR DISCUSSION AND WRITING

The following questions can be used for class discussion, for individual or group writing assignments, and for entries in a reading journal. Follow your teacher's instructions.

1. In "Addiction is a Family Disease," Doctors Robert and Mary McAuliffe discuss a particular kind of addiction, chemical dependency. What definition of chemical dependency does Bob McAuliffe give? What is the trade-off in the relationship between the person and the chemical?

2. Does Dr. McAuliffe claim that all chemical use is poisonous or that a person cannot have a casual relationship with a mood-altering chemical?

3. Below are a number of statements about addiction. After each statement, put a W if there is evidence that Marie Winn would endorse the statement, an M if there is evidence that the McAuliffes would endorse the statement, both a W and an M if all would endorse the statement.

Example: Addiction affects not only the addicted person but his relationships to other people. ___W and M___

a. The main attractiveness of an addictive agent (a substance or experience) is the intense pleasure it gives. ___________

b. Addicts often blame others for their problem. ___________

c. Addicts have an unrealistic view of their control over the addictive agent. ___________

d. The word "addiction," besides referring to chemicals, can refer to compulsive, destructive patterns of behavior. ___________

e. Addicts become unable to function well without the addictive agent. ___________

f. Addiction distorts a person's thinking and grasp of reality. ___________

g. The original amounts of an addictive substance or experience no longer satisfy the addict as use continues. ___________

h. In the early stages of addiction, addictive agents blot out the unpleasant aspects of life. ___________

i. In later stages, addicts use the addictive agent to blot out their shame and their negative emotions concerning their addiction. ___________

The McAuliffes have some do's and don'ts to help relatives of an addict keep their own emotional and mental health and to help the addict come to grips with the problem.

4. Name three don'ts:

5. Name two do's:

WRITING PRACTICE

To help you pull together what you've read so far about addiction, write a light-hearted paper about a non-serious addiction you might have. Examples of non-serious addictions might include addictions to chocolate, the color purple, to a particular team, soap opera, or activity like aerobic dancing. Put in as many characteristics of addiction as you can.

"For Whom the Pasta Boils" by Lloyd Thomas models the light-hearted tone and the evidence of addiction that this assignment calls for.

FOR WHOM THE PASTA BOILS

Lloyd Thomas

I love pasta. Actually, this is a polite way of saying that I am addicted to pasta. I like nothing better than to set a huge pot of water boiling on top of the stove, pour in several handfuls of spaghetti, vermicelli, linguine, or fettucine, and stir them reverently. While the pasta boils, I brew a modest sauce to pour over the heavenly noodles. Sometimes I prepare a vibrant green pesto sauce, made of basil, crushed walnuts, olive oil, and Parmesan cheese. At other times I favor a more traditional Alfredo sauce, which is also made of Parmesan cheese, but which adds cream, butter, and a grating of nutmeg. When the pasta is finished cooking, I strain it, spoon it lovingly on a plate, and then cover it with the sauce.

My hobby, though innocent-appearing, compels me to eat pasta continually, day or night, rain or shine, hot or cold, at home or in restaurants. Merely opening a menu and glimpsing items like spaghetti alla carbonara, linguine alla vongole, or tagliatelle con pesto causes my mouth to water and my pulse to thump. At home, late at night, the sight of a cold plate of macaroni, waiting patiently in the refrigerator, makes me automatically reach for a fork. Like a man who hasn't eaten a solid meal in days, I immediately rescue the macaroni from the refrigerator shelf, tear off the plastic wrap, and transfer it to the pan waiting on the stove. In a matter of minutes, the hot noodles and fragrant cheese sauce are ready to be eaten.

I ask for no pity. I will go anywhere, pay any price, run any risk to consume my daily share of pasta. Contemplating hot pasta covered with a spicy cheese sauce moves me to ecstasy. No matter what shape it comes in--fusilli, which are twisted in graceful spirals; farfalle, which are shaped like tiny bow ties; tagliatelle, which are like wide, flat ribbons; linguine, which are flat noodles with a rough edge like the "tongue" which gives them their special name; or the humble spaghetti, which everybody recognizes--I am addicted to pasta. Therefore, never ask for whom the pasta boils; it boils for me.

MANAGING SENTENCES THROUGH SUBORDINATION: ADJECTIVE CLAUSES AND PHRASES

Another way to combine two ideas is to use adjective clauses and phrases. These clauses wedged tightly against a noun allow us to slip an additional thought into a sentence without creating a second sentence. Stylist Sheridan Baker describes it this way:

> It is an adjectival sort of thing, a shoulder-to-shoulder operation, a neat trick with no need for shouting, a stone to a stone with no need of mortar. You simply put clauses and phrases up against a noun. . .
> (**The Complete Stylist and Handbook** (New York: Harper and Row, 1984), pp. 157-58.)

Adjective Clauses

Adjective clauses begin with who (whom, whose) which that, or where

Examples:

1. The prowler, who must have been alarmed by our headlights, fled out the back door.
2. Here is the secret passage that leads to the dungeon.
3. Sometimes I prepare a vibrant green pesto sauce, which is made of basil, crushed walnuts, olive oil, and Parmesan cheese.
4. The husband and wife team of psychologists are founders of the American Chemical Dependency Foundation in Minneapolis, Minnesota, where they operate a clinic treating various types of dependency.

Practice:

In the space below, combine these two ideas into one sentence using which to introduce the adjective clause:

> Caffeine is found in coffee, tea, and chocolate. It is a stimulant type of drug.

Note: Both the combinations below are correct: the first one emphasizes the drug category, the second the foods that contain caffeine.

Caffeine, which is found in coffee, tea, and chocolate, is a stimulant type of drug.

Caffeine, which is a stimulant type of drug, is found in coffee, tea, and chocolate.

Adjective Phrases (Appositive and Participial)

You have probably been using these phrases in your writing without needing to know their names. We will name them here so that we can talk about them.

An APPOSITIVE is a noun or noun phrase explaining the word next to it:

Washington, our first President

anorexia, an eating disorder

Sheridan Baker uses a series of appositive phrases to begin the "adjectival sort of thing"—a shoulder-to-shoulder operation, a neat trick with no need of shouting, a stone to a stone with no need of mortar.

One way to think of appositive phrases is as streamlined or cut-down adjective clauses.

Example 1: Caffeine, ~~which is~~ a stimulant type of drug, etc.

Caffeine, a stimulant type of drug, etc.

Example 2: The series of adjective clauses in this sentence from "For Whom the Pasta Boils" can be changed to a series of appositives.

GRACEFUL, TWISTED
No matter what shape it comes in--fusilli, which are twisted in graceful

SPIRALS TINY BOW TIES
spirals, farfalle, which are shaped like tiny bow ties, tagliatelle,

WIDE FLAT RIBBONS FLAT NOODLES WITH A
which are wide, flat ribbons, linguine, which are flat noodles with a rough

ROUGH-EDGED TONGUE
edge like the "tongue" which gives them their special name, or humble spaghetti—I am addicted to pasta.

Practice:

Use appositives to combine the following:

1. Hunting bargains is her favorite sport. It requires a sharpshooter's eye and much beating of the bushes.

2. Anorexics are victims of an eating disorder. They fast compulsively.

3. I won't be in town until August 13. That's the last day to register.

Combine these sentences in two steps. First combine these sentences using who, whom, or whose; then transform the adjective clause into an appositive phrase.

Example: James Baldwin wrote "Sonny's Blues." He now lives in Paris.

Step 1 James Baldwin, who wrote "Sonny's Blues," now lives in Paris.

Step 2 James Baldwin, writer of "Sonny's Blues," now lives in Paris.

4. Sonny's brother is a high school math teacher. He tries to help Sonny.

   Step 1

   Step 2

5. Willie Ruff is a superb musician. He also teaches classes in musicology and Afro-American history at Yale.

   Step 1

   Step 2

A PARTICIPIAL phrase is a group of words headed by an ING form of a verb (finding) or by its past tense (found).

Example:

Caffeine, found in coffee, tea, and chocolate, is etc.

Finding the road washed out, we took a detour.

Participial phrases can also be thought of as streamlined or cut-down adjective clauses.

Example:

a. The prowler, ~~who must have been~~ alarmed by our headlights, fled out the back door.

The prowler, alarmed by our headlights, etc.

b. pesto sauce ~~which is~~ made of basil, crushed walnuts, olive oil, and Parmesan cheese

pesto sauce, made of basil, etc.

Practice:

1. **Use the participle "thinking" to combine these two sentences:**

   Donna thought she might have a chance. She applied for the special scholarship.

2. **Use the participle "ignoring" to combine these two sentences:**

   The new boat owner ignored the Coast Guard warning. He launched out into the heavy seas.

3. **Use the participle "addicted" to combine these two sentences:**

   I am addicted to potato chips. I cannot stop eating them until I have finished the whole bag.

Combine these sentences in two steps. First combine them using who, whom, or whose; then transform the ADJECTIVE CLAUSE into a PARTICIPIAL PHRASE.

Example:

Recent studies show marijuana to be more harmful than previously thought. These studies describe personality changes and weakened performance levels.

Step 1 Recent studies, which describe personality changes and weakened performance levels, show marijuana to be more harmful than previously thought.

Step 2 Recent studies, describing personality changes and weakened performance levels, show marijuana to be more harmful than previously thought.

4. The Chinese students are listening to jazz for the first time. They responded enthusiastically to the Ruff-Mitchell duo. (William Zinsser)

Step 1

Step 2

5. Creole lays rhythm on his bass fiddle. He has been concentrating on Sonny.

Step 1

Step 2

DRUGS

Gore Vidal

Novelist, playwright, critic, editor, political columnist, and sometime political candidate Gore Vidal (b. 1925) seems to enjoy stirring the winds of controversy with his unconventional but serious views on both contemporary and time-honored topics. Much of his fiction, for example, **Creation** (1981) and **Burr** (1973), is based on historical sources. **Myra Breckenridge** (1968) concerns the plight of modern human beings in their fight for integrity in a valueless society with corrupt institutions. Vidal's work in all genres is known for its irony and urbane wit.

This essay was published in the **New York Times** in 1970 and is typical of Vidal's irreverent thought. His proposal is quite controversial, yet he states it quite matter-of-factly. As you read this essay, note how directly Vidal presents his proposal and how clearly he lists his supporting reasons. Be careful that you do not read too quickly and miss his logical train of thought. Be careful also that you do not fail to understand fully his argument just because you might disagree with it.

It is possible to stop most drug addiction in the United States within a very short time. Simply make all drugs available and sell them at cost. Label each drug with a precise description of what effect—good and bad—the drug will have on the taker. This will require heroic honesty. Don't say that marijuana is addictive or dangerous when it is neither, as millions of people know—unlike "speed," which kills most unpleasantly, or heroin, which is addictive and difficult to kick.

For the record, I have tried—once—almost every drug and liked none, disproving the popular Fu Manchu theory that a single whiff of opium will enslave the mind. Nevertheless many drugs are bad for certain people to take and they should be told why in a sensible way.

Along with exhortation and warning, it might be good for our citizens to recall (or learn for the first time) that the United States was the creation of men who believed that each man has the right to do what he wants with his own life as long as he does not interfere with his neighbor's pursuit of happiness (that his neighbor's idea of happiness is persecuting others does confuse matters a bit).

"Drugs," from Homage to Daniel Shays: Collected Essays 1952-1972 by Gore Vidal. Copyright (c) 1970 by Gore Vidal, by permission of Alfred A. Knopf, Inc.

This is a startling notion to the current generation of Americans. They reflect a system of public education which has made the Bill of Rights, literally, unacceptable to a majority of high school graduates (see the annual Purdue reports) who now form the "silent majority"—a phrase which that underestimated wit Richard Nixon took from Homer who used it to describe the dead.

Now one can hear the warning rumble begin: if everyone is allowed to take drugs everyone will and the GNP (Gross National Product) will decrease, the Commies will stop us from making everyone free, and we shall end up a race of zombies, passively murmuring "groovy" to one another. Alarming thought. Yet it seems most unlikely that any reasonably sane person will become a drug addict if he knows in advance what addiction is going to be like.

Is everyone reasonably sane? No. Some people will always become drug addicts just as some people will always become alcoholics, and it is just too bad. Every man, however, has the power (and should have the legal right) to kill himself if he chooses. But since most men don't, they won't be mainliners either. Nevertheless, forbidding people things they like or think they might enjoy only makes them want those things all the more. This psychological insight is, for some mysterious reason, perennially denied our governors.

It is a lucky thing for the American moralist that our country has always existed in a kind of time-vacuum: we have no public memory of anything that happened before last Tuesday. No one in Washington today recalls what happened during the years alcohol was forbidden to the people by a Congress that thought it had a divine mission to stamp out Demon Rum—launching, in the process, the greatest crime wave in the country's history, causing thousands of deaths from bad alcohol, and creating a general (and persisting) contempt among the citizenry for the laws of the United States.

The same thing is happening today. But the government has learned nothing from past attempts at prohibition, not to mention repression.

Last year when the supply of Mexican marijuana was slightly curtailed by the Feds, the pushers got the kids hooked on heroin and deaths increased dramatically, particularly in New York. Whose fault? Evil men like the Mafiosi? Permissive Dr. Spock? Wild-eyed Dr. Leary? No.

The Government of the United States was responsible for those deaths. The bureaucratic machine has a vested interest in playing cops and robbers. Both the Bureau of Narcotics and the Mafia want strong laws against the sale and use of drugs because if drugs are sold at cost there would be no money in it for anyone.

If there was no money in it for the Mafia, there would be no friendly playground pushers, and addicts would not commit crimes to pay for their next fix. Finally, if there was no money in it, the Bureau of Narcotics would wither away, something they are not about to do without a struggle.

Will anything sensible be done? Of course not. The American people are as devoted to the idea of sin and its punishment as they are to making money—and fighting drugs is nearly as big a business as pushing them. Since the combination of sin and money is irresistible (particularly to the professional politician), the situation will only grow worse.

* * *

QUESTIONS FOR DISCUSSION AND WRITING

The following questions can be used for class discussion, for individual or group writing assignments, and for entries in a reading journal.

1. What is Gore Vidal's solution to the problem of addiction?

2. What argument does Vidal use to overcome the reader's objection that making drugs available (legal) and cheap will only increase drug abuse?

3. What do you think of Vidal's idea that labeling drugs with a precise description of their harmful effects would keep all reasonably sane people from using them? (For more discussion of this, see the Inference section which follows.)

4. What do you think of Vidal's idea that once drugs were no longer "forbidden," they would no longer be attractive to people? What attractive features of drugs, mentioned by the other writers, does Vidal fail to mention? (For more discussion of this question, see the Inference section.)

5. Unlike Winn and the McAuliffes, Vidal does not discuss the nature of addiction, nor the extent of the problem. What he says is that he has tried once almost every drug and not become addicted and that many drugs are bad for certain people.

- o Are you convinced by the evidence that Vidal gives of one person, himself?

- o What questions would you like to ask Vidal about the certain people for whom many drugs are bad?

6. Vidal's attitude toward drug addicts and alcoholics is that some people will make these unfortunate choices and it's just too bad. He is able to write these people off. What is your attitude? Do you feel that society should try to help these people recover? Should society try to prevent their addiction?

7. Vidal supports his position that drugs should be legalized by citing the principle from the Declaration of Independence that we "are endowed by our Creator with certain inalienable rights, that among these are Life, Liberty, and the Pursuit of Happiness." The exercise of these rights has always been limited when such exercise interferes with the rights of others. (Your right to extend your fist ends where my nose begins.)

   - o How does this apply to drug addiction? Is the harm limited to the addict?

   - o Suppose you could isolate all addicts from their families and society. How then would you feel about letting them "do their own thing"?

8. Vidal points out that forbidding the sale of alcohol (Prohibition) was not effective in eliminating abuse of alcohol. Has legalization of alcohol made it so unattractive that alcohol abuse is no longer a significant problem? Is the comparison of alcohol and today's hard drugs really a valid one in that more people seem to be able to tolerate moderate amounts of alcohol than they can hard drugs?

9. Vidal's strongest and last point is that crime would be reduced if there were no profit in drugs: no more Mafia influence, pushers or addicts committing crimes to pay for their next fix. His point seems undeniable. Perhaps the only qualification here is that some drug crime would still exist since sheer craziness is the motive of some addict crime and that no matter how cheap drugs were, some would still steal for their fix as evidenced by people robbed for a ninety-nine cent bottle of wine.

INFERENCE

Sometimes in encountering an argument, we respond with a mixed reaction. We have to admit that the argument sounds logical, but something doesn't seem just right to us. Although we can't put our fingers on it immediately, something is making us uncomfortable.

These cases often have one part of the argument missing or suppressed. The parts that are supplied seem logical enough, but if we could figure out the missing assumption, we would see what was making us uncomfortable. This special kind of reading or thinking is called **inferring.**

For example, Gore Vidal gives us part of an argument:

Major Premise:	
Minor Premise:	Drugs should be taken out of the "forbidden" category.
Conclusion:	Therefore, if drugs were taken out of the "forbidden" category, they would no longer be attractive to people.

The missing part of his argument is:

"Drugs are attractive to people because they are forbidden."

There is some truth in this premise; we all know people who try drugs as an act of rebellion. But the premise is false in that it does not take in the major attractions of drugs: the "high" or pleasurable feelings, or the temporary relief, especially in the early stages of use, from emotional and physical pain.

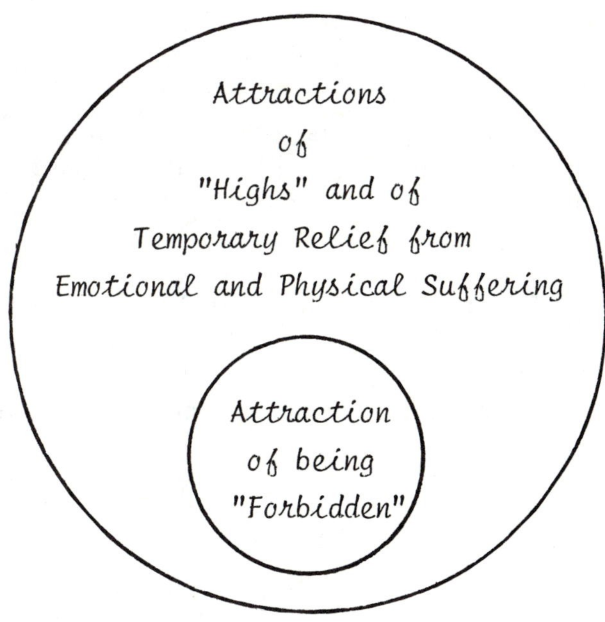

Figure A. The Attractions of Using Drugs

Figure A shows that the attraction of being "forbidden" is not the only or the main attraction that drugs provide. It shows clearly that making drugs legal would not eliminate all the attractiveness of taking drugs.

Two more of Vidal's arguments are based on a "questionable" premise. See if you can supply the missing premise in these arguments.

ARGUMENT 1

Major Premise: In ordinary intellectual decisions, a person is as free to use or not to use something the fiftieth time as he was the first.

Minor Premise: ______________________ is an ordinary intellectual decision.

Conclusion: Therefore, a person is as free to use or not use an addictive substance the fiftieth time as he was the first time.

ARGUMENT 2

Major Premise: In making ordinary intellectual decisions, sane people when informed about the destructive effects of a product, choose not to use the product.

Minor Premise: ______________________ is an ordinary intellectual decision.

Conclusion: Therefore, sane people, when informed about the destructive effects of using addictive substances, choose not to use them.

In both of these arguments, as you have probably already inferred, the missing premise is:

> **"Choosing to use or not use an addictive substance is an ordinary intellectual decision."**

But is this premise true? Once there is a chemical bonding between the addictive substance and the body's cells with a resulting physical craving, does an intellectual decision have much part to play? Once there is an emotional or physical dependence on a substance, is there the same freedom of choice? Once a person's sense of reality concerning himself and the addictive substance is distorted, what kind of objective, intellectual decision can he make?

Consider the role of information or labeling here. How effective has labeling been in getting chronic smokers to quit?

PRACTICE WITH INFERRING

Marie Winn claims that under certain circumstances an ordinarily harmless pursuit of pleasure can be considered a serious addiction, for example, watching television.

By making inferences, you can establish that another ordinarily harmless pursuit of pleasure can, under certain circumstances, be considered a serious addiction.

Write a paragraph describing a person's "eating disorder" as an addiction. Support your position by naming at least four or five facts or results of the person's eating disorder that would demonstrate your case. (Your discussion question notes following the Winn from pages 175-176 article may be helpful.)

SENTENCE COMBINING

(from Gore Vidal's "**Drugs**")

Make a single sentence out of each cluster of sentences, deleting words, changing their form, or adding connectors.

1. Don't say that marijuana is addictive or dangerous.
   It is neither.
   Millions of people know.

2. It is unlike "speed."
   "Speed" kills most unpleasantly.
   It is unlike heroin.
   Heroin is addictive and difficult to kick.

3. For the record, I have tried almost every drug.
I have liked none.
I tried them once.

4. This disproves the popular Fu Manchu theory.
A single whiff of opium will enslave the mind.

5. Americans reflect a system of public education.
It has made the Bill of Rights, literally, unacceptable.
The Bill of Rights is unacceptable to a majority of high school graduates.

6. These graduates now form the "silent majority."
The silent majority is a phrase which Nixon took from Homer.
Homer used the phrase to describe the dead.

"SONNY'S BLUES"

In preparation for Major Writing Assignment #2, reread "Sonny's Blues" (Chapter Two), especially the conversation about drugs between Sonny and his brother.

MAJOR WRITING ASSIGNMENTS

Directions: Choose Assignment 1 or Assignment 2

1. Suppose that Gore Vidal has managed to put a proposition on the state ballot for this June. His proposition (#23) states that "The over-the-counter sale of mood-altering drugs such as heroin, cocaine, marijuana, amphetamines and sedatives shall be legal in this state. The price for these drugs shall be set by the State Board of Pharmacists at a dollar amount close to their actual manufacturing cost."

It is your job to write both the "Argument for Proposition 23" and the "Argument against Proposition 23" for the ballot measures booklet that voters receive along with their sample ballot. Your arguments urging voters to vote for and against Proposition 23 should each be about 300 words.

It is not easy to argue convincingly on both sides of a question, but it is worth the effort. When you write arguments for freshman English or other college courses, you need to know the opposition's ideas as well as your own.

Guidelines

Start out with your positions which might be "Proposition 23 will solve the drug problem" for one position and "Proposition 23 will intensify the drug problem disastrously" for the other. Next, back up your positions with reasons. Do more than just plunk down a reason; expand on the reason by giving examples, instances, explanations; explore the reason for implications, results. Save your strongest reason for the last.

2. At the end of the story "Sonny's Blues," Sonny is drug-free. He tells his older brother that he won't die trying not to suffer but he also admits that his drug use can come again. Since Sonny's future in relationship to drugs is indefinite, the reader can take either the view (a) that Sonny is likely to go back on drugs, or (b) that Sonny is likely to remain off drugs.

Write two papers, one taking view (a) and the other taking view (b).

Guidelines

To support view (a), mention at least four things that may make it impossible for Sonny to stay drug-free. Use quotations from the story and what you have learned about Sonny's attitudes, environment, personality, etc.

To support view (b), give at least four reasons why you think Sonny is now likely to lead a drug-free life. Mention all the things he now has going for him that he did

not have when he turned to drugs and all the things and relationships that have changed.

In writing your response, use what you have learned about addiction from Winn, Vidal, and Cavnar to support your points.

CHAPTER 5

ETHNIC IDENTITY AND AMERICANIZATION

by

Jo An Simmons

Contributor:

Rose Najar

OVERVIEW

This chapter explores the question of ethnic identity, looks at the immigrant experience, and examines various versions of being "American." "The Melting Pot or the Rainbow" raises the question of how much "Americanization" is desirable. "Los Angeles, City of New Beginnings" describes the early and recent ethnic mix of this magnet city for people from across the country and from all over the world. The rest of the chapter describes and analyzes the immigrant experiences of an early American in Mexican California, an Italian family in Los Angeles, and a Chinese family in San Francisco. All of this leads up to a three-stage paper on "My Family's Version of Being American" which is described in the Major Writing Assignment section.

WHAT TO LOOK FOR

By looking at the description of the Major Writing Assignment, you will be able to focus your reading on the issues, analyses, and facts that will help you write your long paper.

CHAPTER PLAN

"The Rainbow or the Melting Pot: A Question of Ethnic Identity," by Jo An Simmons

"Los Angeles, City of New Beginnings," by Jo An Simmons

"Home-Grown Italian Clan Survives LA," by Estelle Roberts

"Puritans from the Orient," by Jade Snow Wong

Major Writing Assignment

THE RAINBOW OR THE MELTING POT:

A QUESTION OF ETHNIC IDENTITY

Jo An Simmons

Jingling in our pockets and purses is a statement of one American ideal: the E pluribus unum stamped on our coins inscribes our goal of being one nation out of many nationalities, and ethnic groups. In a country composed entirely of immigrants and descendants of immigrants, what does being one mean? The answer is constantly being refined by old and new Americans, by those assimilated into our culture for generations and by ethnic minorities in various stages of assimilation. (Assimilation is the process of acquiring the culture of a country.) The edges of the answer get stretched by an opposing American ideal: diversity. The unity of being one certainly can't mean "uniformity" because we also recognize the many. Indeed, we boast of our plurality of religious beliefs, our diversity of political opinions, and our individuality.

Tension results from the pull of these ideals in opposite directions. In order to be a nation, we need consensus about our national purpose, even if we disagree on how to achieve it. For democracy to work, we need an informed, literate citizenry who can communicate with each other in one language. To be a society, we need a common culture: a pool of ideals, traditions, memories, loyalties, attitudes, mores, and customs. Commonality binds the seams of our society; diversity that pulls us in too many directions can tear apart the fabric of society.

Yet within that commonality, we have tremendous variety and freedom. We aren't bound to a single set of values and customs. Americans of various ethnic descent—Scots, Blacks, Greeks, American Indians, Jews, Poles, Swedes, Koreans—enjoy their own ethnic foods, celebrate their own special holidays, preserve their own dances, music, games, and belong to special clubs—Sons of Italy, etc. We have multiple lifestyles, cherish a range of values, speak several dialects, hear many accents, and maintain regional traits. Our only national costume is blue jeans.

In America today, nearly 30% of the population could be considered "ethnic minorities." As defined by David Alloway, an ethnic minority is

> a group of people who differ in language, race, or color or in national, religious, or cultural origins from the . . . majority population of the

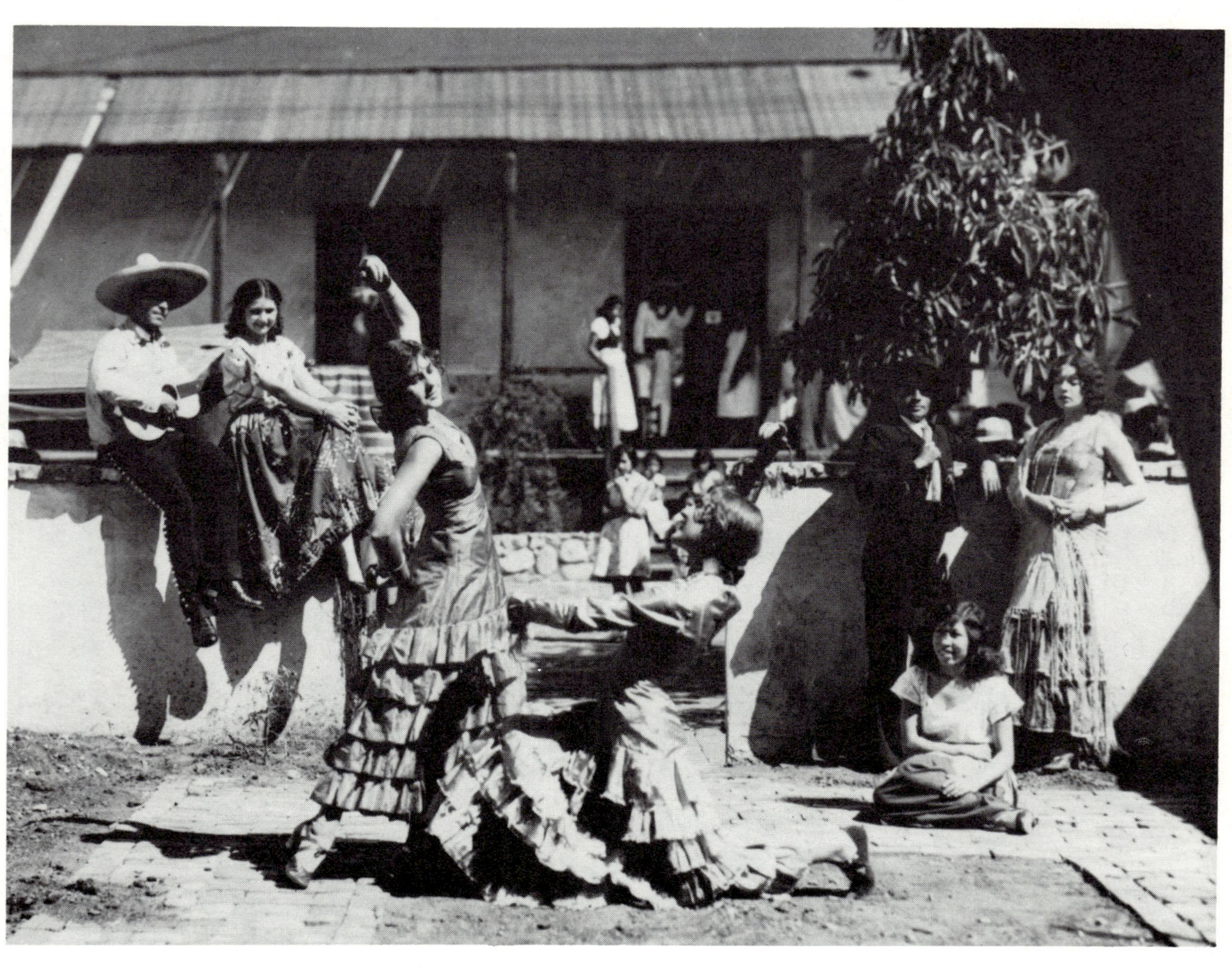

Spanish Dancers. Descendents of the Original Pioneers in Olvera Street
(Special Collections, University Research Library, UCLA)

> country in which they live. The differing identity may be displayed in any number of ways, ranging from distinctive customs, life-styles, speaking accents, dress, or food preferences to particular attitudes, value systems, and economic or political beliefs. (p. 255)

Of the other 70%, many Americans are interested in their ethnic roots and in defining their own version of being "American." A people on the move, we are constantly adapting to life in new surroundings, to becoming at home in new regions, cities, and neighborhoods. Many know the feelings of being a "stranger" or "newcomer."

The tension between assimilation (being one) and ethnic separation (being many) can be seen as a choice between the melting pot and the rainbow, as the image for the degree of Americanization we think of as desirable.

The melting pot dissolves distinct ethnic identity; the cultural ingredients of many different immigrants are blended to produce a strong, homogenous alloy. For most of our history, it was assumed that immigrants wished to assimilate as quickly as possible, to become as "Americanized" as possible. For over a hundred years, the melting pot image prevailed. David Alloway describes a general pattern of immigrants arriving from the 1840's to the 1960's:

> First generation ethnics, those born abroad, of peasant and working-class families, usually arrived in North America penniless and had to concentrate on surviving economically. They usually spoke little or no English and lived in ethnic enclaves, or GHETTOS, avoiding contact with the dominant culture. They tended to be very ethnocentric.
>
> Second generation ethnics, the first generation born in the New World, attended public schools and learned English. Many concealed the fact that they still spoke the language of the old country. This generation sought to come to terms with the dominant culture in order to gain a secure place in the society. Its members were often about equally American (or Canadian) and Old World in outlook.
>
> Third generation ethnics were inclined to slough off their old world roots entirely and to become as Americanized as possible. They often dropped the use of the old language and thought of themselves simply as Americans or Canadians. Many Anglicized the pronunciation of their names or translated them into English. Many also rejected most of native culture and moved away from the ethnic neighborhoods of their parents." (p. 256)

Subsequent generations became increasingly assimilated. As they moved into the mainstream of American society, they lost or rejected much of their old country heritage. Their increased Americanization, prosperity and social status went hand in hand. Once these were attained, some renewed their interest in their ethnic heritage and first language and took greater pride in their origins.

Outside of this pattern were groups who wished to maintain their separateness, for example, groups who fled to America to maintain significantly different religious beliefs. And not all groups were eager to identify themselves with American culture, for example Blacks who came here involuntarily as slaves and groups like American Indians, Mexicans, and Eskimo who were displaced from their lands.

The pattern which David Alloway describes applied to the predominantly European immigrant who came to America before 1965. With quotas removed by the 1965 Immigration Act, a new kind of immigrant appeared. The new immigrants often come from the nations on the rim of the Pacific Ocean; Asians and Latin Americans predominate. The new immigrants, from whatever source, are not always poor. Middle-class immigrants, bringing skills, capital, and a strong work ethic, often prosper in one generation. They can retain their ethnic culture and succeed at the same time. In regard to recent immigrants, Peter Rose, Professor of Sociology at Smith College, says, "America is much more of a pluralistic society now. You don't hear much talk about the melting pot today. The old ideology, the concerted effort to make people the same, has been taken over by reality" (Friedrich, p. 33).

An alternative image to the melting pot is the rainbow which grew out of pride in one's roots, popularized in the 1960's. At that time American Blacks, Hispanics, Indians, and others expressed the importance of ethnic identity to their self-image. Those who favor the rainbow image think of ethnic groups as separate bands of color joined together in one bow. This image preserves ethnic identity yet suggests unity. Ethnic pride differs from "ethnocentrism." The extremists of "ethnocentrism" turn their backs on the larger society and prefer their apartness and their original culture, language, and customs exclusively, often as a result of not feeling welcomed by the larger society.

A recent definition of what being <u>one</u> means in our nation of <u>many</u>, is offered by Brandeis Professor Fuchs:

> What binds Americans to one another, regardless of ethnicity or religion, is an American civic culture. It is the basis for the <u>unum</u> in <u>E pluribus unum.</u> It is a complex of ideals, behaviors, institutions, symbols and heroes connected by American history and its great documents, the Declaration of Independence, the Bill of Rights, the Gettysburg Address. It is backed by a civil religion giving transcendent significance to those ideals. And it is the basis for accepting ethnic diversity while protecting individual rights. An

> American can be as ethnic as he or she wishes in private actions, but in public actions, the rules of the civic culture are binding. (Friedrich, p. 33)

Our ethnic identity is certainly only one of our many selves; we are a great deal more than a member of an ethnic group. Yet whether we favor the melting pot, the rainbow, or some compromise (the pot of gold at the end of the rainbow?), we are all living our own version of being "American." The rest of this chapter looks at a city of ethnic minorities and analyzes the experiences of several immigrants in becoming assimilated.

* * *

LOS ANGELES, CITY OF NEW BEGINNINGS

Jo An Simmons

Since its inception, Los Angeles has been a place where people can start anew. Whether under Spanish, Mexican, or American government, it has drawn those hoping for a fresh start, a better life, and more freedom. Today, Los Angeles is a metropolis of minorities in the sense that no one ethnic group comprises over 50% of the population and it has been called the new Ellis Island because of the thousands of immigrants who have recently chosen it for their new beginnings.

In the beginning was the pueblo, <u>Nuestra de Senora de Los Angeles</u>. Its founding fathers and mothers arrived here on September 4, 1781, after a seven-month trek from Mexico. The pioneer group, in its ethnic diversity, forecast the future cosmopolitan nature of Los Angeles. Historical records show that

> Of the forty-four <u>pobladores</u> (founders), the only people of unmixed Caucasian race in the whole community were two Spanish men. The settlers, who represented a mixture of Indian and Negro, with here and there a trace of Spanish, can be broken down into four racial strains:
>
> 3 Indian families: 8 people
> 2 Indian-Caucasian families: 8 people
> 4 Negro families: 15 people
> 2 Negro-Caucasian families: 13 people
> (Weber, p. 8)

This analysis shows that "though not widely known or emphasized, the overwhelming majority of the founders of the Pueblo de Nuestra Senora de Los Angeles were Catholics of Negro racial strain" (Weber, p. 9).

It took a year for Captain (Don) Fernando de Rivera to recruit the original settlers. He had to find family men who were men of the soil, "healthy, robust, and without known vices or defects," and families who would be willing to leave their homes and villages for the unknown. Once recruited, the families journeyed from Alamos, Mexico, to the Gulf of California, sailing up the Gulf to Mission Santa Maria. From there they went by land through Mission San Diego to Mission San Gabriel, and on to the pueblo site. An early setback was the news that the livestock and supplies which Captain de Rivera had been bringing by separate route had been raided by Indians and that all the soldiers had been massacred. Like the many immigrants who would follow them, these settlers faced both hardship and opportunity, as they created a community from its bare beginnings. This early description recognizes their courage: "These noble pobladores sprang from hardy stock and the blood of true pioneers coursed through their veins" (Weber, p. 9).

An Early Immigrant

Joseph Chapman, an American and one of the pueblo's earliest immigrants, experienced an unusual but successful new beginning in Hispanic California. The circumstances of his arrival were enough to brand this man as an undesirable alien. Joseph Chapman was a boat person, but not in the modern sense of the word. He rowed ashore at Monterey on November 12, 1818, from a pirate ship disabled during the battle between the defending California cannon and the raiding Argentine pirate ships. But if Chapman wasn't an ordinary boat person, he also wasn't an ordinary pirate. Previously in Honolulu as a crew member of an American whaling ship, he had been captured by the pirates and forced to serve as a member of their crew. When the pirates abandoned the disabled Santa Rosa for its sister ship, Chapman used this chance to escape. Once on California shores, he surrendered to Governor Sola.

Despite his unorthodox entry and questionable past, Joseph Chapman would eventually become a favorite adopted son among the Californians. He was first taken captive but had the good fortune of being put under the charge of Sergeant (Don) Antonio Lugo, a kind-hearted man. Under orders to bring him to Los Angeles, Lugo soon befriended the tall stranger from Maine. From captor-captive, trying to

Los Angeles: Old Plaza and Church

(Special Collections, University Research Library, UCLA)

Chapman would have a language-teacher, protector, and sponsor. Chapman's own good will, his amazing ability with tools and skill in building, and his considerable strength and hard work would win him favor not only with Lugo but with others.

On orders from the Governor, Lugo and Chapman went to Santa Inez Mission. Here, handyman Chapman built a grist mill. Each Sunday at the mission, Chapman would see the beautiful Senorita Guadalupe Ortega at the services, she and her family journeying to the mission from their vast land holdings, Rancho Nuestra Senora del Refugio. Chapman secretly fell in love with her and confided to Lugo his dream of marrying her one day. The governor next asked Chapman to help the Franciscan padres of Mission San Gabriel with their mill. It was during this year (1821) that Chapman was granted amnesty by the King of Spain. Chapman's ingenious solution to the mill problem won him the gratitude of Padre Sanchez who would later commission him to build the first ship in Southern California, a sixty-ton schooner. Its parts were built at mission workshops and transported by ox-carts to San Pedro where they were assembled.

Like any stranger, Chapman became an the object of fear and discomfort in the eyes of some people. As an ex-pirate, he was a curiosity, a scary sight to be glimpsed at by children in the safe company of their parents. But his very accomplishments became suspicious; the superstitious explanation of his achievements was that they were performed in league with the devil.

The account of Chapman's help with the Los Angeles Plaza Church below shows how the Indians got this impression and how Lugo countered the charges:

> Chapman said that if he was supplied with some Indian workmen and tools, he would go up in the mountains, and get out some large timbers for the church—and to the great astonishment of the Angelenos, he actually succeeded in doing this, and it was considered a wonderful feat in those early days, in view of the almost complete absence of transportation facilities. . . .
>
> Chapman took his Indian laborers and departed for the mountains, and there performed veritable marvels that made all Southern California wonder; and indeed, they suspected him of being a master of black magic—indeed, the nickname they gave him was Diablo Chapman--Chapman the Devil!
>
> The Indians themselves could manage to cut down a tree by hacking it in irregular fashion, but it was liable to drop anywhere, either smashing into other trees, or over rocks and thus destroying its value as large timber. Chapman, however, who was a good timberman, knew how to line, score, and hew, marking the line along the ground where the tree was to fall; and,

as the trees always fell in the places he pointed, he was looked upon as a demon in disguise.

Chapman managed to have his timbers dragged down by himself and his Indians' own strong arms from the upper canyons by using skids and ropes. Once down below they were dragged on the road to Los Angeles by the aid of rawhide ropes lashed around the horns of oxen. . . . . . As the heavy timbers slid along the ground, upon their faces which Chapman had rough hewed, they were turned from time to time, and thus scoured clean as if they had been planed. Arrived at the road, they were loaded into heavy carretas (oxcarts) and thus were hauled down to the Los Angeles River to the Plaza. . . .

Indeed, this gave rise to great discussions concerning the demoniac nature of this tall American, until Lugo finally said: "Who can manage Indians as he does? I know the padres consider him as a man of good character, and as for his being a wizard, has not all of his work gone to the benefit of the holy church?" And when the other Californians urged against this Chapman, the almost unpardonable crime in their eyes of not being able to ride a horse, Don Antonio Lugo would say: "Yes, he can, too ride a horse now, without falling off of his horse more than twice in one day!" (Kirkman, p. 11)

Meanwhile, back at the ranch (the 48,000 acre Ortega rancho), the Ortega family entertained no suspicions about Chapman. Little did they realize that he was in love with Guadalupe or that Don Antonio Lugo had determined to help him marry her. Lugo had decided that Chapman was an asset to Southern California and that he ought to settle here permanently by marrying into a fine family. Experienced in these matters, Lugo got a letter of recommendation from the priest at the Plaza Church and rode north with Chapman, stopping en route at a mission to have him baptized a Catholic. Once in Santa Barbara, Don Lugo introduced him as an eligible bachelor among his friends there, a worthy suitor for the hand of the loveliest senorita. Thereafter, Lugo and Captain Ortega, the head of the family, agreed upon a match between Chapman and Guadalupe. But would Guadalupe agree? Though marriages in that society were arranged by elders, the young women had the final say in the matter. Chapman proposed to Guadalupe but she refused. Fortunately for both of them, she changed her mind just as he was about to ride away. Thus Chapman married his heart's desire at the old Mission in Santa Ynez and it was reported that "theirs was one of the happiest marriages on record" (Kirkman, p. 11).

In the years that followed, Chapman bought a house and land in Los Angeles from Agustin Machado on which he planted 4,000 grape vines. He applied for naturalization as a Mexican citizen in 1829, receiving it two years later. Then Don Jose Chapman built a home in old Santa Barbara where he and Guadalupe raised their five children. In 1838 he was granted a sobrante (remainder) of some five thousand acres in the Santa Barbara District. He died in 1849 much at home in his adopted country.

Analysis of this Early Immigrant Experience

Chapman was certainly an exceptional immigrant from his unfortunate illegal entry to his eventually fortunate status as a California Don. Although Chapman's immigrant experience was in some ways easier than that of later immigrants, it illustrates some points about the mutual adjustment between an immigrant and his host country. Like his happy marriage to Guadalupe, Chapman's marriage to Mexican California was a combination of good luck, his willingness to take on a new culture, and openness on the part of his new countrymen. Chapman had the luck of bringing skills needed in the development of the country and its economy; his timing was right. Americans were not yet coming to California in threatening numbers. By 1846 the situation would have changed. "We find ourselves suddenly threatened," said the last Mexican governor, Pio Pico, "by hordes of Yankee emigrants." Assimilation into the culture was not a problem for Chapman; he was willing to learn the language of the country, to work hard, to contribute to the common good, to become a citizen and obey its laws, to adopt some of its values and customs (being a Catholic), and to marry a local girl (hardly a sacrifice). Though he experienced some prejudice, his host society was generally an open society and welcoming to him. He was especially blessed in having a native sponsor, friend, and protector in Antonio Lugo, and in having Ortega consider his character and accomplishments, rather than his pirate past.

Today's Ethnic Composition

Like the Pueblo of 1781, Los Angeles in 1985 is home to a high percentage of ethnic minorities and new home to large numbers of immigrants. Within the 464 square miles of the City of Los Angeles, the population is 48% Anglo, 27% Spanish, 17% Black, and 6.6% Asian and Pacific Island in origin (U.S. Census, 1980). Los Angeles is residence to more people of Mexican origin than any city outside of Mexico City, more Koreans than any location outside of Korea, more American Indians than anywhere else, and more Samoans than in the Samoan Islands (Rolle, pp. 77, 81, 83, 82). This ethnic diversity is also true of Los Angeles County (4,083 square miles):

Anglo	3.4 million	46 %
Hispanic	2.5 million	34 %
Black	1.0 million	13 %
Asian	400,000	5 %
Other non-white	140,000	2 %

(Rolle, p. 82)

This diverse population is partially the result of a continuous migration of Caucasian and Black Americans from other states. While there has also been continuous migration from other countries, it was relatively small in the past. In 1940, only one out of eight Californians was foreign born. Today in the Los Angeles/Long Beach metropolitan area alone, one out of four residents is foreign born. Of the 7,477,503 people in this statistical area, 1,644,793 are immigrants or refugees and 26.7% speak a language other than English at home (U.S. Census, 1980).

"Los Angeles," says Rand Corporation Demographer Kevin McCarthy, "has become the natural embarkation point in the U.S. There is no question that it is the new Ellis Island" (Andersen, p. 18). Today's immigrant is more likely to arrive by jumbo jet at LAX (Los Angeles International Airport) than by steamer in New York Harbor and to originate from Central or South America and Asia than from Europe. The immigrants' aegis has shifted from the symbolic Lady Liberty with her lighted torch to the pueblo sponsor, Our Lady Queen of the Angels.

ETHNIC EXPLOSION

	1983	1970
Mexicans	2,100,000	822,300
Iranians	200,000	20,000
Salvadorans	200,000	*
Japanese	175,000	104,000
Armenians	175,000	75,000
Chinese	153,000	41,000
Koreans	150,000	8,900
Filipinos	150,000	33,500
Arab Americans	130,000	45,000
Israelis	90,000	10,000
Samoans	60,000	22,000
Guatemalans	50,000	*
Vietnamese	40,000	*

TIME Chart *Fewer than 2,000

Los Angeles County

(Courtesy of Time magazine)

If the immigrant arrives by night flight, he cruises over a city not only of myriad sparkling lights, but of myriad nations under heaven. In addition to the groups listed on the chart above are Cambodians, Canadians, Chileans, Croats, Ecuadorians, French, Germans, Greeks, Italians, Laotians, Lithuanians, Poles, Puerto Ricans, Russians, Scots, Thais, and others both newly arrived and descended from previous generations.

* * *

HOME-GROWN ITALIAN CLAN SURVIVES L.A.

Estelle Roberts

Mama was making ravioli in the kitchen. Sleeves rolled up and elbows deep in flour, her fingers sticky with the mixture of chopped spinach and parsley from the garden, grated Romano cheese and sausage, she was almost finished. She had only to roll the wooden ravioli presser into the last square of filled dough.

The smell of nutmeg and thyme, anise and cheese filled the house this Saturday in the spring. A coconut cake was on the sideboard, boiled eggs were cooling on the small bleached wooden sink and bottles of wine had been brought up from the cellar.

Papa was in the field next to our house gathering mushrooms. Papa kept a tin tub beside him and with only a glance or a touch of his fingertips, he picked only those that were safe to eat. After washing them, he put them in a pot of water on the old black stove in the shed behind the house. As insurance against a poisonous one, Papa threw in a silver dollar, kept for that purpose only. If the dollar turned gray while the mushrooms boiled, they were to be thrown away. It never did. We always ate the mushrooms. While he waited for the water to boil, he sat on a bench

---

Estelle Roberts' article, "Home-Grown Italian Clan Survives L.A.," appeared in the View Section of the **Los Angeles Times** on February 2, 1984, and is reprinted here with the author's permission.

under the fig tree that grew in the middle of the yard, lit a cigarette and hummed a theme from "La Traviata."

Blossoms fell from the olive trees that lined the driveway. Peach, plum, and apricot scented the air. The tiger cat lay in the shade nursing her kittens. A neighbor called to my father. Leaning on the fence that held up grape vines, they drank red wine and cursed Mussolini.

Memories of Childhood

These are my earliest memories of childhood in Los Angeles in the 1930s. I was the youngest of seven children and we lived almost in sight of the Los Angeles City Hall. We were nourished by an ancient culture, yet we aspired to the ideals of the American mainstream. These ideals included living in a democracy where the class system was less structured, and where there was greater educational and economic opportunity and freedom to pursue individual goals. Our parents, who had come from Italy, admired America for these possibilities, became citizens and observed all the rules.

However, they were loath to embrace much of the culture--in particular, the lack of formality in social behavior, dress and public entertainment. My father abhorred movies, considering them the devil's own handiwork and a bad influence on young people. Casual behavior between young men and women was considered improper. My parents did not approve of the easy give and take in social situations that even then characterized the Southern California "laid-back" style. My father was opposed to any of his daughters working during our school years. Many of the restrictions applied mainly to the females in the family, my mother included. The boys were given more latitude, in the Italian tradition.

The circumstances, ones all immigrants face, led to contradictory modes of behavior. Though we might have fresh figs and homemade sausage for breakfast, and dance the tarantella on the Fourth of July, we were never taught the Italian language. My parents considered that un-American. On the other hand, though it was OK to dance barefoot on Muscat grapes to help make the wine, it was not OK to go roller-skating. That was considered a vulgar recreation.

Armed with little more than an education--he had studied for the priesthood in Naples but changed his mind--my father arrived here at the turn of the century. He spoke English, had read the classics and either had or developed skills in horticulture and construction. His belief in the teachings of the Bible and the stoic humanitarian philosophy of Marcus Aurelius, and my mother's strong sense of duty and devotion to her family, formed the basis of our moral upbringing. My father also pointed out to us that we were the possessors of a great heritage—referring to Dante, Galileo, Da Vinci, et al.—and that we should live up to that heritage. A combination of the traditional Italian primacy of family, plus the cooperation, discipline and delegation of duties that is imperative in a large family, created strong feelings of loyalty and a common sense of achievement in work and creativity.

My father was outgoing, debonair, quick to show affection and anger. He dressed up and visited friends most afternoons. My mother was shy with anyone outside the home, and in those days did not display affection openly. But her love for her family was felt in many ways. Her only outing was a Saturday morning trip to the Grand Central Market downtown. Far too busy with the housework and multiple jobs associated with caring for seven children, she did not spend much time cajoling us.

My mother came to this country with her family under reasonably comfortable circumstances when she was a very young girl before 1900. She grew up in New Orleans where her family owned a bakery. She and my father were married there and began their family. After a time, they were lured by the golden tales of California, and they traveled across the country by train in 1915. At first they rented but eventually saved enough money to buy a small house in Los Angeles, where I was born. My father worked for a time as a landscape designer for several Los Angeles business people and later took on part-time jobs.

No After-School Activities

For many years, our mother did not allow us to participate in after-school activities—no sports, dramatics or special sessions. Attendance at school was a legitimate necessity, but most social activities were not worth the "dangers" involved in crossing the street, riding in a car. . . . She seemed most content when she had her children in her physical presence, just as a mother hen might. As we grew older, 13 or 14, we hardly made it outside the front gate except to sweep the sidewalk. We were allowed to go to the small L.A. County branch library near school and to the grocery store.

My sisters and I preened on the front porch every Sunday afternoon, ostensibly reading, but hoping for adventure from every passing car. The proximity of Hollywood was not lost on my mother. She hinted that if we sat there on the porch we might be spotted for the movies by a passing film producer. Her ruse worked. We did not seriously rebel. We had time to read and to draw, to watch chicks and kittens being born, and time to play with a pet goat a neighbor gave me.

We were close to being self-sufficient, existing primarily on foods grown in our gardens and processed in our home. My father maintained a garden in every inch of available space on our small lot. We harvested everything from onions and garlic to exotic quince, kumquats and persimmons. We had olive, fig, walnut, almond, peach, plum and apricot trees, grapes and pomegranates. In season we had asparagus, tomatoes, celery, lettuce, spinach, cucumbers, squash and many herbs. We had our own chickens and eggs, and enjoyed herbed mushroom omelets during the depths of the Depression.

We cured our own olives, made our own catsup, vinegar, relishes, sausages, bread, pies, root beer and wine. Despite this bountiful diet, I would have gladly traded a piece of Italian bread warm from the oven for a slice of Wonder Bread, which seemed ever so much more glamorous and which my mother scorned.

We designed, made patterns and sewed our own clothes. Papa gave us all haircuts, put new soles and heels on our shoes, and made all home repairs. My mother practiced home medicine: senna tea for fever, a slice of raw tomato bandaged over an infection to draw it out, Sloan's liniment for aches, plenty of Castor oil and Ex-Lax. Doctors' services were reserved for broken bones only--and only if the break didn't heal itself in a few days. We made our own games. A ball tied to a piece of string attached to the clothesline pole became a tether ball, kites were made from twigs and newspapers, paste from flour and water, paints from beet juice, onions and tea.

After graduation from high school, the boys went to work in civil service jobs or banks. The girls did the same. We had all been directed to take business courses in high school despite any individual proclivities. My father was more or less retired by the late '30s, and the older boys supported the household.

Since ours was a self-contained family, each member took over a necessary function. One brother was the historian. He kept the records and took the family pictures. Another was the economist. He managed the money that they all contributed to running the household. Another brother became the medical expert.

Another brother was transportation director and looked after the automobiles each brother and my father owned. I ended up being the sweeper. At least I remember sweeping (endlessly) the front yard, the driveway and the backyard, in constant rotation as the many trees dropped their blossoms and leaves. Later I was promoted to secretary and wrote notes and sent greeting cards for my mother.

As we grew older, we gradually joined the greater society. In time we chose our own clothes, made suggestions about how they should be made or shortened them, participated in high school activities, wore makeup, tasted junk food.

The Gradual Change

The changes took place gradually. Mother began to find it convenient to buy prepared foods like bread and cake, to use the services of a laundry, to sing the popular songs heard on the radio, to allow us to visit friends at their homes, to wear slacks. None of these small changes were significant by themselves, but our parents' acceptance of them represented their adaptation to the American culture. In many cases, my older brothers and sisters fought the important battles for more freedom and the right to make decisions, which we became heir to.

The old neighborhood has disappeared, replaced by the arrival of new ethnic groups, and the building of Los Angeles County buildings. Sociologists tell us the Italians in America have successfully assimilated, particularly in Southern California, where tradition is not strongly valued. However, the culture and values that came to many of us whose parents immigrated from Italy, have remained durable and greatly rewarding.

* * *

ANALYSIS OF A LATER IMMIGRANT'S EXPERIENCE

Estelle's family arrived in Los Angeles in 1915 under favorable circumstances: both parents spoke English and had skills. Estelle's father was educated and had a skill (landscape design) needed in the growing city; Estelle's mother had strong nurturing and coping skills. Their fellow Italians had been coming to Los Angeles in easily absorbable numbers.

Instead of a local sponsor such as Joseph Chapman had, Estelle Roberts' family had each other; the old-country value of the family's coming first enabled both the family as a whole and the individual members to succeed. The "cooperation, discipline and delegation of duties" which Roberts describes made outside help unnecessary. The family became its own corporation with each wage earner contributing; it supplied its own services like home repair, sewed its own clothing, raised and processed its own food, and created its own fun. Each member worked hard. The value of individual fulfillment took second place to the good of the whole family. Perhaps individual children would have preferred to major in a subject other than business. Perhaps they would have preferred careers in areas other than civil service and banking. Lack of self-fulfillment seems to have been overbalanced by the self-worth that came from having an important role to play and by the family's "common sense of achievement in work and creativity." Such family teamwork is typical of some immigrant groups and situations.

Becoming assimilated Americans and yet retaining ethnic identity was a neat balancing trick accomplished by Estelle's family. The family balanced pride in their Italian heritage with admiration for American political and social ideals. The children were taught to revere both their Italian culture and the American dream.

But the family didn't accept every aspect of the American dream or life-style (as many American families don't). The parents didn't adopt those American customs that they didn't approve of or that they, at first, feared. Ideas about life-style such as child-raising and standards of behavior, food preferences, and customs were from their own culture. Over a period of time, more American customs were accepted. The family also blended customs, for example, celebrating the Fourth of July with Italian dancing and food. Estelle Roberts's family embraced the English language and American citizenship with all it entailed and made their own contribution to the Los Angeles community.

QUESTIONS FOR DISCUSSION AND WRITING

The following questions can be used for class discussion, for individual or group writing assignments, and for entries in a reading journal. Follow your teacher's instructions.

1. Estelle's older brothers and sisters went to American high school but were not allowed full participation in the teenaged life-style of the times. If you had been one of them, what would you have missed the most?

2. What could you envy about their home life?

3. Do you know of any families that have the tight teamwork that Estelle's family had? Did your family ever have this pattern in past generations in farming or urban situations?

4. What are the losses and gains for the individual family member?

5. Does your family have any blended customs such as Estelle's Fourth of July celebration? Do you retain anything from another region of the U.S. or from another country?

6. Which aspects of the American life-style do you or your parents reject?

VOCABULARY

Directions: **Supply the missing forms of the words in the boxes as directed on page 60.**

1. **Migrate** (verb) to go from one country, region, or locale to settle in another; to pass periodically from one region to another, e.g., The Canadian geese migrate southward in the winter

Verbs	Noun	Adjective
Migrate	a.________tion	b.________tory

Emigrate (verb) — to leave one's own country and take up residence in another. Many people emigrated from Ireland to America in the 1840's.

—a person who **emigrates** is an **emigrant**; an **emigré** is a person who flees his country because of political conditions

3. **Immigrate** (verb) — to enter and settle in a country not one's own, e.g., The California Gold Rush motivated many fortune-seekers to **immigrate** to the United States.

—**Immigration** and **Immigrant** are noun forms.

4. **Enclave** (noun) — this French word means a country within another country or mostly surrounded by another country, e.g., The Korean enclave in Los Angeles is located near Olympic Boulevard.

5. **Ghetto** (noun) — originally a section of a city (European) in which all Jews used to be required to live; a section predominantly inhabited by Jews; a thickly populated section of a city predominantly inhabited by Negroes, Puerto Ricans, and any other minority group because of social or economic conditions

6. **Ellis Island** — an island in Upper New York Bay formerly used as an immigrant examination station.

7. **Myriad** (adj.) — an indefinitely great number, e.g., The myriad stars in the Milky Way; having innumerable characteristics, e.g., the myriad mind of Leonardo da Vinci.

8. **Cajole** (verb) — to persuade by flattery or promises

9. **Debonair** (adj) — pleasant-mannered, gracious, courteous and charming, e.g., a debonair and well-dressed gentleman.

10. **Loathe** (verb) — to feel disgust for, to abhor, e.g., I loathe mashed yellow turnips.

Verbs	Nouns	Adjectives	Adverbs
Loathe	**Loathing** (a strong dislike)	**Loath** (unwilling or reluctant to do something)	

11. **Ostensible** — this word from the root **show** means apparent, seeming, e.g., His ostensible motive was to meet the guest of honor; he really came to see Antonia.

Verbs	Nouns	Adjectives	Adverbs
		Ostensible	c.________
	ostentation (showiness)	d.________tious	

12. **Proclivity** (noun) natural tendency, inclination, bent

13. **Proximity** (noun) nearness in place, time, order of occurrence or relation, e.g., I can't even be in the proximity of a chocolate chip cookie, without devouring it.

14. **Ruse** (noun) trick, stratagem

15. **Slough off** (verb) to shed or cast off as a snake disposes itself of its slough (outer layer of skin)

16. **Vestiges** (noun) traces, surviving evidence. After ten years in the North, Lucille has just the vestiges of a Southern accent.

BIBLIOGRAPHY

Alloway, David. "Ethnic Minorities." **Academic American Encyclopedia.** Danbury, CT: Grolier, 1984. Quotations reprinted by permission.

Andersen, Kurt. Reported by Benjamin W. Cate. "The New Ellis Island." **Time,** 13 June 1983, pp. 18-25.

Friedrich, Otto. Reported by Douglas Brew/Los Angeles and Sidney Urquhart/New York. "The Changing Face of America," **Time,** 8 July 1985.

Kirkman, George Wycherley. "The Ex-Pirate Chapman." **Los Angeles Times,** 19 August 1928, p. 11. Quotations reprinted by permission of the **Los Angeles Times.**

Rolle, Andrew. **Los Angeles from Pueblo to City of the Future.** San Francisco: Boyd and Fraser, 1981.

Weatherwax, John M. **The Founders of Los Angeles.** Los Angeles: Bryant Foundation, 1954.

Weber, Msgr. Francis J. **The Old Plaza Church: A Documentary History.** Libra Press, 1980 (350 copies).

PURITANS FROM THE ORIENT:
A CHINESE EVOLUTION

Jade Snow Wong

Jade Snow Wong, the daughter of Chinese immigrants to San Francisco, has recorded both the treasures and the tensions of growing up in a dual culture, Chinese and American. She broke family tradition by attending a junior college and later Mills College. Her knowledge of her native language and culture has contributed to her success both as an artist and a writer.

. . . .From the village of Fragrant Mountains in southern Canton, my father had immigrated as a young man in 1903 to San Francisco. Many years later when I was a grown woman, he told me with sadness that when he had asked his mother, whom he adored, for permission to come to the United States, she had expressed her reluctance. When this only son had insisted that he must leave her, she had cursed him "Go! Go! You will have the life to go, but not the life to return!"

Trained in his father's rice and lumber business, he had been offered a position as accountant for an importer of rice and other staples needed by the Chinese in San Francisco. The inhabitants of the new Chinatown clustered together for mutual protection and a degree of social life, even though most of them were employed outside the community, serving Westerners as laborers, laundrymen, waiters, cooks, or in other occupations not requiring much knowledge of the American language they hadn't mastered. It was a predominantly male group of bachelors and married men who had left their families behind while they sought fortunes in the new land, then and now dubbed in Chinese, "Old Golden Mountains," for the legend of the Forty-niner Gold Rush days had been grossly exaggerated in Canton to lure railroad workers to California. . . .

It was the ambition of most of these men to work and save in the United States and return to China to marry or rejoin a waiting wife, buy property in the village, and enjoy rents for lifelong income. Many succeeded in doing so. But my father happened to combine free thinking with Chinese conservatism. While attending night classes at the Methodist Chinese Mission in San Francisco to learn English, he was exposed to Christian theory and the practical kindness of Christian Westerners. The Golden Rule did not conflict with the Confucian doctrines which he had carefully retained. The measure of human dignity accorded to Western women particularly impressed him. He was contemporary with Sun Yat Sen, founder of the new Chinese Republic in 1910, born in the same village district, and a follower of the new Christianity in China. As part of his revolutionary demands in forging a new nation, Dr. Sun had advocated the elimination of the bound feet that had kept Chinese women crippled house slaves.

My father's motherland was in the grip of military and political upheaval. My father wrote to his family, "In America, I have learned how shamefully women in China have been treated. I will bleach the disgrace of my ancestors by bringing my wife and two daughters to San Francisco, where my wife can work without disgrace, and my daughters shall have the opportunity of education." He was beginning his own domestic revolution. For fifty-five years, my father was to remain in San Francisco. He retained a copy of every letter he wrote to China.

To support the family in America, Daddy tried various occupations—candy making, the ministry to which he was later ordained--but finally settled upon manufacturing men's and children's denim garments. He leased sewing equipment, installed machines in a basement where rent was cheapest, and there he and his family lived and worked. There was no thought that dim and airless quarters were terrible conditions for living and working, or that child labor was unhealthful. The only goal was for all in the family to work, to save, and to become educated. It was possible, so it would be done.

My father had had only a few years of formal Chinese schooling. He taught himself garment manufacturing, from cutting the yardage in five-dozen-layer lots to fixing the machines when they broke down. A Western jobber delivered the yardage to him and picked up finished garments for sales distribution to American retailers. My father figured his prices to include thread, machine use, labor, and his overhead-profit. He was a meticulous bookkeeper, using only an abacus, brush, ink, and Chinese ledgers. Because of his newly learned ideals, he pioneered for the right of women to work. Concerned that they have economic independence, but not with the long hours of industrial home work, he went to shy housewives' apartments and taught them sewing.

Only the ambitious but poor gather their courage and tear up their roots to journey across the seas, in the hope of bettering their living abroad. In China, the winds of popular discontent were blowing, caused by the decaying old empire and the excessive concessions granted to various European powers. My father used to tell us of insults and injuries suffered by ordinary Chinese at the hands of East Indian mercenary police, employed by the British in Hong Kong.

My mother still talks of the poverty in Fragrant Mountains. If they had rice, they were fortunate. It there was salt, or oil, they were even more fortunate. Tea made the fourth absolute necessity; anything more was luxury. Meat and fish were rarities. Sometimes a relative would bring some fresh green vegetables. Sometimes they bought a penny's worth of salted olives or thick, red soy, to steam on the rice for a change of flavors. On a birthday or a feast day, there might be a chicken. For annual grave pilgrimages to pay respect to the dead, roast pig was first offered to the departed souls; later the meat was enjoyed by the worshippers.

My earliest memories of companionship with my father were as his passenger in his red wheelbarrow, sharing space with the piles of blue-jean materials he was delivering to a worker's home. He must have been forty. He was lean, tall, inevitably wearing blue overalls, rolled shirt sleeves, and high black kid shoes. In his pockets were numerous keys, tools, and pens. On such deliveries, I noticed that he always managed time to show a mother how to sew a difficult seam, or to help her repair a machine, or just to chat.

I observed from birth that living and working were inseparable. My mother was short, sturdy, young looking, and took pride in her appearance. She was at her machine the minute housework was done, and she was the hardest working seamstress, seldom pausing, working after I went to bed. The hum of sewing machines continued day and night, seven days a week. She knew that to have more than the four necessities, she must work and save. We knew that to overcome poverty, there were only two methods: working and education. It was our personal responsibility. Being poor did not entitle us to benefits. When welfare programs were created in the depression years of the thirties, my family would not make application.

Having provided the setup for family industry, my father turned his attention to our education. Ninety-five percent of the population in China had been illiterate. He knew that American public schools would take care of our English, but he had to be the watchdog to nurture our Chinese knowledge. . . . When the two oldest girls arrived from China, the schools of Chinatown received only boys. My father tutored his daughters each morning before breakfast. In the midst of a foreign environment, he clung to a combination of the familiar old standards and what was permissible in the newly learned Christian ideals.

My eldest brother was born in America, the only boy for fourteen years, and after him three daughters—another older sister, myself, and my younger sister. Then my younger brother, Paul, was born. That older brother, Lincoln, was cherished in the best Chinese tradition. He had his own room; he kept a German Shepherd as his pet; he was tutored by a Chinese scholar; he was sent to private school for American classes. As a male Wong, he would be responsible some day for the preservation of and pilgrimages to ancestral graves--his privileges were his birthright. We girls were content with the unusual opportunities of working and attending two schools.

For by the time I was six, times in Chinatown were changing. The Hip Wo Chinese Christian Academy (in the same building as the Methodist Mission) had been founded on a coeducational basis, with nominal tuition. Financial support came from three Protestant church boards: the Congregational, Presbyterian, and Methodist churches contributed equal shares. My father was on the Hip Wo School Board for many years. By day, I attended American public school near our home. From 5:00 p.m. to 8:00 p.m. on five weekdays and from 9:00 a.m. to 12 noon on Saturdays, I attended the Chinese school. Classes numbered twenty to thirty students, and were taught by educated Chinese from China. We studied poetry, calligraphy, philosophy, literature, history, correspondence, religion, all by exacting memorization. The Saturday morning chapel services carried out the purposes of the supporting churches.

Daddy emphasized memory development; he could still recite fluently many lengthy lessons of his youth. Every evening after both schools, I'd sit by my father, often as he worked at his sewing machine, sing-songing my lessons above its hum. Sometimes I would stop to hold a light for him as he threaded the difficult holes of a specialty machine, such as one for bias bindings. After my Chinese lessons passed his approval, I was allowed to attend to American homework. I was made to feel luckier than other Chinese girls who didn't study Chinese, and also luckier than Western girls without a dual heritage.

We lived on both levels of our factory, which had moved out of the basement to street level. . . .

Bedrooms were upstairs, both in the front and rear of the factory, to be where there were windows. Between front and rear bedrooms were more machines and the long cutting tables, which were partially lit by the skylights. I shared a room with my younger sister, and later with my baby brother, too. Windows were fitted with opaque glass to eliminate the necessity for curtains, and iron bars were installed by Daddy across the entire length of those upstairs windows to keep out intruders and keep in peeping children. . . .

. . . There was little time for play and toys were unknown to me. In any spare time, I was supplied with embroidery and sewing for my mother. . . .

Yet there was little reason for unhappiness. I was never hungry. Though we had no milk, there was all the rice we wanted. We had hot and cold running water--a rarity in Chinatown, as well as our own bathtub. Others in the community used the YWCA or YMCA facilities, where for twenty-five cents, a family could draw six baths. Our sheets were pieced from dishtowels, but we had sheets. I was never neglected, for my mother and father were always at home. During school vacation periods, I was taught to operate many types of machines--tacking (for pockets), overlocking (for the raw edges of seams), buttonhole, doubleseaming; and I learned all the stages in producing a pair of jeans to its final inspection, folding, and tying in bundles of a dozen pairs by size, ready for pickup. Denim jeans are heavy--my shoulders ached often. My father set up a modest nickel-and-dime piecework reward for me, which he recorded in my own notebook, and he paid me regularly.

On Sundays, we never failed to attend the Methodist Church, as my father's belief in the providence of God strengthened with the years, and his wife and family shared that faith. My father's faith in God was unwavering and unshakable. . . . I suppose that for him, the Christian faith at first comforted him far from his loved ones. Secondly, it promised him individual worth and salvation, when all his life in China had been devoted only to his family's continuity and glorification. Third, to this practical man who was virtually self-taught in all his occupations, Christianity suggested action on behalf of others in the community, while Confucianism was more concerned with regulating personal relationships. Daddy seldom hesitated to stick his neck out if he thought social action or justice were involved. For instance, he was on the founding board of the Chinese YMCA and fought for its present location, though he was criticized for its being on a hill, for being near the YWCA, for including a swimming pool. . . .

My mother dutifully followed my father's leadership. Because of his devotion to Christian principles, she was on the path to economic security. She was extremely thrifty, but the thrifty need pennies to manage, and the old world of Fragrant Mountains had denied her those. Upon arrival in the new world of San Francisco, she accepted the elements her mate had selected to shape her new life: domestic duties, seamstress work in the factory home, mothering each child in turn, church once a week, and occasional movies. Daddy frowned upon the community Chinese operas because of their very late hours (they did not finish till past midnight) and their mixed audiences.

Very early in my life, the manners of a Chinese lady were taught to me. How to hold a pair of chopsticks (palm up, not down); how to hold a bowl of rice (one thumb on top, not resting in a open palm); how to pass something to elders (with both hands, never one); how to pour tea into the tiny, handleless porcelain cups (seven-eighths full so that the top edge would be cool enough to hold); how to eat from a center serving dish (only the piece in front of your place; never pick around); not to talk at table, not to show up outside of one's room without being fully dressed; not to be late, ever; not to be too playful—in a hundred and one ways, we were molded to be trouble-free, unobtrusive, quiescent, cooperative.

We were disciplined by first being told, and then by punishment if we didn't remember. Punishment was instant and unceremonious. At the table, it came as a sudden whack from Daddy's chopsticks. Away from the table, punishment could be the elimination of a privilege or the blow on our legs from a bundle of cane switches. My father used the switch, but mother favored a wooden clotheshanger. Now that I have four children myself, I can see that my parents' methods insured "domestic tranquility." Once, when I screamed from the sting of his switch, my father reminded me of my good fortune. In China, he had been hung by his thumbs before being whipped by an uncle or other older family member, called to do the job dispassionately.

Only Daddy and Oldest Brother were allowed individual idiosyncrasies. Daughters were all expected to be of one standard. To allow each one of many daughters to be different would have posed enormous problems of cost, energy, and attention. No one was shown physical affection. Such familiarity would have my parents and endangered the one-answer authoritative system. One standard from past to present, whether in China or in San Francisco, was simpler to enforce. Still, am I not lucky that I am alive to tell this story? Mother used to point out to me one of the old women seamstresses, tiny of build, with bound feet. She came from another village which practiced the killing of unwanted newborn females, and admitted that she had done so herself in China. But a daughter was born here to her, and I remember her. She was constantly cowed by her mother's merciless tongue-lashings, the sounds of a bitter woman who had not been blessed by any son.

Thirty-five years later, I have four children, two sons and two daughters. In principle we remain true to my father's and mother's tradition, I believe. Our children respect my husband and me, but it is not a blind obedience enforced by punishment. It is a respect won from observing us and rounded by friendship. My parents never said "please" or "thank you" for any service or gift. In Chinese, both "please" and "thank you" can be literally translated as "I am not worthy" and naturally, no parent is going to say that about a service which should be their just due. There is no literal translation for "sorry" in Chinese. If someone dies, we can say, "It is truly regrettable." But if we regret an act, we say again, "I am not worthy." Now I say "thank you," "please," and "sorry" to my children, in English, and I do not think it lessens my dignity. The ultimate praise I ever remember from my parents was a single word, "good."

We do not abhor a show of affection. Each child looks forward to his goodnight kiss and tuck-in. Sometimes one or more of them will throw his arms around one of us and cry out, "I love you so."

My son, Mark, has completed more than eight years of night Chinese school, the same one I attended. I have also served on that school board, as my father before me. Unlike my well-attended Chinese classes—nearly every Chinese child in the community of my childhood was sent to night school for some years—Mark's last Chinese grade included only a handful of students. . . . The movement of second-generation Chinese Americans has been to the suburbs or to other parts of San Francisco, and it is no longer practical to send their children, the third generation, to Chinese school in Chinatown. My husband and I cherish our Chinese ties and knowledge, and waited many years to purchase a home which would be within walking distance of Chinatown. If a child has difficulty with homework, Chinese or American, he or she can come to see us at our office-studio, and we drop everything to help.

As in my own dual education, the children are learning Chinese history, culture, or what being a member of the Chinese race means. The six-year-old learns one new ideograph a day. After a week, he knew that one writes Chinese from top to bottom, from left to right. They do not lack time for playing, drawing, reading, or TV viewing. Sometimes they do complain, because Chinese is not taught as pleasurably as subjects at American school. When they ask why they must attend Chinese school, I say firmly, "This is our standard. If you lived in another home, you could do as they do." Our children chatter among themselves in English, but they can understand and speak Chinese when desired. It is a necessity when with their grandmothers. Even this simple ability contrasts with some children of Chinese ancestry. As my mother exclaimed in dismay when such a grandchild visited her, "We were as a duck and a chicken regarding each other without understanding."

As a wife and mother, I have naturally followed my Chinese training to wait on my husband and serve my children. While ceramics is my career, the members of my family know they come first, and they do not pay any penalty for my work. Chinese men expect to be family heads, and to receive loving service from wife and children, but they are also marvelously helpful as fathers, and nearly all Chinese men I know enjoy being creative cooks on occasion. If you visit the parks of Chinatown, you are likely to see more men than women overseeing the laughing children. If you shop in Chinatown, you find as many men as women choosing the groceries. My husband has given our children from birth more baths and shampoos than I have. He has also been their manicurist and ear cleaner, for once a week, when they were smaller, there were eight ears to swab clean and eighty nails to trim.

Selective self-expression, which was discouraged in my father's household, has been encouraged in our family. About two years ago, my husband established this tradition: every Sunday evening each child presents an original verbal or verbal-visual project, based on a news article, a school project, a drawing (since the youngest can't read yet), a film. We correct diction, posture, presentation, in the hope that each will be able to think aloud on his feet someday. Each of the three older children has one or more special friend. I have met these friends at our home, preferring that they be invited here rather than have our children leave home. Seldom do we plan children's parties, but when we entertain our adult friends, our children are included. How else would they learn correct etiquette and expect to fit into an adult world some day? . . .

Traditional Chinese parents pit their children against a standard of perfection without regard to personality, individual ambitions, tolerance for human error, or exposure to the changing social scene. It never occurred to that kind of parent to be friends with their children on common ground. Unlike our parents, we think we tolerate human error and human change. Our children are being encouraged to develop their individual abilities. . . .

In the next part of this selection Jade Snow Wong tells us of her increased responsibilities as an eleven-year-old, her growing awareness of the difference between the culture of her home life and that of the public school, and of an incident that raised the question whether this difference meant inferiority.

As I advanced in American high school and worked at those jobs, I was gradually introduced to customs not of the Chinese world. My American teachers were mostly kind. I remember my third-grade teacher's skipping me half a year. I remember my fourth-grade teacher--with whom I am still friendly. She was the first person to hold me to her physically and affectionately--because a baseball bat had been accidentally flung against my hand. I also remember that I was confused by being held, since physical comfort had not been offered by my parents. I remember my junior high school principal, who skipped me half a grade and commended me before the school assembly, to my great embarrassment. . . .

In contrast, Chinese schoolteachers acted as extensions of Chinese parental discipline. There was a formal "disciplinarian dean" to apply the cane to wayward boys, and girls were not exempt either. A whisper during chapel was sufficient provocation to get called to the dean's office. No humor was exchanged; no praise or affection expressed by the teachers. They presented the lessons, and we had to learn to memorize all the words, orally, before the class. Then followed the written test, word for word. Without an alphabet, the Chinese language requires exact memorization. No originality or deviation was permitted and grading was severe. One word wrong during an examination could reduce a grade by 10 percent. It was the principle of learning by punishment.

Interest and praise, physical or oral, were rewards peculiar to the American world. Even employers who were paying me thanked me for a service or complimented me on a meal well cooked, and sometimes helped me with extra dishes. . . . I perceived a difference between two worlds.

The difference was not always lovely. One day after junior high school classes (I was one of only two Chinese faces there), a tormentor chased me, taunting me with "Chinky, chinky, Chinaman . . ." and tacked on some insults. Suddenly, I wondered if by my difference, I was inferior. This question had to be resolved again and again later: when I looked for my first job, when I looked for an apartment, when I met with unexplained rejection. It was a problem I felt that I could not discuss with my parents.

It is a problem which has not diminished with the years. Only a few days ago, my two youngest children came home from their walk to the neighborhood library with the story that some boys had physically attacked them as they passed the schoolyard, insulting them because they were Chinese. Immediately I took them with me and looked for the schoolyard's director, who called the culprits. There were defensive denials and looks of surprised guilt. But our children will not be wondering for years if being Chinese means being inferior.

The author then explores the conflict she feels between the contradictory values of her two cultures and her struggles to mediate between the two.

By the time I was graduating from high school, my parents had done their best to produce an intelligent, obedient daughter, who would know more than the average Chinatown girl and should do better than average at a conventional job, her earnings brought home to them in repayment for their years of child support. . . .

But having been set upon a new path, I did not oblige my parents with the expected conventional ending. At fifteen, I had moved away from home to work for room and board and a salary of twenty dollars per month. Having found that I could subsist independently, I thought it regretful to terminate my education. Upon graduating from high school at the age of sixteen, I asked my parents to assist me in college expenses. I pleaded with my father, for his years of encouraging me to be above mediocrity in both Chinese and American studies had made me wish for some undefined but hopefully brighter future.

My father was briefly adamant. He must conserve his resources for my oldest brother's medical training. Though I desired to continue on an above-average course, his material means were insufficient to support that ambition. He added that if I had the talent, I could provide for my own college education. When he had spoken, no discussion was expected. After his edict, no daughter questioned.

But this matter involved my whole future—it was not simply asking for permission to go to a night church meeting (forbidden also). Though for years I had accepted the authority of the one I honored most, his decision that night embittered me as nothing ever had. My oldest brother had so many privileges, had incurred unusual expenses for luxuries which were taken for granted as his birthright, yet these were part of a system I had accepted. Now I suddenly wondered at my father's interpretation of the Christian code: was it intended to discriminate against a girl after all, or was it simply convenient for my father's economics and cultural prejudice? Did a daughter have any right to expect more than a fate of obedience, according to the old Chinese standard? As long as I could remember, I had been told that a female followed three men during her lifetime: as a girl, her father; as a wife, her husband; as an old woman, her son.

My indignation mounted against that tradition and I decided then that my past could not determine my future. I knew that more education would prepare me for a different expectation than my other female schoolmates, few of whom were to complete a college degree. I, too, had my father's unshakable faith in the justice of God, and I shared his unconcern with popular opinion.

So I decided to enter junior college. I lived at home and supported myself with an after-school job which required long hours of housework and cooking but paid me twenty dollars per month, of which I saved as much as possible. The thrills derived from reading and learning, in ways ranging from chemistry experiments to English compositions, from considering new ideas of sociology to the logic of Latin, convinced me that I had made a correct choice. I was kept in a state of perpetual mental excitement by new Western subjects and concepts and did not mind long hours of work and study. I also made new friends, which led to another painful incident with my parents, who had heretofore discouraged even girlhood friendships. . . .

She then describes her defiance of her parents concerning a movie date with a Chinese-American boy and the aftermath of challenging her parents' values.

That stormy disagreement climaxed my departure from total acceptance of my parents' ideas and authority. In the thirty years which have intervened, my receptiveness to Western ideas has not meant my unequivocal acceptance. Each situation which arises requires its own evaluation. Sometimes the Western assumption is rejected; sometimes Chinese caution is discarded.

My present standard of values was remarkably amplified at Mills College, which offered me a general scholarship because of a good junior college scholastic record. Mills is primarily a residence college for women, and I was given a chance to live on campus by working for room and board in the home of the dean. Additional duties at her office enabled me to earn money for books and necessities.

Many classes were small in number, with less than ten students. The professors' methods here were the opposite pole from the Chinese. No longer did I memorize wise echoes of the past. The emphasis was on originating, creating, articulating. I was awkwardly unsuccessful at first. But I groped, was made to express my thinking aloud, and had my ideas discussed, rejected, or commended by an audience. I learned too to make and fire pottery and copper enamels, an art that was to become my work. My two years there for completion of my B.A. degree convinced me that education in the liberal arts was a lifetime prize well worth my four years of struggle. . . .

The rest of the article describes her experience at Mills College, some early jobs, finding her present vocation, which combines pottery-making with writing, and her marriage.

Just about the time I had started the pottery business, I received letters of inquiry from Harper & Bros., signed by a woman editor who had read some magazine articles, expanded, actually, from college papers, which I had written about Chinatown. She asked me to think about writing an autobiography, and when I consulted with my junior college English teacher, I received further encouragement on the project from her. The timing of our wedding was two months before the publication of my book, Fifth Chinese Daughter, in 1950. That book's rapid initial sales amazed us. It had been dedicated to my mother and father, and when the first royalty check came six months after publication, my reaction to its amount was to want to share it with my parents. Though my ways were different from those of their other children, I was no less filial and grateful. First, I asked my husband for permission. His reply was, "You don't have to ask me about anything which is right." He, too, is a Chinese son in a big family.

I telephoned my father to say we would come home to him for dinner. He wondered why. I replied, "I have something for you."

He was suspicious, "What is the something?"

I was secretive, "A surprise—you must wait."

Daddy and Mama were both in the kitchen, preparing the dinner. My gifts had been properly wrapped in red paper, as at New Year's, for presentation. My father opened his envelope at once, beamed in excitement, and gave his hundred-dollar bill an American kiss. My mother continued to cook, and ignoring her envelope on the stove top, murmured a rare "Thank you." Later, she left the kitchen with it, but made no additional comment.

Sometimes my father's grace was routine, sometimes it was a silent moment, sometimes it was to ask forgiveness for our sins. But tonight, it had a different tone. As my younger sister and two younger brothers, my husband, my mother, and I bowed together with him, he said, "We are gathered here because of a book about which fellow villagers, merchants, and friends on the street have been congratulating me. For this book was written in America by a Chinese, not only a Chinese, but a Chinese from San Francisco, not only a Chinese from San Francisco, but a Wong, not only a Wong, but a Wong from this house, not only a Wong from this house, but a daughter, Jade Snow. Heavenly Father, this accomplishment was not mine but yours. From your many blessings, this girl, raised according to your commandments, was able to do this work."

My father, mentioning me in a prayer for the first time, had accepted me, and a part of him had accepted America. At the age of seventy plus, after years of attending night classes in citizenship, he became naturalized. He embraced this status wholeheartedly. One day when we were discussing plans for his birthday celebration, which was usually observed the tenth day of the fifth lunar month by the Chinese calendar, he announced, "Now that I have become a United States citizen, I am going to change my birthday. Henceforth, it will be on the Fourth of July."

If you would like to read the whole article, see "Puritans from the Orient: A Chinese Evolution," by Jade Snow Wong, from The Immigrant Experience, edited by Thomas C. Wheeler. Copyright (c) 1971 by The Dial Press. Excerpt reprinted here by permission of Doubleday and Company, Inc.

* * *

VOCABULARY

Directions: **Supply the missing forms of the words in the boxes as directed on page 60.**

1. **Conservatism** (noun) — the tendency to preserve what is established and to promote gradual development, rather than abrupt change.

2. **Retain** (verb) — keep, hold, preserve; **retainer** fee to keep services, a device to hold teeth in position.

Contemporary

(noun) — a person nearly the same age as another or living at the same period of time as another. Winston Churchill was a contemporary of Franklin Delano Roosevelt.

(adj) — of the same time; of the present time

The root tempus, meaning time, gives us many words:

Tempo	musical time, characteristic beat
Temporal	enduring for a time only, as opposed to eternal
Temporary	existing for a time only; not permanent
Temporize	try to gain time or stall for time
Extemporize	to speak or compose on the spur of the moment

Verbs	Nouns	Adjectives	Adverbs
	Tempo	**Temporary**	a.__________
Temporize			
Extemporize		**Extemporary**	
		Extemporaneous	**Extemporaneously**

4. **Meticulous** (adj) — exact, precise; extremely or excessively careful about minute details

5. **Abacus** (noun) — a device for making arithmetic calculations, consisting of a frame set with rods on which balls or beads are moved

6. **Concession** (n) (concede) (v) — concede—to yield or grant: The Mets finally conceded defeat. —the act of conceding or yielding; a space within certain premises for a subsidiary business: They had the coke concession at the arena.

7. **Nominal** (adj) — a trifling cost in comparison with the actual value

8. **Calligraphy** (noun) — fine, beautiful, or fancy handwriting; a script produced chiefly by brush, esp. Chinese, Japanese or Arabic writing of high artistic value

9. **Fluently** (adv) with an easy or ready flow, to speak or write fluently

The root flux, meaning flow or flowing, gives us many words:

Affluence an abundant supply or flow; abundance of money, property, etc.

Fluidity flow or state of flowing

Influx a flowing in

Verbs	Nouns	Adjectives	Adverbs
Flow	**Fluid** **Fluidity** **Affluence** **Influx**	c.__________	

10. **Opaque** (adj) not transparent; hard to understand

11. **Unwavering** (adj) steady, without doubts, indecisions, or swaying back and

12. **Unobtrusive** (adj) not thrusting oneself forward, being pushy, calling attention to oneself

The root trude, meaning thrust, gives us many words:

Obtrude to thrust forward or call attention to

Intrude to thrust or bring in without reason, permission, or welcome

Protrude to project, thrust forward

Extrude to thrust out, to expel, e.g., to extrude molten rock

Verbs	Nouns	Adjectives	Adverbs
Obtrude	**Obtrusion**	d.________	**Obtrusively**
Intrude	e._______	intrusive	intrusively
Protrude	f._______		
Extrude	g._______		

14. **Idiosyncrasies** (noun) individualities, peculiarities, quirks

15. **Abhor** (verb) despise, hate; loathe

16. **Provocation** (noun) annoyance, aggravation

17. **Conventional** (adj) ordinary, customary

18. **Adamant** (adj) utterly unyielding in attitude or opinion in spite of all appeals, urgings, etc.; as hard as a diamond

19. **Edict** (noun) any authoritive command; a decree issued by a sovereign or other authority

20. **Unequivocal** (adj) simple, direct, obvious, unmistakable; having only one possible meaning or interpretation

21. **Filial** (adj) pertaining to or befitting a son or daughter; filial obedience

QUESTIONS FOR DISCUSSION AND WRITING

The following questions can be used for class discussion, for individual or group writing assignments, and for entries in a reading journal. Follow your teacher's instructions.

1. Jade Snow Wong's father had already adopted some Western ideas before he sent for his family to join him in San Francisco. What revolutionary opportunities did he offer his wife and daughters? How did he help his older daughters before coed Chinese schooling was available?

2. What were some of the reasons the Wong family left China?

3. Once they were here, what methods did the Wongs use to overcome poverty?

4. How did young Jade Snow Wong feel about having both American and Chinese studies?

5. In what ways did the oldest son receive special treatment? What would be his special responsibility?

6. Jade Snow was taught the manners of a Chinese lady. Which rules of etiquette would you find hard to follow? Which rules sound like good ideas to you?

7. There were two steps to the Wong family's disciplining of children. What were they? How does Jade Snow's method of disciplining her own children differ from her parents'?

8. In what other ways do Jade Snow's child-raising practices differ from her parents'?

9. What important family tradition has she kept?

10. Jade Snow's husband is a second generation Chinese-American. What special things does he do in his role of husband and father?

11. What incident made Jade Snow wonder whether her being different from other Americans might mean that she was inferior? How did she handle the situation when her children were attacked by prejudiced schoolboys?

12. How was her American schooling different from her Chinese schooling in teaching methods, discipline, and the relationship between teacher and student?

13. What decisions did Jade Snow make that departed from her parents' ideas about her future?

14. In the end, how did she exceed her parents' standards for her and bring them unexpected honor?

15. **Comparison Question:**

On your own paper, make a chart with four columns: **Points of Comparison; Estelle Roberts' Family; Jade Snow Wong's Family; My Family.** In the family columns, describe each family in regard to the various points of comparison. These descriptions will help you write Paper 2 (page 252) and will clarify your thinking about the two readings.

Points of Comparison

1. Pride in family's original culture and how it was encouraged
2. Family's attitude toward the continued use of their native language
3. The family's functioning as an economic unit
4. The common good vs. individual fulfillment or expression
5. Work and education valued as ways of rising in the world
6. Some aspects of American life-style rejected by parents
7. Some American ideas accepted by parents
8. Some restrictions on children's full participation in American life
9. Some restrictions exclusively for daughters
10. Similarities between the two fathers
11. Similarities between the mothers
12. Evidence that parents gradually accepted some American values or ways
13. Blended customs

ACQUIRING STYLE THROUGH CREATIVE IMITATION

The sentences below, written by Jade Snow Wong, are followed by an imitation. Add your own imitation in the space provided.

1. I observed from birth that living and working were inseparable.

   I observed from birth that growing and taking risks were inseparable.

2. The only goal was for all in the family to work, to save, and to become educated.

   The only goal was for all in the crisis to stay calm, to cooperate, and to figure a way out of the problem.

3. When he had spoken, no discussion was expected. After his edict, no daughter questioned.

   When he finished, no one spoke. After his announcement, no one moved.

4. Only the ambitious but poor gather their courage and tear up their roots to journey across the seas, in hope of bettering [themselves.]

   Only the burdened but determined work part time and deprive themselves of leisure to attend community college, in hopes of bettering themselves.

   Note: This beautiful sentence is hard to imitate in its entirety; the sample sentence is a partial imitation.

   Only the calm but efficient can work in an emergency room.
   Only the brave but foolhardy
   Only the tough but gentle
   Only the flabby but determined
   Only the guilty but forgiven

Follow Lloyd Thomas' model paragraph in doing the writing practice described below.

Writing Practice

The "melting pot" image has been used repeatedly to describe the presence of diverse ethnic groups with their own language, culture, and traditions contributing harmoniously to our American society. Think of another image such as a patchwork quilt, a garden, a rainbow, a salad, to better portray this ethnic diversity. Using analogy, show how each element reflects the ethnic mix of Los Angeles or of your own city or locality.

L.A.'s Ethnic Diversity

The various ethnic groups in Los Angeles fit together like pieces in a vast patchwork quilt. Just as distinctive, brightly colored pieces of cloth can be sewed together to create a beautiful and useful patchwork quilt, so the diverse elements of Los Angeles' pluralistic population fit together to create a cosmopolitan city. Viewed from the air, this ethnic patchwork quilt might seem stitched together by our freeway system. Of course, the fit of the pieces isn't perfect; we notice great agglomerations of Latins in East Los Angeles, Asians in Monterey Park, and Blacks in South-Central Los Angeles. However, these groups are also spread throughout many other geographical areas, lending their distinctive culture and traditions to the entire city. The most beautiful patchwork quilts exhibit a heterogeneous and harmonious blend of color, fabric, and shape. In the same way, Los Angeles' beauty as a city will increase as it learns to appreciate and embrace its ethnic diversity.

MANAGING SENTENCES THROUGH SUBORDINATION
ADVERB CLAUSES

The previous chapter showed one way to fit two ideas into a sentence when one idea is more important than the other. Chapter Four demonstrated how to tuck a minor idea into a major idea by using an adjective clause:

Major idea: The prowler fled out the back door.

Minor idea: He must have been alarmed by our headlights.

Sentence: The prowler, who must have been alarmed by our headlights, fled out the back door.

This chapter offers another way of expressing two related thoughts while emphasizing one thought over the other. In this case, the two thoughts are placed side by side and the less important thought begins with a SUBORDINATING CONJUNCTION **(although, as,because, even if, even though, if, since, though unless, when, whenever, where, while, etc.)** The subordinating conjunctions create an adverb clause which can be hitched to either end of the sentence carrying the major idea.

Minor Idea — Major Idea

sub. conj. ~~~~~~~~~~, ____________________
(adverb clause) (sentence)

If my paycheck arrives tomorrow, I shall survive.

OR

Major Idea — Minor Idea

____________________ sub. conj. ~~~~~~~~~~
(sentence) (Adverb Clause)

I shall survive if my paycheck arrives tomorrow.

Let's look at some of the relationships we can express with this type of sentence.

CAUSE AND EFFECT

Our main idea is PRIDE IN ONE'S ETHNIC HERITAGE HELPS A PERSON ASSIMILATE. By adding a because, since, or as clause, we can tell why this is true; we can show the cause and effect relationship between ethnic pride and the confidence needed for assimilation.

Because self-confidence is needed in taking on another culture, pride in one's ethnic heritage helps a person assimilate.

OR

Pride in one's ethnic heritage helps a person assimilate since self-confidence is needed in taking on another culture.

CONTRAST

By adding a clause beginning with although, even though, though or while, we can contrast our major idea with what one might expect or fear.

Though some fear ethnic pride as a threat to unity,	pride in one's ethnic heritage helps a person assimilate
Although you might expect the opposite,	
Even though this truth may surprise you,	

CONDITION

Suppose now our main idea is A PERSON WILL GRADUALLY TAKE ON NEW CUSTOMS AND VALUES. By adding an adverb clause to this sentence, we can state under what conditions a person will take on customs and values by adding conjunctions like if, even if, unless, provided that, until, when.

If he feels welcome in the new country, a person will gradually take on its customs and values.

A person will gradually take on new customs and values if he approves of them.

Unless
or
Until } he feels welcome, an immigrant may cling to his old culture.

TIME SEQUENCE

Subordinating conjunctions also allow us to express the time relationship between two ideas:

Before a person can speak the language of a country, he feels isolated.

While a person is learning a new language, he may feel unsure about his pronunciation.

After people can speak the language of a country, they feel more at home there.

Whenever we encounter something strange, our first reaction may be fear.

When a family has been in a country for many generations, its primary roots are there.

LIST OF SUBORDINATING CONJUNCTIONS

after	if	till
although	in order that	unless
as	lest	until
as . . . as	now that	when
as if	provided (that)	whence
as though	since	whenever
because	so as (so . . . as)	where
before	so that (so . . . that)	wherever
even if	that	while
even though	though	whither

(Michael Kammer and Charles Milligan, **The Writing Handbook** (Chicago: Loyola University Press, 1963), p. 50.)

TIPS ON USING SUBORDINATE CONJUNCTIONS

1. While can express contrast:
   Jack Sprat can eat no fat, while his wife can eat no lean.

   While can mean at the same time as:
   While I was trying to remember her name, she asked me mine.

2. As can mean since or because:
   The seniors voted for Ann as she was our first choice.

   As can mean while:
   We reached the bus stop as the bus was pulling away.

3. Subordinating conjunctions turn perfectly good sentences into adverb clauses:

Perfectly good sentence:	The coach liked the idea.
Adverb clause:	Although the coach liked the idea

   Adverb clauses are desirable and perfectly good in their own right when they are connected to a sentence:
   Although the coach like the idea, it came too late in the season.

   By themselves, adverb clauses are dreaded fragments:
   Although the coach like the idea

4. When subordinating clauses come before the main idea, they are following by a comma.

Practice

Write your own sentences with your own content patterned after the models provided.

1. As we grew older, we gradually joined the greater society (Estelle Roberts).

   As we grew older, we ____.

2. When you are oppressed, as any immigrant can tell you, you fight back if you can or dare; if you cannot and you have the means, you leave. (John Williams, "Time and Tide: Roots of Black Awareness")

   When you are ______________________, you ____________________;
   if you cannot and have the means, you ______________________________.

3. Whenever our whole family gets together, everyone talks at once.

   Whenever our whole family gets
   together, ____.

4. Though we had no milk, there was all the rice we wanted (Jade Snow Wong).

   Though we had no ________, there ______________________________.

5. Though my ways were different from those of their other children, I was no less filial and grateful (Jade Snow Wong).

   Though my ways were different from those of the other children,
   I ____
   ____.

6. After I grew up, I became interested in my family's history.

   After I grew up, I ____.

7. Since ours was a self-contained family, each member took on a necessary function (Estelle Roberts).

   Since ours was a ________________ family, each member __________________

   ____.

8. If they had rice, they were fortunate. If there was salt, or oil, they were even more fortunate (Jade Snow Wong).

   If ____________________________, they were fortunate; if __________

   ____________________________, they were even more fortunate.

9. As long as I can remember, I had been told that a female followed three men during her lifetime: as a girl, her father; as a wife, her husband; and as an old woman, her son (Jade Snow Wong).

As long as I can remember, I ____

______________________________.

BOOKS FOR FURTHER READING

The books below recount other immigrant experiences from a variety of ethnic groups. These books may describe conditions similar to those of your forbears. Choose a book for your own pleasure or as an assignment given by your teacher.

Galarza, Ernesto. **Barrio Boy.** South Bend, IN: University of Notre Dame, 1971.

Gamio, Manuel. **The Life Story of the Mexican Immigrant.** New York: Dover Press, 1972.

Kazin, Alfred. **A Walker in the City.** New York: Harcourt Brace Jovanovich, 1951.

Kingston, Maxine Hong. **The Woman Warrior.** New York: Random House, 1977.

Lous, Anne B. **Immigrant Speaks.** New York: Vantage, 1981.

Malamud, Bernard. "Jewbird." In **The Stories of Bernard Malamud.** New York: Farrar, Straus & Giroux, 1983.

Marshall, Paule. **Brown Girl, Brown Stones: A Novel.** Old Westbury, N.Y.: Feminist Press, 1981.

Rodriguez, Richard. **Hunger of Memory.** Boston: David R. Godine, 1981.

Santiago, Danny. **Famous All Over Town.** New York: New American Library, 1984.

Seller, Maxine, ed. **Immigrant Women.** Philadelphia: Temple University Press, 1980.

Wheeler, Thomas C. **The Immigrant Experience.** New York: Penguin Books, 1972.

Selected readings from this book:

Agueros, Jack. "Halfway to Dick and Jane: A Puerto Rican Pilgrimage."
Alfred, William. "Pride and Poverty: An Irish Integrity."
Boe, Eugene. "Pioneers to Eternity: Norwegians on the Prairie."
Milosz, Czeslaw. "Biblical Heirs and Modern Evils: A Polish Poet in California."

Pryce-Jones, Alan. "The Center of Impermanence: New York in the Eyes of an Englishman."
Puzo, Mario. "Choosing a Dream: Stations in Hell's Kitchen."
Roskolenko, Harry. "America, the Thief: A Jewish Search for Freedom."
Williams, John A. "Time and Tide: Roots of Black Awareness."

Wong, Jade Snow. **Fifth Chinese Daughter.** New York: Harper and Row, 1950.

Yep, Lawrence. **Child of the Owl.** New York: Harper and Row, 1977.

Yung, Judy, ed. **Island: Poetry and History of Chinese Immigrants of Angel Island, 1910–40.** San Francisco: San Francisco Study Center, 1982. (1982 Amerian Book Award.)

MAJOR WRITING ASSIGNMENTS

This assignment consists of three separate papers written over a three- to four-week period which can add up to one long paper on "My Family's Version of Being American." (Please follow your instructor's schedule for rough drafts and final copies.)

Paper 1: "My Roots"

Gather as much of the following information as you can about your parents and previous generations.

Note: You aren't expected to write a lengthy genealogy (though this assignment may inspire you to do one on your own). Do what is reasonable. If you have information on only one side of the family, use that. If you were adopted or raised by foster parents, work out an alternate assignment with your teacher.

Information:

1. Where they were born
2. When they came to U.S. (or your home state)
3. Why they came
4. How they came
5. Where they first settled
6. How they coped in the new situation (any sponsors, friends, relatives or community to help)
7. What kind of life they led
8. Anything special that you learned about your origins

Present this information chronologically beginning with the first generation to arrive.

Paper 2—"My Ethnic Heritage"

In describing your ethnic heritage, cover at least six of the items below, taking at least one from each category:

Customs/Family Traditions

1. Special celebrations or ways of celebrating holidays or holydays
2. Food preferences—special dishes, kinds of foods
3. Family traditions
4. Traditional music, dances, games, folktales, folkart
5. Traditional dress
6. Special courtship customs
7. Family fun
8. Special ways of observing births, marriages, deaths
9. Other customs or traditions

Language, Dialect, Family Expressions

1. Use of another language at home
2. Use of a dialect, like Black English, at home
3. Retention of any accent in speech
4. Particular expressions that may have originated in another country or region of the U.S., e.g, calling a milkshake a frappé

Values/Attitudes

1. Some aspects of American life-style rejected by parents
2. Some aspects of American life-style accepted by parents
3. Priority given to good of family as a whole or good of individual members?
4. Values important to your family—education, work, religion, etc.
5. Ideas on child-raising, e.g, disciplining, treatment of male and female children
6. Ideas about proper wife and husband roles
7. Ideas about what is polite and impolite, funny and not funny
8. Other values or attitudes

Paper 3: "My Heritage and I"

Describe what you think you will drop from your heritage and why you will not pass this particular custom, attitude, etc., on to your children and describe what you cherish from your heritage and plan to pass on. Give your reasons for these choices.

Long Paper—"My Family's Version of being American"

Put your three papers together, following any instructions your teacher may give about a general introduction and transitions between the three parts of your long paper.

EVALUATION

We value your opinion. By filling out this evaluation, you can advise us on what to keep or drop from future editions of the book. Please send your evaluation to:

Dean Juan Francisco Lara
Office of Academic Interinstitutional Programs
1332 Murphy Hall
University of California, Los Angeles
Los Angeles, California 90024

Please rate the reading selections on a scale from 1 (poor) to 5 (great); if a selection was not assigned, circle or underline 0.

"The Library Card"	0	1	2	3	4	5
from Hunger of Memory	0	1	2	3	4	5
"Learning to Listen"	0	1	2	3	4	5
"What is Known about Learning to Write"	0	1	2	3	4	5
"Jazz: A Study in Black and White"	0	1	2	3	4	5
"Shanghai"	0	1	2	3	4	5
"Sonny's Blues"	0	1	2	3	4	5
"How to Mark a Book"	0	1	2	3	4	5
from Uses of Enchantment	0	1	2	3	4	5
"Television Addiction"	0	1	2	3	4	5
"Addiction is a Family Disease"	0	1	2	3	4	5
"Drugs"	0	1	2	3	4	5
"The Melting Pot or the Rainbow"	0	1	2	3	4	5
"Los Angeles: City of New Beginnings"	0	1	2	3	4	5
"Home-Grown Italian Clan Survives L.A."	0	1	2	3	4	5
"Puritans from the Orient"	0	1	2	3	4	5

Please rate the major writing assignments:

Reading Plan for One's Children and Its Rationale	0	1	2	3	4	5
Analysis of Reading Experiences of Wright, Rodriguez, Welty						
Short version	0	1	2	3	4	5
Long version	0	1	2	3	4	5

Disc Jockey Assignment	0 1 2 3 4 5
The Connection between Blues and American Blacks	0 1 2 3 4 5
Applying Bettelheim's Ideas to a Specific Fairy Tale	0 1 2 3 4 5
Ballot Measure Argument	0 1 2 3 4 5
Sonny's Prospects of Being Drug-Free	0 1 2 3 4 5
My Family's Version of Being American	0 1 2 3 4 5

Please rate the helpfulness of these reading features:

Overview pages	0 1 2 3 4 5
Anticipation-Response Guides	0 1 2 3 4 5
Graphic Organizers, Charts, Figures	0 1 2 3 4 5
Summaries	0 1 2 3 4 5
Reading Journals	0 1 2 3 4 5
Marking a Book Technique	0 1 2 3 4 5
Future Reading Lists	0 1 2 3 4 5

Please rate the usefulness of these writing features:

Paragraph assignments	0 1 2 3 4 5
Questions for Journal Entries and Writing Practice	0 1 2 3 4 5
Imitation of Larger Writing Units	0 1 2 3 4 5

Please rate the usefulness of these features for fluency, correctness, and style:

Managing Sentences sections	0 1 2 3 4 5
Creative Imitation of Sentences	0 1 2 3 4 5
Sentence-Combining	0 1 2 3 4 5

Please rate the book as a whole: 1 2 3 4 5

Any general comments or suggestions?

____

____

____

Questions for Students

1. Do you think this textbook has helped your reading and writing skills?

   ____

2. Was this textbook less grim than other composition texts? ____________

3. Has this text in any way changed your attitude toward reading and writing? _______ How? ________________________________

Questions for Teachers

1. Do we have enough material for a one- or a two-semester class? __________
2. Did you assign any full-length books like **Willie and Dwike** in addition to this book? ______________________________
3. Did your class meet for three or five hours a week? ____________
4. At the end of the semester, did you see improvement in students' skills? ________________________________
5. Did you see any improvement in class morale? ______________
6. Would you recommend the book? ________________

A 6
B 7
C 8
D 9
E 0
F 1
G 2
H 3
I 4
J 5